Cool Christianity

Cool Christianity

Hillsong and the Fashioning of Cosmopolitan Identities

CRISTINA ROCHA

OXFORD
UNIVERSITY PRESS

OXFORD
UNIVERSITY PRESS

Oxford University Press is a department of the University of Oxford. It furthers
the University's objective of excellence in research, scholarship, and education
by publishing worldwide. Oxford is a registered trade mark of Oxford University
Press in the UK and certain other countries.

Published in the United States of America by Oxford University Press
198 Madison Avenue, New York, NY 10016, United States of America.

© Oxford University Press 2024

All rights reserved. No part of this publication may be reproduced, stored in
a retrieval system, or transmitted, in any form or by any means, without the
prior permission in writing of Oxford University Press, or as expressly permitted
by law, by license, or under terms agreed with the appropriate reproduction
rights organization. Inquiries concerning reproduction outside the scope of the
above should be sent to the Rights Department, Oxford University Press, at the
address above.

You must not circulate this work in any other form
and you must impose this same condition on any acquirer.

Library of Congress Cataloging-in-Publication Data
Names: Rocha, Cristina, author.
Title: Cool Christianity : Hillsong and the fashioning of cosmopolitan
identities / Cristina Rocha.
Description: New York, NY, United States of America : Oxford University Press, [2024] |
Includes bibliographical references and index.
Identifiers: LCCN 2023033951 (print) | LCCN 2023033952 (ebook) |
ISBN 9780197673201 (paperback) | ISBN 9780197673195 (hardback) |
ISBN 9780197673225 (epub)
Subjects: LCSH: Fashion—Religious aspects—Christianity. |
Clothing and dress—Religious aspects—Christianity. | Clothing and dress—Australia. |
Clothing and dress—Brazil. | Pentecostal churches—Australia. |
Pentecostal churches—Brazil. | Hillsong Church.
Classification: LCC GT521 .R58 2024 (print) | LCC GT521 (ebook) |
DDC 391.00981—dc23/eng/20231016
LC record available at https://lccn.loc.gov/2023033951
LC ebook record available at https://lccn.loc.gov/2023033952

DOI: 10.1093/oso/9780197673195.001.0001

Paperback printed by Marquis Book Printing, Canada
Hardback printed by Bridgeport National Bindery, Inc., United States of America

Contents

Preface   vii
Acknowledgments   xi

Introduction   1

1. Cool Christianity   24
2. Fandom   52
3. Resting in God   75
4. Living the Dream   98
5. Transnational Infrastructures of Circulation   123
6. The Return   143
7. Taking Root and Spreading Shoots   163

Conclusion   186

Notes   197
References   205
Index   221

Preface

As I was finalizing this book, the trickle of sexual abuse and money scandals at Hillsong Church in the United States and Australia became a flood that finally engulfed its founder and Senior Global Pastor Brian Houston. After taking leave to fight criminal charges for covering up child sexual abuse committed by his late father, Frank Houston, in January 2022, Brian Houston was forced to resign for breaching the Hillsong code of conduct three months later. In a meeting with all the Hillsong staff in Sydney, the interim (and since February 2023, permanent) Global Senior Pastor Phil Dooley revealed that Houston had been the subject of an internal investigation for texting a woman in 2013 and spending time with another in a hotel room under the influence of alcohol and medication in 2019. Unfortunately for the megachurch, Houston's resignation came a day before the American streaming service Discovery+ released a negative documentary series focusing on Hillsong's scandals. This series came after an equally critical BBC series on Hillsong in 2021. In the fallout, nine of the sixteen churches that had joined Hillsong in the United States cut ties with the megachurch.

Houston's case followed a string of US megachurch pastors and evangelical Christians, such as Jerry Farwell Jr (Liberty University), Mark Driscoll (Mars Hill), and Bill Hybels (Willow Creek), among others, who have resigned amid sexual abuse and bullying scandals. Abuse (sexual, physical, and psychological) in majority and minority religious and spiritual communities is not new. Scholars (Lofton 2018; Orsi 2017; Johnson 2018; Goodwin 2020; Blyth 2021) have been increasingly paying more attention to this difficult issue.[1] John of God, the Brazilian faith healer and leader of a global spiritual community that was the subject of my previous book (2017), was charged and jailed for sexual crimes in 2019. During fieldwork, I did hear several rumors of sexual abuse of women, but no one would confirm them, as I detailed in my book (2017: 159–162). After many of his victims came forward with their stories, Kathleen McPhillips, a scholar who had been writing on abuse in the Australian Catholic Church, and I (Rocha and McPhillips 2019) reflected on the power of charismatic male leaders over spiritual communities. These leaders not only derive their authority from patriarchy but also from their charisma, that is, their believed supernatural powers or qualities (Weber [1922] 1968: 48).

As for Hillsong, I am not aware of allusions to abuse at the megachurch by the many scholars who have researched it (Goh 2008; Riches 2010; Riches and Wagner 2017; Yip 2015; Wagner 2020, among others) but for Klaver's (2021: 143–150) analysis of how Brian Houston framed learning about his father's pedophilia and his testimony at the Australian Royal Commission into Institutional Responses to Child Sexual Abuse in 2014. To be sure, Maddox (2013a: 23) has written on the culture of male headship at Hillsong, something that can easily lead to abuse, since it means that "wife submits to husbands, laity submits to pastors, and junior pastors submit to senior pastors." The lack of scholarship on abuse at the megachurch until the scandals broke on the media could be explained by Hillsong's culture of secrecy, where power is concentrated at the very top, and Hillsong's efforts to protect the brand by silencing people (Hardaker 2021; Hardy 2022, 2023). In addition, there has not been a thorough ethnography of the New York branch, where Cool Christianity—with its celebrity culture, greenrooms, VIP privileges, and consumerist excesses—is much more developed than in other campuses of the Hillsong global network.

How these scandals will play out for Hillsong globally in the long run is still unclear. So far, the fallout has been mainly in the United States and Australia, where revenue and attendance have fallen. Despite being frequently on the news globally (particularly cover stories in the *New York Times* and *The Guardian*), things have been more subdued in Brazil. The story was reported by the Brazilian secular media only as reviews of the Discovery+ documentary, but even then the documentary was criticized for not being balanced and excessively critical of the megachurch (Feltrin 2022). The evangelical online media did report it, but the news did not get much traction with just a couple of comments for each story.

I suggest that there are several reasons why Hillsong continues to thrive in Brazil. These have to do with the central argument of this book: Hillsong offers young middle-class Brazilians an alternative geography of belonging and the possibility of a cosmopolitan life. It also creates loyal subjects through its exciting, less authoritarian, and what Brazilians deem a more ethical style of Pentecostalism than that in their homeland. The position of Brazil in the Global South and its aspiration for cosmopolitan modernity (Rocha 2006) play a strong role here. The things that make Hillsong appealing to this cohort—its origins in the Global North, use of the English language, the constant stream of foreign pastors at the services whose preaching is translated live on the platform, its high production values, and a focus on excellence, in addition to a more egalitarian relationships between pastors and followers—will not change with the church's fallout.

Another reason for Hillsong's survival is that it is much smaller in Brazil, with only two branches and no independent churches joining in as it happened in the United States. Hillsong is able to control the message within its own branches. In addition, congregants have a close relationship with their local Brazilian pastors, not Brian Houston, who visited Brazil only once, before it was even an established church. Thus, the Houstons and the scandal-ridden American celebrity pastor Carl Lentz are not so well known to Brazilians.

In a way, things have not changed much for Brazilian followers who accept the narrative of the church headquarters that they are going through "a difficult season," and that "the church never said it was perfect." If anything, many have praised the church for being transparent and taking responsibility for its errors. They reasoned that a Brazilian church would cover up any scandals and a pastor would keep working, as it has happened so many times. For instance, *Renascer* church pastors were jailed by the FBI as they entered the United States carrying large undeclared sums of money hidden in a hollowed-out Bible (FBI Arrests Two Brazilian Bishops in Miami 2007). As they left jail, they returned to preaching in their Brazilian megachurch. Here again, in their admiration of Hillsong's supposed accountability, they display a desire for "excellence" and the rule of law that they imagine exists in the Global North but not in their own country. Others offered the Pentecostal belief in the "spiritual battle" as an explanation for these scandals. For them, it was Hillsong's success that had led to the devil's attack.

All in all, this book shows the importance of place and class for the expansion of Cool Christianity. As the reader will see in the many stories of fandom and dreams, travel and return, Brazil's location in the Global South was generative. It made them aspire for a different life that they believed Hillsong and Australia could give them. As they returned, they dreamed of transforming their own churches and the country, while at the same time strengthening their overseas networks. Hillsong continues to offer Brazilians the possibility of being co-present at home and overseas, and I do not see this changing in the short term.

Acknowledgments

This book was supported by many people and institutions. First and foremost, I am thankful to the Australian Research Council Future Fellowship for the large research grant that allowed me to conduct research in Australia and in Brazil over many years. The support of the School of Social Sciences at Western Sydney University was fundamental for this project to become a book, for which I am indebted. I am also grateful to the Department of Religious Studies at Utrecht University. There, Birgit Meyer, Katja Rakow, and other scholars and students welcomed me as a Visiting Researcher in 2017 and again in 2019. Martijn Oosterbaan at Utrecht University, Miranda Klaver at the Free University of Amsterdam, and Linda van de Kamp at the University of Amsterdam were also wonderful dinner hosts, friends, and sounding boards for early chapters of this book. The degree to which our discussions inspired my work is clear in the pages of this book. The Brazil Institute at Kings College, University of London, offered me another stimulating site to write and discuss my work.

I am especially indebted to the Paris Institute for Advanced Study (IAS) for a year-long fellowship in 2021–2022. Over wonderful lunches, seminars, and coffees, I was able to discuss the book and other fellows' exciting projects. At the Paris IAS, I thank the Director Saadi Lahlou and the Scientific Director Simon Luck, who did all they could to get me there during a period few people were able to leave Australia due to the COVID-19 pandemic. And also the lovely IAS staff (Claire Jeandel, Nadège Bourgeois, Cécile Durant, Bertrand Pouvesle, Geneviève Marmin, Christopher Boulhares, Lisette Winkler, and Sandrine Morvan), who supported me at the Institute and with advice on best cafes in Paris, where to buy kitchen supplies, get vaccine boosters, and so many other little things that living in a new city entails. The IAS fellows were supportive, witty, and clever. Our long morning walks to the IAS, when we chatted and witnessed the city waking up for the day, made all the difference to my stay. They are too numerous to mention here, but especially Pamela Surkan, Sheldon Garon, Susan Clayton, Paul Emmelkamp, Jim Hollifield,

Emmanuelle Honoré, Thiago Chacon, Raul Matta, Sonia Gentili, Nassima Neggaz, Marylin Booth, and David Kanter. In Paris, Stefania Capone at the Centre D'études en Sciences Sociales du Religieux (César), EHESS, was a wonderful colleague and dinner host. Clara Saraiva welcomed me at the ICS, University of Lisbon, and took me on a delightful walk through the hills of Sintra, where she did fieldwork.

In Brazil, I am indebted to Paul Freston, Brenda Carança, Paulo Barrera, Alberto da Silva Moreira, Ricardo Mariano, Rodrigo Toniol, Ronaldo de Almeida, Carlos Steil, Cristina Maria de Castro, Nina Rosas, Joana Bahia, Dilaine Sampaio, and Leonardo Cavalcanti for their friendship and invitations to give seminars and master classes that provided opportunities to receive feedback for early drafts.

Special thanks to Mark Hutchinson and Kathleen Openshaw for our discussions on Pentecostalism in Australia, and convening with me a series of symposia and co-editing a book on this topic, where I presented and published some of the ideas contained in this book. My colleagues at the Sydney Women Anthropologists Group, Kalpana Ram, Diane Losche, Gillian Cowlishaw, Alison Leitch, Heidi Norman, Kim Paul, and Jennifer Newman, were also wonderful sounding boards for some of the chapters.

At Hillsong, I must thank the lovely Tanya Riches, whose enthusiasm for scholarly work and social justice was infectious. Also Hillsong São Paulo pastors Pedro and Thiciane Albuquerque were kind to welcome me and patient enough to answer my many queries. Pastors at CJC church Sydney and at Brazilian churches affiliated with Hillsong Network and Family were also generous with their time when we sat for interviews. I am grateful to Alphacrucis scholars who made time to be interviewed for the project. My biggest thanks go to the Brazilian community at Hillsong. Although they must stay anonymous, they were always open for me to join them in church activities and talk to me about their experiences and dreams for their lives, church, and country.

At Oxford University Press, I am grateful to my editor, Theo Calderara, for his expert guidance and support, and the anonymous peer reviewers who were generous with their time and offered excellent suggestions.

As always, I thank my partner, George Morgan, and my family in Brazil, who have been supportive and patient over the many years it took to write this book.

Parts of this book have appeared before in the following publications. I am grateful for the publishers for permission to use this material:

Rocha, C. 2017. "The Come to Brazil Effect": Young Brazilians' Fascination with Hillsong. In T. Riches and T. Wagner (eds.), *The Hillsong Movement Examined: You Call Me out upon the Waters*, pp. 125–141. New York: Palgrave Macmillan.
Rocha, C. 2019. "God Is in Control": Middle-Class Pentecostalism and International Student Migration. *Journal of Contemporary Religion* 34 (1): 21–37.
Rocha, C. 2020. "Living the Dream:" Post-Millennial Brazilians at Hillsong College. In C. Rocha, M. Hutchinson, and K. Openshaw (eds.), *Australian Pentecostal and Charismatic Movements: Arguments from the Margins*, pp. 217–235. Leiden: Brill.
Rocha, C. 2021. Cool Christianity: The Fashion-Celebrity-Megachurch Industrial Complex. *Material Religion* 17 (5): 580–602.
Rocha, C. 2021. Global Religious Infrastructures: The Australian Hillsong Megachurch in Brazil. *Social Compass* 68 (2): 245–257.

Introduction

Every Sunday, the Hillsong bus does the rounds driving congregants before and after each service between Sydney's Central Station and the Hillsong church nearby. The red bus displays a large Hillsong logo and the †=♥ (cross equals love) symbols that have become an integral part of the Australian megachurch global brand. One Sunday in the summer of 2016, as I walked toward the bus amid a crowd of young people, I saw Marta standing by the bus. Marta was a young Brazilian woman and a Hillsong College student. She was looking hip in her blue-and-white-striped maxi-dress and top-knot hairdo. She greeted me with kisses on both my cheeks, as it is common among Brazilians, and told me that she was in charge of the "bus ministry" (i.e., welcoming churchgoers onto the bus).

On the bus, it was standing room only. Some American girls near me were chatting about the Great Barrier Reef and other places to visit in Australia. Behind me there were four young Brazilians discussing their romantic lives. Suddenly, the bus made a sharp turn and the Asian girl, who was standing next to me and texting on her phone, fell backwards onto other people. Everybody laughed, including her, and we all helped her stand up again. The atmosphere was buzzing with loud conversation and laughter. Ten minutes later, we arrived at the church where a throng of people was waiting on the sidewalk to take the bus back to Central Station. The crowd parted as if it were the Red Sea, and we got off the bus and found our way toward the church.

As I entered the church, I saw Marcos and Paula standing by the front desk where translation devices are picked up. They told me that tonight they were volunteering to translate the service into Brazilian Portuguese for those who had not yet mastered English. Many young Brazilians were talking animatedly next to them by the desk. They all looked fresh, young, and excited to be there. As I said hello to everyone, Patrícia invited me to get a drink of water before the service. But before we reached the water fountain, the doors suddenly opened for the next service. We gave up on the water and rushed into the auditorium among the crowd to find seats. Thankfully, we walked in fast enough and the three central rows marked "Reserved for the

Brazilian Community" were still mostly empty but for a few seats covered with bags and jumpers. We took our seats on the first row. Patrícia's friends, Claudia and Rafaela, arrived soon after and sat with us. Claudia was a 19-year-old from São Paulo; she was clearly upper-middle class from the way she spoke, dressed, and her manners. She told me that this was her first visit to Hillsong and she was thrilled. She had been to Bola de Neve church in Brazil (a Pentecostal church that targets young people) but did not like it. She thought it was too boring and full of rules. "They kept telling me what to do!," she explained. Rafaela was 23 years old, also middle class and from São Paulo. They told me that they shared a flat. Rafaela had come to service last weekend—Easter time. She was blown away: "It was amazing! There is nothing like this in Brazil!" She used to go to a Brazilian Spiritist center in Sydney but was now going to come to Hillsong.[1] While we were talking, other Brazilians arrived and filled the three rows. Paula and Marina waved and came up to give me a hug. They were from my Hillsong connect group, a fortnightly Brazilian meeting group I had been participating in for the past year. We were all there, and in expectation of "what God is going to do today," as Hillsong pastors often say.

Soon the lights were dimmed, and black-and-white images of nature and cities started being projected on the large screens on stage to the sound of drumming. As the images started changing faster and faster, the drums reached a crescendo, and then the music and lights were cut off. We were left in silence and total darkness for a few seconds. We all knew this routine at the start of every service, but the crowd still loved the theatricality and drama, and so they screamed and clapped. "Welcome to cool church," I thought to myself. When the lights came back again, many people rushed to be close to the stage. The band was now in full force playing worship songs: "There is no other name; there is no other name; Jesus, Jeeesusss!" Everyone was singing, clapping, swaying side to side; a few others jumped up and down or opened their arms in the shape of the cross as a sign of surrender. Halfway through the worship songs the tattooed gym-junkie-looking guy in the next row knelt on the floor, nested his head in his hands, and cried. He was soon sobbing uncontrollably. I felt like asking whether he was okay but decided not to as nobody else really paid attention to him. Strong emotions performed publicly in the privacy of the dark theater were expected. "This is between him and God" was the attitude of those attending. Everyone continued to sing, clap, and sway side to side, and at times raised hands in the air.

I noticed that Claudia got her phone out of her bag and started filming the service. Patrícia noticed me watching Claudia and explained: "She is WhatsApping! She is sending the video to her friends in Brazil." I nodded in understanding. Over the many years that I had been researching Brazilians at Hillsong I have learned that they have a fandom-like relationship with the megachurch and its worship bands. By sending them the video in real time, Claudia was sharing with them the experience and excitement of actually being here, a place where many of them desire to be. She was also following in the footsteps of some Brazilian celebrities such as the soap opera star Bruna Marquezine, who had shared her visit to Hillsong in Los Angeles on Instagram with her 43 million followers. Like Marquezine, Claudia was spreading the particular affective aesthetics of Hillsong services to Brazilians. Such is the immediacy of the digital world in creating an aesthetic and affective transnational community.

* * *

Cool Christianity is an ethnographic account of the creation of a transnational Pentecostal field between Brazil and Australia, two countries that have been peripheral in the history of Pentecostalism but which more recently have been at the forefront of new forms of global Pentecostalism. This book tells the story of how the style of the Australian megachurch Hillsong— which has expanded globally through music, digital media, branding, and celebrity culture and which elicits strong emotions of excitement, pleasure, and pride—was adopted by the Brazilian middle classes as a way of becoming cosmopolitan and performing social distinction within Brazilian social hierarchies (Bourdieu 1984). Here, I am interested in how young Pentecostal Brazilians forge cosmopolitan identities through everyday practices and an orientation toward the (Pentecostal) lifestyles of the English-speaking world, particularly the United States and Australia. The literature on cosmopolitanism in the social sciences is vast (Vertovec and Cohen 2002; Beck and Sznaider 2006; Rovisco and Nowicka 2011). Here, I take a grounded approach. In this, I follow many other scholars, among them Glick Schiller et al. (2011: 399), who define cosmopolitanism as "a simultaneous rootedness and openness to shared human emotions, experiences rather than tolerance for cultural difference." Like them (2011: 402), I endeavor to "ground the relatively abstract notion of cosmopolitanism within a study of concrete social practices and 'ways of being.'"

Cosmopolitanism is multiple, lived, and situated. It takes place within historical and global structures of domination. For these young Brazilians, who are rooted in their national and Pentecostal identities, cosmopolitanism is about a dream of transformation—of themselves, their churches, and their country. While born-again Christians are usually concerned with transforming the world, these Brazilians desired to transform their Brazilian churches to make them moral and accountable, and thus positive examples for the country. For them, cosmopolitanism was not only about engaging with Cool Christianity, the trendy and modern sensational form of the Global North. It was also about becoming open to "better" forms of being Christian. It was about learning to be rational, autonomous, responsible adults who are able to challenge what they see as the authoritarian, anti-ethical, money-focused, and excessively emotional styles of Brazilian Pentecostal churches. As such, they move away from following the traditional external authority of the pastor to become reflexive modern subjects (Giddens 1991).

Pentecostalism is the fastest-growing religion in Brazil. The country has also its own share of Pentecostal megachurches that have expanded overseas among the urban poor (Almeida 2009; Openshaw 2018; Oro 2014a; van de Kamp 2016; van Wyk 2014). Although in the past two decades Pentecostalism has made inroads among the aspirational lower-middle and middle classes, among the youth (Dantas 2010; Maranhão 2013), and even if the Pentecostal caucus in congress is growing at each election[2] and some Ministers of the former President Bolsonaro's government were Pentecostal, it is still the case that it is more prevalent among the poor. Indeed, the latest Datafolha poll (Balloussier 2020) has found that currently around 30% of the Brazilian population is Protestant and a large majority of them are Pentecostal, an increase from 22% from the 2010 census. It also found that the majority of Pentecostals are women (58%), Black (59%), young (40% are between 16 and 34 years old), and poor (50% of Pentecostals earn up to twice the monthly minimum wage, equivalent to US$215).

Having been a slavery-based society, Brazil still suffers from enormous social inequality and violence against the poor and Black[3] (Alves 2018). This is so pervasive that scholars have characterized class distinction in the country as "segregation" and "social apartheid" because it overlaps with race (O'Dougherty 2002: 173–174; Pinheiro-Machado and Scalco 2014; Alves 2018; Souza 2018). While the wealthy and the middle classes are white, the poor are overwhelmingly Black. Featherstone and Lash (1995: 10) compared São Paulo (the country's largest city and one of the largest in the world) and Delhi and described them as "global colonial cities which have long ago undergone . . . class polarization." They (1995: 3) coined the term "Brazilianization" to account for "the re-emergence of fortress motifs and the spatial segregation of various social groups in global cities." For Brazilian anthropologist Teresa Caldeira (2000: 2–4), São Paulo city epitomizes life in Brazil:

> Fortified enclaves are privatized, enclosed, and monitored spaces for residence, consumption, leisure and work.... Both symbolically and materially, these strategies operate by marking differences, imposing partitions and distances, building walls, multiplying rules of avoidance and exclusions, and restricting movement.

This segregation is still present. In his *The Anti-Black City*, anthropologist Jairo Alves (2018: 2) investigated São Paulo slums in the city periphery and found that "spatial segregation, mass incarceration, and killings by the police are all constitutive dimensions of the reproduction of the urban order."[4] Moreover, a 2021 study found that residents of São Paulo's upmarket suburbs lived 22 years longer than those who inhabited its poorest suburbs. Poorer areas had much worse standards of education, health, housing, and mobility and suffered from high levels of violence. Thus, the gap in life expectancy can be neatly mapped on geography and race—white Brazilians resided in wealthier areas and lived longer than Black Brazilians who resided in poorer areas in the city outskirts (Rede Nova São Paulo 2021).

Anthropologist Maureen O'Dougherty (2002: 6) researched how the Brazilian middle-class "materially and symbolically attain and perform their class" through education and international consumption and travel. Similar to my findings, she (2002: 11) demonstrated that "the class project to attain social distinction and global modernity through consumption engages middle-class people in the local reproduction of inequalities." Poor Brazilian youth in the peripheries of the large cities try to resist this imposed class distinction by consuming designer clothes. However, they do so within capitalist structures that keep them poor. In their study of this phenomenon, Pinheiro-Machado and Scalco (2014: 12) observed:

> This is a reflection of Brazilian apartheid that separates, as if they were two distinct planets, the sociability space of the "Europeanized" Brazilians of

the middle class, and Brazilians perceived as "barbarians" from the popular classes.

Accordingly, the upper and middle classes constantly patrol and reinforce symbolic class borders by denigrating the tastes of the poor. Religion can also be mobilized for this endeavor, as I have shown elsewhere in regard to Buddhism and Spiritism (Rocha 2006a, 2006b, 2017b). This is also true of Pentecostalism. Since many of its traits in Brazil go against middle-class sensibilities, it is stigmatized by the Brazilian media, intellectual elites, and the (upper) middle classes (Lehmann 1996: 203; Freston 1997; Mariz 1996; Martin 2006; Rocha 2006b). The large majority of Pentecostal churches subscribe to the Theology of Prosperity, concentrate heavily on tithing, spiritual warfare, magic, healing, glossolalia, and exorcism. The strong focus on money and practices of exorcism (including physically holding down those supposedly possessed) often embarrass middle-class followers and some resort to mocking these practices. As Freston (1997: 188) has argued in regard to middle-class Pentecostals in Brazil, "the search for respectability would not be served by appearing too Pentecostal." In his research on middle-class Pentecostalism in Argentina, Köhrsen (2016: 41) found similar issues:

> The educated middle class shows a critical attitude towards Pentecostalism. Embracing characteristics—such as exorcisms, prosperity gospel, faith healing, emotional outbursts, etc.—perceived as inappropriate, and being regarded as a religion of the ignorant and poor, Pentecostalism does not fit well with the representations of the educated middle class. Therefore, middle-class actors tend to avoid Pentecostalism.

Martin (2006: 138) has noted that even among academics researching the subject in Latin America, there is an "intellectual and aesthetic disdain for the movement" regarded as in "bad taste." That many megachurch pastors have become seriously wealthy by exploiting the poor (Antunes 2013), and some have been engulfed in fraud and corruption scandals and jailed (FBI Arrests Two Brazilian Bishops in Miami 2007; Peres 2020), has not helped their cause. Neither have pastors in Rio de Janeiro who associated with narcotrafficking mafias in exchange for funding and assistance in expelling Afro-Brazilian religious communities from their neighborhoods (Pinezi and Chesnut 2019). In addition, pastors entering into the political arena and their close association with the far-right former Brazilian President Jair Bolsonaro have also been criticized (Almeida 2019; Burity 2020).

Hence, among the (upper) middle classes there is an element of shame and stigma in being Pentecostal. This is something that all of my interviewees alluded to. Indeed, one interviewee told me that he had lost most of his friends when he converted to Pentecostalism as a teenager. Another told me that her parents were upset when she told them about her conversion upon arriving as a student in Australia, and sarcastically asked her whether she was going to give all her money to the pastor. A young man told me that he would be happy if churches like the Brazilian megachurch Universal Church of the Kingdom of God or UCKG (which is notorious for preying on the poor) would go bankrupt because it gives such a bad name to Pentecostalism.[5] Similarly, I frequently met awkward pauses and bewildered looks whenever I explained to friends and family what I was researching. Why then would these young people be attracted to Pentecostalism and Hillsong?

In analyzing Hillsong's appeal to middle-class youth in Brazil, this book investigates the ways in which Christianity is changing in a global, digital, and postsecular age (Casanova 1994; Habermas 2006). The explosion of Pentecostal and Charismatic churches, particularly in the Global South, is simultaneously shifting the geographies of Christianity away from the West (despite the enduring influence of the Global North) (Anderson 2013; Coleman 2000; Coleman and Hackett 2015; Jenkins 2002; Martin 1990, 2002; Miller and Yamamori 2007), and creating porous cultural and religious communities and imaginaries across borders (Adogame 2013; Butticci 2016; van de Kamp 2016; Rocha et al. 2020). New and reconfigured forms Christianity in both the Global North and South are increasingly digitally mediated, engaged with youth and popular cultures, and involve new forms of consumption, branding, and identity (Johnson 2018; Gauthier et al. 2013; Sanders 2014; Sandler 2006; Sargeant 2000; Twitchell 2007; Ward 2020).

I grapple with these transformations by investigating Hillsong's aesthetic style as a sensational form that creates an affective religious community for young middle-class Brazilians. For Meyer (2010b: 742), sensational forms are authorized religious forms that are spectacular and appeal to the senses. They organize followers' access to the divine. In doing so, I draw on the work of scholars of aesthetics of religion and material religion who argue for an understanding of aesthetics as *aisthesis*, that is, the ways in which humans make sense of themselves and the world through their bodily senses and things (Arweck and Keenan 2016; Grieser and Johnston 2017; Martin 2006; Meyer

2009, 2010b; Meyer and Verrips 2008; Vásquez 2011). These scholars approach religion "as a sensory and mediated practice" (Grieser and Johnston 2017: 1). I am interested in how Hillsong's aesthetic style is created, branded, marketed, and consumed both online and offline; and how it shapes and binds particularly young Brazilians as they transition into adulthood. In doing so, I respond to Meyer's (2009: 10) call for scholars 'to pay close attention to the specific ways through which particular religions and religious forms and elements feature in the making of communities via distinct aesthetic styles."

Furthermore, I expand on Meyer's work to focus on how particular sensational forms and aesthetic styles are associated with social class and are mobilized for social distinction purposes. In doing so, this book engages with Bourdieu's (1984) work on class-based taste, habitus, and social distinction. Performing class distinction (via the cultural capital and practices adopted from the Global North) and aspiration to modernity go hand in hand in Brazil. Throughout much of Brazilian history, there has been a pervasive anxiety regarding where Brazil stands in relation to modernity (Oliven 2000; Ortiz 2000; Souza Martins 2000). Historically, elites have associated the poor with whatever they deem premodern and backward in the country, while they strive for the modernity that they believe is located in the Global North. Such a view rests on a set of historicist assumptions according to which modernity is understood as "something that became global over time" and that certain cultures and societies can only ever experience a belated modernity, having been consigned to "an imaginary waiting room of history" (Chakrabarty 2000: 7–8).

I perceive Hillsong's aesthetic style as part of a "Cool Christianity" trend (Rocha 2021). This kind of Pentecostalism has its distant origins in the late-1960s' Jesus People but consolidated in the twenty-first century as a way to reach the unchurched at a time of dwindling church participation (Johnson 2018; McCracken 2010; Sandler 2006). In order to make Christianity relevant to new generations, particularly the middle-class youth, "Cool" churches appropriate elements of secular youth and popular cultures, be it dress style, body decoration, trendy graphic design, social media aesthetics, pop music, celebrity culture, and the methods of the entertainment industry.

Scholars have used the terms "New Paradigm" (Miller 1997) or "Seeker" (Sargeant 2000) to designate churches that "tailor their programs and services to attract people who are not church attenders" (Sargeant 2000: 2–3). They do so by creating an informal atmosphere, using contemporary language and technology, and focusing on religious experience. Seeker churches borrow from secular models of business and entertainment, use marketing and branding principles, and use innovative methods. According to Miller and Yamamori (2007: 27), they "are at the cutting edge of the Pentecostal movement: they embrace the reality of the Holy Spirit but package religion in a way that makes sense to culturally attuned teens and young adults, as well as upwardly mobile people who did not grow in the Pentecostal tradition." As a rule, their services are entertaining (featuring a live band, professional lighting and sound, large screens) and address people's everyday lives (with topical messages on practical concerns).

However, in this book I chose to use the concept of "Cool Christianity" rather than "New Paradigm" or "Seeker" to analyze the Hillsong style for several reasons that have to do with my grounded approach. First, this is how again and again young Brazilians referred to the megachurch and its aesthetics in our conversations (using the English word). Second, the concept of "Cool" helps us understand *how* these churches engage with youth through affect—it elicits imagination, desire, and dreams of a life that can be otherwise. Rather than the usual detachment associated with the term "cool" (Frank 1997; Pountain and Robins 2000), Cool Christianity propels young people to action, makes them want to change their lives and that of their local churches. This is so because the term "cool" is also inflected by asymmetries of power—there are things, people, and places that are not cool. Hence, it can be mapped onto geopolitical inequalities where those in the Global South believe cool things, peoples, and places are located in the Global North. In brief, the concept of Cool Christianity allows us to understand the embodied appeal of Hillsong and Australia to young middle-class Pentecostal Brazilians (and others from the Global South; see Rocha et al. 2021) and how it is related to dreams and aspirations.

Hillsong

Established in Sydney, Australia, by Brian and Bobby Houston in 1983, Hillsong is a global religious phenomenon (Goh 2008; Klaver 2021; Riches and Wagner 2017; Rocha 2017b, 2019, 2020b; Wagner 2020). Before the sexual abuse and money scandals that broke in late 2020, it had American celebrities among its followers, a global audience to its cable TV channel, and the music of its award-winning worship bands sung weekly by an estimated

50 million people in 60 languages. Despite the mounting scandals since then, in May 2022, four out of the ten most popular worship songs were by Hillsong worship bands, according to the Christian Copyright Licensing International Top 100 (McGinnis 2022). Hillsong's social media following has continued to grow. Presently, Hillsong has 3 million Instagram followers, while its band, Hillsong United, has 4.3 million YouTube subscribers. This does not include media presence for its other bands and global campuses. Since the start of the twenty-first century, it has "planted campuses" (as the church calls its branches in a nod to corporate and university cultures) in most global cities. Many of the pastors in these campuses are locals who have studied at Hillsong College and have returned home. This is the case of Brazil as well, where the church established a campus in an upmarket neighborhood of São Paulo City in late 2016, after years of pleading by Brazilian fans of the church and its bands.

As Hillsong grew extraordinarily around the world and its style became a template to other churches in the United States (Bowler and Reagan 2014) and elsewhere—a process Martí (2017: 382) has called the "Hillsongization of Christianity"—scholars have analyzed different aspects of this phenomenon. Many have understandably focused on music since it is key to its sensational form and global expansion. Music meditates people's relationship with God, thus authenticating the church's spiritual authority (Abraham 2018; Evans 2017; Jennings 2014; Porter 2017; Riches 2010). Others have investigated Hillsong's strategic uses of branding and marketing and its engagement with consumer capitalism (Maddox 2012, 2013b; McIntyre 2007; Shanahan 2018; Wagner 2017, 2020; Yip 2015). Goh (2008) explored the megachurch's semiotics and spatial practices as media that materialize the Christian experience, while Connell (2005) sought to understand how its first location in Sydney's suburbia appealed to its young residents who lacked places to congregate. Some have investigated gender relations at the megachurch (Maddox 2013a, 2013b; Riches 2017). Wade and Hynes (2013: 173) have employed affect theory to understand how "Hillsong produces and mobilizes affect" to generate "subjects who are at once comfortable, enthusiastic and loyal." Miller (2015) investigated the history of Pentecostal Charismatic Christianities in Australia and why Hillsong and other local megachurches grew in the twenty-first century. More recently, Klaver (2021) has conducted fieldwork at Hillsong churches in Amsterdam and New York to investigate the role of global cities and mediatization of society in the ways in which Hillsong and Pentecostalism expand globally.

Grounded Imaginaries

Most research on Hillsong has been conducted in the Global North. And much focuses on the church as an institution. This book builds on this literature to consider the grounded, everyday imaginations of and experiences with Hillsong for youth hailing from the Global South. Hillsong has standardized and authorized sensational forms through which it spreads globally. However, Brazilian middle-class youth engage with Hillsong in particular ways because they have different dreams and aspirations from their peers in the Global North. This book follows this cohort as they dream of a life that can be "otherwise" (Willis 1990; Allen et al 2016; Hodkinson 2016)—where they are fluent in English, have friends from all over the world, and feel that they belong to a kind of Christianity that is modern, successful, sophisticated, ethical, and cool. We will see how they become fans of the megachurch and make efforts to travel to its headquarters in Australia. There, they learn to be modern autonomous subjects at church while transitioning to adulthood. As they frequently told me, they "learned a different way of doing church." We then follow them on their return and their (mostly unsuccessful) attempts to transform their own churches and their country in light of the Cool Christianity style they learned at Hillsong. Lastly, we explore the challenges Hillsong faced in establishing the São Paulo campus. While some aspects of its style were easily accepted and copied by other Brazilian churches (such as music and exciting services), its engagement with secular youth cultures, toleration of other religions, and more egalitarian power relations between members and pastors (at least by Brazilian standards) did not sit well with the Brazilian Pentecostal style.

The key questions this book poses are as follows: What is the role of affect and aesthetics in Hillsong's appeal? How does Pentecostalism assist young Brazilians spiritually and materially in their everyday lives as international students and migrants? What are the infrastructures that sustain the transnational Pentecostal field between the two countries, and thus afford Brazilians in Brazil a sense of "co-presence" (Madianou 2016) with Hillsong in Australia and its global community? What happens to their church adherence when they return to Brazil? And why are some Brazilian churches joining the Hillsong network, while others are copying Hillsong's Cool Christianity style of church buildings, services, music, clothing, social media use, and even its logo?

I argue that Hillsong offers an appealing space for young middle-class Brazilians to perform their faith in the postsecular age. This is so for several reasons. First, the Cool Christianity style adopted by Hillsong—with its high production values that communicate success, excitement, and modernity—generates particular affect (pride, desire, excitement, and pleasure) that plays an important role in how the megachurch is able to bind this cohort. By contrast, Brazilian churches are criticized for their poor aesthetics, lack of excellence and ethics, authoritarianism, and long "old-style" boring services that have little connection with their lives. Second, as a Seeker church, Hillsong focuses much less on spiritual battle, exorcism, and conservative values, and more on attracting people to church through informal, fun, and exciting services. Hillsong values inclusivity and tolerance of people's behaviors in hope that, as they go through the church's doors, the Holy Spirit will change them, and they will convert. As a result, in contrast to most Brazilian Pentecostal churches, churchgoers enjoy some personal freedom—they are allowed to dress as they please, listen to secular music, and participate in youth culture. My interlocutors also told me that Hillsong is less sexist than many Brazilian churches in the sense that women are able to become leaders.

Third, Hillsong relies on volunteers to support its services and a lot of its day-to-day management. While many former Hillsong College students and media stories have criticized this practice as exploitative (Frishberg 2020; French and Adler 2021), it gives young Brazilians a degree of autonomy they never had at their own churches. Volunteers are allowed to choose where they want to work, and later can become leaders in many areas of the church. As a consequence, young Brazilians feel much more invested in the church than in Brazil, where the church hierarchy is more rigid. As such, volunteering gives young people, who are on the brink of adulthood, tools to become adults and self-reflexive modern subjects (Giddens 1991). In interviews, they said how significant the volunteering experiences at the church have been in their lives. They learned punctuality, reliability, and excellence in their work practices, and how to become leaders in any area of work they chose.

Fourth, the Hillsong College appeals to middle-class Brazilian youth who can afford to take time out from their university studies. In addition to offering student visas, its focus on "leadership" and creative industries (dance, music, singing, live audio production, film and TV) rather than straight theology makes it exciting. Finally, Brazilians desire to join Hillsong church and College because of the cosmopolitan possibilities they afford them. As I have shown elsewhere (2006a, 2013, 2017b, 2020b), Brazilians rate highly ideas, practices, and commodities that come from the Global North, particularly if they are communicated in English. At Hillsong they are able to study in English, make friends from all over the world, and be part of global youth and celebrity cultures.

Hillsong not only gives middle-class Brazilians a home to practice their religion but also allows them to create an "alternative geography of belonging" (van de Kamp, 2017: 2) through which they are able to leave the country's peripheral position behind and feel they belong to the spiritual, aesthetic, and physical center of Christianity, as well as to the secular centers of world power because of its location in global cities such as Sydney, London, and New York. This alternative belonging is created through particular materialities and infrastructures—Hillsong's smart church buildings; its hip soundscapes; its pastors' dress style, books, and recorded preachings; the use of English language; global services and events; and the intense use of digital media, network programs, and teaching resources. Such aesthetic infrastructures allow Brazilians to achieve a sense of "co-presence" (Madianou 2016) with other congregants elsewhere in the world. It is through these materialities and standardized sensational forms that Hillsong's "Cool Christianity" circulates.

Multisited and Digital Ethnography

This book builds on the methods I employed on my previous monographs on religious globalization and transnationalism (2006a, 2017a)—multisited ethnography combined with analysis of traditional and digital media (websites, blogs, and social media). In doing so, I follow Coleman and Hackett (2015: 15) who have noted that because Pentecostalism is a global heterogeneous movement and it affects "local" cultures differently, it forces anthropologists "to consider using 'multi-sited' ethnography to capture the ways P/e often connects people from different parts of the world through use of mass media, religious imagination, and ritual events." Here, I tracked online and offline flows between Brazil and Australia in both directions, and also monitored other influences on the field, particularly those from the United States, a central node in an open-ended network of sites from which Pentecostal flows arrive in Brazil. Australian Pentecostalism is just the latest in a long line of influences in the Brazilian field. From its inception with Italian and Swedish missionaries who established the Christian Congregation and Assemblies of God, respectively, in the early twentieth century, Brazilian Pentecostalism has been heavily influenced by overseas Pentecostal cultures (Mariano 2014: 39–40). While foreign missionaries have continued to arrive in the country in larger numbers, Brazilians have started to travel to study in Bible colleges and participate in conferences overseas, mostly in the United States. The circulation of media, in the form of translated books, taped seminars, conferences, and other resources, and more recently, social media, has also contributed to the porosity of Brazilian Pentecostalism.

Certainly, the emergence of new media such as social networks sites, instant messaging, apps, webcam, texting, and email in conjunction with the creation of ever more powerful portable devices has revolutionized the ways in which people live and establish (transnational) relationships online and offline. Mediatization—as a means to keeping transnational relationships, by imagining and participating in a larger world—has become all-pervasive. Madianou and Miller (2012) have coined the concept of "polymedia" for this new environment where communication does not take place over a single technology but by choosing between and combining a variety of platforms. Moreover, polymedia also allows people to achieve a sense of "co-presence" (Madianou, 2016:1), an intense awareness of the lives of others "made possible through the affordances of ubiquitous media." While Madianou and Miller deploy the concepts of polymedia and co-presence to analyze transnational families, here I will show that they can be used with regard to members of religious communities, as this new digital environment allows them to participate in rituals and communicate with other members in real time.

The affordances of polymedia in creating a sense of co-presence became clear in the first year of the COVID-19 pandemic. When churches were closed in Australia to curb the spread of COVID-19 in mid-March 2020, the Hillsong headquarters in Australia, its overseas campuses and congregations, and my own fieldwork moved swiftly online. In many ways, COVID-19 has shed a new light on "immobile transnationalism," that is, the ways in which people are still connected when they are not traveling, previously studied by Levitt and Glick Schiller (2004) as those who stayed behind when family and friends migrated. The difference now is that we are all mostly immobile and transnational if we have access to the Internet. It is noteworthy that online and offline practices are complementary; they work in tandem, one reinforcing the other (Campbell 2012; Fewkes 2019). Thus, here I respond to Cool's (2012) call to scholars to investigate physical and virtual interactions as parts of the same social site, which she called "colocation." An advantage of following churches and congregants on digital media is that it allowed me to track interactions and influences on the field that reflect real-life situations as young participants were constantly both online and offline. It also expanded my understanding of the networks that comprised the field, something that I would have missed had I focused solely on the offline multisited interactions.

I conducted six years (2015–2020) of multisited ethnography (participant observation and interviews) in Australia and Brazil, as well as an analysis of the flows of people, ideas, practices, objects, images, and (old and digital) media between the two countries. After that, I continued to follow services online in Brazil and Sydney after COVID-19 made it difficult to travel and to join services, and to follow the media reports on the megachurch. In Sydney, I conducted participant observation at Hillsong city campus, and to a lesser extent, in two churches which follow a similar style to Hillsong—Australian megachurch C3, which also has branches in Brazil, and CJC, a Brazilian migrant church. I did so because young Brazilians strategically circulated among them, although Hillsong was their central focus. I participated in these churches' weekly services, fortnightly connect groups and annual conferences, and external activities such as parties and barbeques. At Hillsong, I also took its 10-week Alpha course together with a group of Brazilians. There we discussed basic tenets of Christianity and how they connect with our own lives. This was a good opportunity to better understand young Brazilians' values and whether they differed from what was explained to us during the course.

Moreover, I conducted open-ended interviews with the Hillsong City College Principal, a C3 College manager, and Alphacrucis College teachers (the official college of the Australian Christian Churches, previously known as AOG in Australia, where many Brazilians continue their theological education after studying at Hillsong College). I was interested in the challenges Brazilians faced as they encountered less-conservative theologies and social mores in these colleges and churches, and what impact these had on their beliefs and practices. I also interviewed young Brazilians who studied at these colleges, and those who participated in services and connect groups at these three churches. Interviews were focused on life histories spanning the reasons why they traveled to Australia, their conversion narratives, how they saw the role of Pentecostalism in their everyday lives as international students, and their "religious remittances," that is, their transnational connections with family, friends, and church pastors in Brazil.

In Brazil, I spent three periods of three to four months (in 2015, 2016, 2018) conducting fieldwork in São Paulo, Campinas, São Jose dos Campos, Curitiba, Belo Horizonte, Brasília, and Natal. In addition to the São Paulo Hillsong branch, I conducted participant observation and interviews at the churches that are part of the Hillsong Network and Family, and those whose pastors had traveled to Australia to participate in Hillsong, C3, and CJC conferences and services. I was interested in how these pastors made sense of their experiences in Australia, which features their churches had adopted or rejected from the Australian megachurch, how they saw the establishment of Hillsong in Brazil, the international church networks they were part of (including those that sent them teaching resources), and whether their vision for their own churches had similarities to how they perceived the Australian megachurches.

Furthermore, I interviewed Brazilians in the music industry who first introduced Hillsong United music into Brazil in order to find out how the culture industry was able to make Hillsong so famous at a time when Australia and its cultural products were virtually unknown. I also tracked and interviewed Brazilians who had returned home after being part of these churches' congregation and/or studying at their colleges in Australia. Some of them I had previously met and interviewed in Australia. I explored how they coped with the challenges of returning to their local churches, and whether and how they kept their links with their friends and churches in Australia. Here, their online and offline lives merged deeply, as they dealt with the difficulties of adapting to the homeland and nostalgia for Australia and their experiences at Hillsong. In total, I conducted 60 interviews. Interviewees were recruited through a snowballing method or people volunteered for interviews during participant observation. Interviews were conducted in Portuguese or English, depending on the interviewees' preferences (I am originally from Brazil and have lived in Australia for over 20 years); they were recorded, transcribed, and translated.

At the same time, I followed these churches and their congregations online on their social media accounts. Hillsong church engages intensely with social media: its pastors, bands, college, TV channel, and kids/youth/women's programs, as well as the church headquarters and each of the Australian and global branches, post multiple times a day on various media (Facebook, Instagram, Twitter). This gave me an appreciation for how content and styles traveled and were translated from the Hillsong headquarters to the Brazilian campus. It meant that I could observe followers in Brazil interacting with the local branch and watching streamed services and events from the headquarters in Sydney.

Learning Christianities

In writing this book, I had much to learn about Christianity. I was not brought up in a religious family. In fact, one could say that my family became anti-religious over time. The alliance between sectors of the Catholic Church and the 1964 military coup in Brazil, its staunch patriarchy, and the power it held over Brazilian society put my parents off it for good. I also studied in progressive schools, so my friends were not religious. Thus, I approached this study as I did previous research projects on Buddhism (Rocha 2006a; Rocha and Barker 2010) and spiritual healing (2017a) in that I had to learn not only how and why people lived their religions the way they did but also the tenets of their religions. Furthermore, while Buddhism and spiritual healing and the New Age movement were not controversial among my middle-class peers, since it is usually the middle classes in the West that have an interest in them, Pentecostalism is a different proposition.

In the now classical 1991 essay, anthropologist Susan Harding analyzed how the media, progressives, and also anthropologists constructed Christian fundamentalists in the United States as "the repugnant cultural other." As she researched them, Harding was constantly interrogated why she was doing so and whether she was a fundamentalist herself. The anthropology of Christianity (Cannell 2006; Coleman and Hackett 2015; Engelke and Robbins 2010; Robbins 2003, 2007, 2014) as a field of research has grown considerably in the past two decades as processes of globalization have accelerated, and now around 60% of the 2.5 billion Christians in the world live in the Global South. However, the historical anthropological engagement with Christianity and theology has been fraught as they have different "ethical orientations to the world" (Coleman 2015: 278). Indeed, Fenella Cannell (2006: 4) has posited that Christianity "was the repressed of anthropology over the period of formation of the discipline." Anthropology asserted its credentials as a rational and empirically based science; thus, it made an effort to differentiate itself from and reject Christian theology. In addition, the discipline originally focused on cultural difference, and Christianity was an integral part of Western culture. Accordingly, while anthropologists have perceived the study of other religions as part of the discipline's remit, this was not so in regard to Christianity. Furthermore, Christian missionaries trod the same territory as anthropologists as they did fieldwork in the peripheries of the world and had an impact on the local cultures. At the same time, Christians were powerful advocates for their anti-modern beliefs in the West. Given such tense history, Cannell (2006: 5) has exhorted anthropologists to "set aside the assumption that we know in advance what Christian experience, practice, or belief might be."

Like Harding (1991) and Cannell (2006) before him, anthropologist Simon Coleman (2015: 275) also felt the same pressure to explain to other scholars why he was "studying such crap" when he researched Pentecostalism and Prosperity Gospel in Sweden. In a 2015 article, he used this constant questioning to discuss anthropologists' ethical practices regarding conservative Christians (2015: 277). Building on Harding's article, he asked whether the two ethical positions that Harding referred to—(1) "engagement as opposition," that is, subscribing to a project of political opposition through a complex and nuanced understanding of the Other; and (2) the self-reflexivity of anthropologists as they "see aspects of the self in the Other"—can be held by the same scholar. He argued for a reflection on the borders as productive sites to think of ethical engagements with the Other. Coleman showed that Christians are interested not only in engaging with other cultures in an effort to convert them. More importantly, as they produce borders between themselves and nonbelievers, they are consolidating and performing their own identity as Christians. As such, these borderlands are constantly produced and reproduced. Thus, Coleman (2015: 295) cautions anthropologists not to accept this totalizing dichotomy that constructs fundamentalist Christians as a homogeneous community, if we want to:

> produce nuanced ethnography or even effective activism. . . . Ironically, such an approach would be to accede to the power of Pentecostal language, while also deploying an older anthropological language of encompassing whole peoples within notions of a single "culture."

He suggests that ethnography is more productive if it holds a double position of engagement and skepticism. At any rate, Coleman notes that there are gaps in the borderlands created by Pentecostals. Some may be dogmatic, but others venture into very diverse worlds. This is true of the megachurch Hillsong and its followers, as we will see in this book. In fact, it is Hillsong's engagement with the secular world (through branding, social media, fashion, music, etc.), and opening up to contemporary social movements such as Black Lives Matter and the LGBTQI+ communities that have attracted many middle-class young Brazilians.

Following Coleman's admonition, here I engage with these young Christians in what I hope is a productive way. For instance, as part of the Brazilian middle class, I could easily relate to my interlocutors' aspiration to live in the Global North, learn English, and have a life that could be otherwise. I was able to empathize with young Brazilians as they dealt with culture shock while endeavoring to put down roots and become citizens in Australia. Their struggles as they transitioned to adulthood in a new land reminded me of my own struggles when I left Brazil on my own for the first time as a 17-year-old to study in the United States. In addition, their desire for a better world in which all peoples were offered love and respect, and where hierarchy was not so prominent as in Brazil, also struck a chord. Equally, my research on spirituality and the New Age prepared me to appreciate their beliefs that God had prepared a life path for them; that He watched over and protected them at all times; and that they were able to receive the Holy Spirit in their own bodies and speak in tongues. Many of the people I engaged with for my previous book on followers of the Brazilian faith healer John of God (2017a) also thought the God/the Universe/spirits of light were protecting them and showing them the right path in life. They affirmed that they received spiritual messages from their higher self or spiritual entities, and some were mediums for these entities and spoke in their voices. I would not say that these life-worlds are the same, of course. But they facilitated the "negotiation of a multiplicity of ethical positions" (Coleman 2015: 277) between myself as an anthropologist and the community I studied, between engagement and skepticism. While I was able to engage with some aspects mentioned earlier, as a secular and progressive anthropologist, I have been taken aback by some of the community's values and practices, such as gender roles and their missionary work. I still remember revulsion on hearing an Elder of one of the churches in which I conducted research explaining to me how proud he was of having "planted" many churches among Indigenous peoples in the Global South. The horror of the Yanomami genocide in the Amazon, perpetrated by miners and missionaries supported by the Bolsonaro government (Pacheco 2023), came to light some years after this interview, but many fellow anthropologists, friends, and the media (Angelo 2017) knew of similar issues with other Indigenous groups before that.

Hence, I understand why my friends and the media in Australia and Brazil have a negative perception of Pentecostals as much as I understand why and how young people are attracted to megachurches like Hillsong and C3, and migrants bounce between smaller migrant churches and these megachurches. It is my hope that this ethnography helps the reader hold a position between engagement and skepticism as well.

Book Structure

Although the sequence of chapters seems to suggest a linear progression in the flows of Pentecostalism between Australia and Brazil, in fact, the flows examined here are circular and coeval. Hillsong's Cool Christianity is constantly moving in and out of Brazil and Australia through music, digital media, material culture, international visiting pastors to the São Paulo branches, and Brazilians returning from Hillsong Australia (and from other branches in the United Kingdom, Europe, and the United States). At the same time, Brazilians in Australia are always in touch with family, friends, and their own churches in Brazil, sending them religious remittances and inspiring others to follow in their footsteps. I chose to order the chapters as a journey from Brazil to Australia and back simply to help readers make sense of this complex assemblage of intersecting flows.

In Chapter 1, I set the context for this book by investigating Hillsong's adoption of "Cool Christianity" as a "sensational form" (Meyer 2009, 2010b) that binds particularly young people as they transition into adulthood. I focus on how religious aesthetics, branding, and celebrity culture play an important role in community creation and identity formation for young people. I argue that, for young middle-class Brazilians, Cool Christianity generates a sense of belonging not only to the global Christianity community (as it is usual for Christians) but also to a cosmopolitan community based in the Global North. This chapter also shows how this cohort deploys their privilege of class and race through affect as they reject the Pentecostalism of poor "backward" Brazilians. As such, this chapter sets the scene for us to understand how social class, affect, and a global power-geometry (Massey 1993) have an important role to play in choice of church style.

Chapter 2 investigates the ways in which Cool Christianity and Hillsong have arrived in Brazil via US popular culture and Christian music. It explores how young Brazilians become fans of Hillsong's worship bands and the megachurch starting in the 1990s. It shows how this fandom expanded to and intertwined with an imaginary of Australia, where the headquarters of the band and megachurch are located. Hillsong and Australia then become places and forms of authority—they exert power and offer hope and optimism as paths to change their lives. This prompts young middle-class Brazilians to travel to Australia to join Hillsong services, conferences, and its worship bands and enroll at Hillsong College. I argue that this relationship of fandom with Hillsong and Australia makes Brazilians yearn to remake Brazilian churches and Brazil in their image.

In Chapter 3, I explore the role of Pentecostalism in the lives of the middle-class Brazilian students who have traveled to Australia and joined Pentecostal churches. There, Brazilian students lead precarious lives. They are transitioning into adulthood and living away from the homeland and without their families for the first time. In addition, they experience downward mobility and are at the mercy of constant changes in the Australian migration policy. Here, I open my focus of analysis to other two churches that adopt similar aesthetic formation to Hillsong's—C3 and CJC, an Australian megachurch and a Brazilian church, respectively—as many Brazilians strategically circulate between these and Hillsong to find a home away from home. I argue that Pentecostalism offers them a framework to make sense of their student migration journey. I show that Brazilian students narrate the governance of mobility (visas, jobs, English language courses, sponsorships for permanent residency) in the language of religion, as exemplifying God's work in their lives. For them, God determines whether they can stay or must return to Brazil. In their lack of control regarding their stay, citizenship in the Kingdom of God gives them a more significant sense of belonging than that of the Australian nation.

In Chapter 4, I discuss young Brazilians' experiences at Hillsong College. I consider the powerful affective and transformational experiences of youth enrolled and housed at Hillsong College and who arrive alone in Sydney. I am interested in how they affectively embed their subjectivity within the church and come to think of their experience of studying and serving full time (thus donating substantial time and energy to the church) as "living the dream." I argue that there are many reasons for them to feel so enthusiastic about the college—its focus on leadership and teaching of punctuality, reliability, autonomy, and excellence; the more egalitarian relationships with pastors and worship leaders; opportunities to make friends with other students from all over the world; and their own subjectivity becoming associated with the church (and brand) they loved. Overall, the Hillsong College elicited deeply affective responses from Brazilian students.

Chapter 5 explores significant infrastructures—smart church buildings and their hip soundscapes, digital media, Hillsong network and teaching programs, and a Brazilian Christian travel agency—that allow Hillsong to expand into Brazil. Importantly, such infrastructures allow people to achieve a sense of "co-presence" (Madianou 2016) with other congregants elsewhere in the world. This was particularly apparent when Hillsong's services and activities went online due to the COVID-19 pandemic. This chapter shows that these infrastructures comprise an architecture through which Hillsong's Cool Christianity circulates. It argues that these infrastructures connect with followers through affect (pride, desire, excitement) as they communicate success, excitement, modernity, and cosmopolitanism to young middle-class Brazilians who aspire to break with the local conservative Pentecostalism that caters to the poor. As such, here I call for a focus on human and non-human actors and infrastructures that move religion across borders, with special attention to how imagination and power differentials shape mobility and immobility.

Chapter 6 follows those Brazilians who have joined Hillsong church and College and the Brazilian CJC in Australia on their return home. I show the difficulties they face in reinserting themselves in their old churches due to different styles of service, church management, and culture. As a consequence, the majority of them leave their old churches and start "church-hopping" in search of churches whose aesthetics styles and values are similar to the ones they learned in Australia. Many never find them and remain churchless. Importantly, their experience in Australia gave them a cosmopolitan outlook on life—all of them kept close contact with their peers in Australia, be they pastors, college teachers, fellow congregants, or other students, and traveled to visit them. Hillsong had become so important in their lives that once the church established a campus in São Paulo in 2016, some of them left jobs and family behind in other parts of Brazil to serve at the church.

In the final chapter, I investigate the establishment of Hillsong São Paulo and how the Hillsong's Cool Christianity style spreads in the country, both online and offline. I am interested in how the challenges the megachurch faced in Brazil bring to the fore not only Hillsong's own problems caused by its global expansion through branding and fandom. They also show the inherent tensions that exist when a global network takes root locally. I contend that as a megachurch with branches in many countries which have different

Pentecostal cultures, the Hillsong aesthetic style needs to be fine-tuned—inclusive enough to be relevant to youth but also conservative enough to allow for its global expansion. Moreover, I contend that the Hillsong's Cool Christianity style is able to flourish in the country and be adopted (and adapted) by other churches because its focus on excellence, excitement, celebrity culture, use of English language, and high production values fit well the imaginary that Brazilians have of the Global North.

In the Conclusion, I consider how the narratives of abuse at Hillsong played out in Brazil in comparison to Australia and the United States. I argue that Brazil (and potentially other countries in the Global South) has been shielded from this turbulent period because Hillsong's appeal there—a focus on grace and love rather than judgment; opportunities to become cosmopolitan, learn English, and attain work skills; and an alternative geography of belonging—has endured. Accordingly, this book shows that the local is key to religious (im)mobility. The social conditions of the local generate affective imaginaries of other places and propel people to action. This could be in the form of fandom, (imaginary or actual) travel, and adoption of new sensational forms from elsewhere. By focusing on how Hillsong's Cool Christian style spreads in Brazil through middle-class aspiration for cosmopolitanism, this volume shows how the work of imagination is mediated by power asymmetries between the Global North and South.

1
Cool Christianity

> Born in Australia, it's now where New York's trendy Gen-Y crowd spend their Sunday mornings. But for ye of little faith, it's hard to make sense of Hillsong. Is it legit? Is it a hipster cult? And why's everyone wearing Saint Laurent? We join the flock to find out if Christianity can be this cool and still be Christian.
> —Brodesser-Akner, *GQ Magazine*, 2016

Until late 2020, when Carl Lentz, the celebrity NYC Hillsong Lead Pastor, was fired for sexual and financial misconduct, American celebrities and the "cool kids" were flocking to Hillsong NYC. Hot on their heels, the secular media sent reporters to understand why celebrities and cool youngsters were going to Hillsong. Wasn't church something just for the old and suburban? Report after report mentioned Justin Bieber and other celebrity followers, and described Hillsong services' clubbing style, excellent production values, good music, and great vibe. Fashion was also always prominent in these reports, as in the *GQ Magazine* article in the epigraph. *Harper's Bazaar* titled its story, "Is This the Most Fashionable Church Ever? A writer goes inside Hillsong—a spiritual refuge for models, editors and Justin Bieber" (Marcus 2015). *Women's Wear Daily* (*WWD*), a fashion-industry trade journal, observed, "'This' is Lentz's uniform: a Saint Laurent leather jacket, ripped jeans and a low-cut T-shirt. It's far from what one might expect a pastor to wear, but Lentz is not a 'normal' pastor. . . . He's a cool pastor" (Tietjen 2017). Even the *New York Times*, while reviewing Lentz's book, focused on what he was wearing: "Mr. Lentz appeared onstage wearing hipster aviator glasses, tight black pants and a black blazer draped open over a low-cut black T-shirt" (Harris 2017). Another journalist summarized the situation with these words: "Fashion is at the forefront of Christianity's image rehab" (Laneri 2019).

While fashion and celebrities occupied center stage at Hillsong New York since consumer capitalism and celebrity culture are much more advanced in the United States, they are also visible across the global Hillsong network. The megachurch pastors are well-known for having a cool look: undercut hairstyle, fedora hats, leather jackets, white T-shirts, sometimes a flannel shirt tied to the waist (a remnant of the working-class dress code from Sydney's Western suburbs where the church originated), skinny ripped jeans, and leather boots or white sneakers. Hillsong's new Global Pastor, Phil Dooley, in his late forties, always wears a woolen beanie over his long wavy blond hair, even in summer. Presumably, it signals his love of surfing. In his forties, Chris Mendez, the Lead Pastor for South America, also follows Hillsong's "look book" of black leather jacket, white T-shirt, and skinny jeans. Youngsters in congregation strive to mirror their pastors. The same reporter for *GQ Magazine* (Brodesser-Akner 2016) noted that pastors are becoming influencers:

> [The hat] is what they're all wearing, like a badge or a uniform. The hat first appeared five or six years ago when Pastor Joel wore it. In his American press clippings, which begin around 2010, the year Pastor Joel (Houston) and Pastor Carl (Lentz) established Hillsong's first American branch, Pastor Joel is basically never not with the hat. And at some point, you have to acknowledge that a large group of people in New York City adopting the fashiony [sic] choices of their spiritual leaders is a peculiar thing, but also an indication that whatever these leaders are doing, they are doing it very effectively. They are leading. They are influencing.

Over the years, other churches have also adopted these Hillsong features. A young Brazilian, who had returned from studying in Australia when I spoke to him, noted a similar phenomenon in Brazil:

> If you go to certain churches here in Brazil, people dress like Australians. Their trousers are this low ... they wear a long necklace, a long T-shirt, or a loose flannel shirt. Sometimes they put on that hat, as if we were in a church in Australia. The trend is to be just like them.

Fashion and celebrity culture are the hallmarks of what can be called "Cool Christianity" or "Hipster Christianity" (McCracken 2010; Sanders 2014; Sandler 2006). This style of Christianity can be traced to the Jesus People movement of the late 1960s, itself a merger of counterculture, communalism, and evangelical orthodoxy (Eskridge 2013; Luhrmann 2012; Schäfer 2020). According to Schäfer (2020: 931):

> Pentecostal and charismatic traditions within evangelicalism were particularly successful in attracting countercultural converts. Rather than stressing doctrinal purity and literalism, they emphasized the personal, therapeutic, and emotional dimensions of the faith. Practices gleaned from Christian primitivism, such as faith healing, laying on of hands, speaking in tongues, and getting filled with the Holy Spirit, appealed to a generation reared in "situation ethics" and "make love not war" rhetoric. Pentecostal ritual resolved the contradiction between fundamentalist absolutes and countercultural permissiveness in the merger of spiritual fervor and moral rigidity. It offered strict normative guidance and moral absolutes based on biblical authority while validating hippie ecstasy, intuited knowledge, and communal relationships.

Although the Jesus People movement died down by the end of the 1970s, its legacy lived on. Many of the characteristics of the Pentecostal and Charismatic Christianity that derived from their involvement with the counterculture—its music and worship style, therapeutic approach, and engagement with youth and popular cultures—continued to assist their growth among young, middle-class, university graduates (Eskridge 2013; Luhrmann 2012; Schäfer 2020). As the number of people ticking "no religion" in censuses increased in many parts of the world in the past decades (Halafoff et al. 2020; Lipcka 2015; Pew Research Center 2021),[1] Pentecostal and Charismatic churches engaged more closely with contemporary youth and popular cultures in an effort to become relevant to young people. As I mentioned in the Introduction, Cool churches blur the sacred and secular by adopting youth styles, marketing and business strategies, and new technologies—from fashion trends to pop music, social media, cool graphic design, creative industries, and services that resemble clubbing. Whether churches should be stylized as "cool" or "hipster" has been contested and the subject of endless discussions among Christian pastors and congregations for the past two decades, as we will see later in this chapter.

Scholars have analyzed the ways in which Christianity has been expanding into youth and popular cultures as a phenomenon pertaining to independent Pentecostal megachurches (Coleman and Chattoo 2020; Johnson 2018;

Klaver 2015b; Sanders 2014; Sargeant 2000). However, elsewhere (Rocha 2021) I demonstrated that this repackaged Christianity directed at middle-class youth is also produced by secular celebrities, the fashion industry, and young Christian entrepreneurs who see their commodities as part of the Great Commission. I argued that this assemblage of different actors generates a "Fashion-Celebrity-Megachurch" industrial complex. The fashion industry and Christian designers create goods and styles that are given to celebrities (secular singers and actors, as well as megachurch pastors and musicians) who endorse them. Such endorsement increases their sales, and for Christian entrepreneurs, their opportunities for evangelizing. As the WWD reporter explained: "He [Carl Lentz] gets most of his clothes—including the Rolex on his wrist—for free because he has generous friends, some of whom happen to be designers, like Jerry Lorenzo of Fear of God [label]"[2] (Tietjen 2017). Similarly, secular celebrities are creating Christian-inspired songs, concerts, and designer clothes that help disseminate Cool Christianity. For instance, Kanye West presented his "Sunday Services" at the Coachella Festival in 2019. There, in addition to singing his Christian songs along with his gospel choir, he launched a new line of streetwear called "Yeezy Sunday Service." This merchandise was sold in a pop-up tent called literally "Church Clothes." Among other items, there were sweatshirts emblazoned with the words "Holy Spirit" and socks with the words "Church Socks" and "Jesus Walks." Later that same year, West released his highly anticipated album *Jesus Is King* and "dropped" an eponymous line of streetwear. Soon after, secular celebrities, such as James Corden, hosted West and his choir on their TV shows. Christians also disseminated the album on social media. At Coachella and at the launch of his new album, spectacle, fashion, celebrity youth cultures, Christianity, and capitalism were tangled in a powerful assemblage, creating a particular aesthetic, sensorial experience of Christianity that can be consumed, enjoyed, and worn. Importantly, this aesthetic experience shapes how these actors understand themselves and generates a sense of belonging to a community of fans and consumers of Cool Christianity.

Hillsong has also been involved in this powerful assemblage. It sells its streetwear line and other accessories at the church shops, in its conferences, online, and until early 2022 when Senior Global Pastors Brian and Bobby Houston were fired, through its "Team Box." Like other secular subscriptions boxes, Hillsong's Team Box is an actual box containing church branded clothing, accessories, music CDs, stickers, pastors' books, and encouraging messages that are "curated" monthly and sold online. The Team Box is supposed to "inspire" consumers to connect with and feel the presence of God in their lives, as well as start conversations about Him. I suggest that the box has an element of surprise, excitement, gift giving, and community building (hence the name "Team" Box). Many Hillsong young followers posted video clips on YouTube of opening their boxes and displaying their excitement by showing the audience each item. Here we can see again Hillsong's engagement with contemporary themes that are dear to young people—fame through social media, consumption, and fashion, all bundled in Cool Christianity. Christian designers' labels, Kanye West's clothes and music, and Hillsong's merchandise create emotional bonds and a common aesthetic vocabulary among consumers. They guide a common orientation to the world.

In this chapter, I analyze Hillsong's "Cool Christianity" as a "sensational form" (Meyer 2009, 2010b) that binds particularly young people as they transition into adulthood. I focus on how aesthetics, branding, and celebrity culture play an important role in community creation and identity formation for them. I argue that, for young, middle-class Brazilians, Cool Christianity generates a sense of belonging not only to global Christianity (as it is usual for Christians) but to a cosmopolitan community based in the Global North. I contend that this cohort associates Cool Christianity with modernity, while rejecting Brazilian Pentecostalism because they associate it with poor "backward" Brazilians and their aesthetics. As such, this chapter sets the scene for us to understand how social class and a global power geometry (Massey 1993) have an important role to play in choice of church style.

Aesthetics of Religion

The scholarship on aesthetics and its connection to religion has grown considerably since the 1990s (Arweck and Keenan 2016; Grieser and Johnston 2017; Martin 2006; Meyer 2009, 2010b; Meyer and Verrips 2008; Vásquez 2011). These scholars understand religion as a practice of mediation that uses the senses, objects, sounds, images, and rituals to engage with the divine. As I briefly mentioned in the Introduction, following this work, I use aesthetics in the broader sense of *aisthesis*, a concept coined by Aristotle to refer to *bodily sensations and knowledge* that help us make sense of ourselves and the world. In this context, the field of aesthetics of religion focuses on the intersection of affect, sensoria, culture, and society. As Grieser and

Johnston (2017: 2) noted, "Aesthetics of Religion focuses on understanding the interplay between sensory, cognitive and socio-cultural aspects of world-construction, and the role of religion within this dynamic." Using the concept of *aesthetics/aisthesis* to study the appeal of Pentecostalism is fitting because, in this form of Christianity, the body and its senses take central stage in how people understand their worlds. It is in people's bodies that the Holy Spirit is made present in their lives, be it through ecstatic experiences, glossolalia, healings, intuitive messages, and prophecy. Hence the fundamental role of music and spectacle as media that make the transcendent immanent.

Thus, here I am not using aesthetics in the sense of a disinterested appreciation of beauty and the sublime, a much later and narrower association advocated by Kant. According to Meyer and Verrips (2008: 23–24), this "bodiless and dematerialized" approach to aesthetics differentiated between mind and body, high and low (mass-produced) art, and art and religion. These binary schemes are hierarchical, in that the first term of the pair is seen as superior to the other. The scholarship of material religion has shown that, in fact, media is inherent to religion as "God . . . needs to be present to believers in some way" (Meyer 2010b: 748). The downplaying of forms, objects, images, and bodily sensations in the study of religion is due to a Protestant bias that saw religion as pertinent to the mind, interiority, and belief. In this context, Protestant Europe constructed belief as a universal category in all religions because of its centrality in Christianity. Meyer and Houtman (2012: 2) posited that:

> Instead of being a universal disposition that, as it were, naturally forms the defining characteristic of religion, "belief" has been "universalized" through scientific, religious, and political practices, such as evolutionary schemes, Christian missionization, and colonial governance.

Historically, scholars of religion have adopted this emic Protestant understanding of religion. Meyer (2010b: 744–746, 749) has shown that Weber was following the evolutionary scheme of the Enlightenment when he differentiated magical religions (those which use rituals, images, objects, etc., such as Catholicism and Indigenous religions) from salvation religions (those which have favored pure meaning, such as Protestantism) and argued for the superiority of the latter. She (2010: 746) notes that "Weber's narrow understanding of and dismissive attitude toward aesthetics, and the privileging of content and meaning above form" still forms the bases of academic work on religion. Scholars of material religion do not wish to dismiss belief, but to decenter it in the social scientific study of religion. As much as belief is part of religion—as "an expectation of the way one's world works" (Meyer et al. 2010: 209)—so, too, are things, shrines, practices, clothes, sensations, bodies, places, and rituals. Accordingly, these scholars seek to understand how these assemblages of subjects and objects coexist and co-constitute one another and are sensitive to regimes of power.

This volume follows this research program. In particular, it draws on Meyer's two interlinked concepts of style and sensational forms. For Meyer (2009: 10–11):

> Style is at the core of religious aesthetics exactly because the adoption of a shared style is central to processes of subjectivation, in that style involves particular techniques of the self and the body that modulate . . . persons into a socio-religious formation. Operating as a marker of distinction . . . , style is central to the making of religious and other kinds of communities.

Over time, shared aesthetic styles—as a way of connecting to others and the transcendental—are sanctioned as truthful and become fixed. They perform boundary work, marking insiders (who are cognizant of this style, language, practices, artifacts, and worldviews) from outsiders. In order to persuade subjects of their validity, they appeal to them emotionally and through their bodily senses. Meyer calls these religious repertoires "sensational forms." For Meyer (2009: 14):

> [Sensational forms] are relatively fixed, authorized modes of invoking and organizing access to the transcendental, thereby creating and sustaining links between believers in the context of particular religious power structures. Sensational forms shape both religious content (beliefs, doctrines, sets of symbols) and norms. These forms are transmitted and shared; they involve religious practitioners in particular practices of worship and play a central role in modulating them as religious moral subjects.

New or unauthorized sensational forms, such as Cool Christianity, are contested and need to be negotiated with established religious aesthetic styles. Importantly, as we will see in this volume, Meyer (2011: 33–34) notes that negotiations about new sensational forms are central to religious transformation and that new media are not simply available as neutral technologies but convey particular visions of the world. This pertains to Cool Christianity. Rather than just a contemporary form to an ancient message, as Hillsong pastors argue, this new sensational form brings with it different norms, ideas of morality, images, and how people relate to Christianity.

Significantly, "a shared religious style—materializing in, for example, collective prayer, a shared corpus of songs, images, and modes of looking, symbols and rituals, but also a similar clothing style and material culture—makes people feel at home" (Meyer and Verrips 2008: 28). This is of particular importance for the argument of this book, that is, that Hillsong's Cool Christian style, not only shapes the subjectivity and aspirations of young middle-class Brazilians but also helps them find a home in the Global North.

Consumer Culture, Branding, Style, and Identity

How can we understand the appeal of Cool Christianity to young people? In the introduction to their book, *Religion and Consumer Society: Brands, Consumers and Marketing*, Gauthier et al. (2013) investigate how consumption and the hypermediatization[3] of culture have become hallmarks of late modern societies and drivers of globalization. Following Bauman (2008), they note that in consumer culture, not only does the market organize social relations but also permeates them to such an extent that society's dominant values derive from it. In this culture, the self (as other areas of social life such as social relations, values, and norms) increasingly becomes a commodity—it needs to be styled, branded, and promoted in "the marketplace of life" (Gauthier et al. 2013: 3). As individuals produce their commodified selves, they tie their choices in consumption—their curated style—to their identity. Importantly, more than satisfying needs, consumer goods "are markers of social relations and socially constructed meanings. Goods are the visible part of culture, and it is through their exchange that social life is made to exist" (Gauthier et al. 2013: 11). In other words, consumption is embedded in a web of social relations and practices. What one consumes not only conveys one's identity, lifestyle, and values but also is meaningful to and establishes connections with one's community and to (now global) society. The market is thus profoundly social.

In *The Conquest of Cool*, Frank (1997) has demonstrated the historical process of how this came about. He argued that AdMen in New York's

Madison Ave co-opted and associated the idea of "cool" or "hip," derived from countercultural youth movements, to consumerism in the 1960s. By doing so, the advertising industry broadened the appeal of cool to society at large. Thus, consuming cool grew into identity creation, personal freedom, nonconformism, and the twin processes of group formation and distinction from "non-cool" others. According to him (1997: 26), "What happened in the sixties is that hip [or cool] became central to the way capitalism understood itself and explained itself to the public." Writing on cool and politics in the United Kingdom, Pountain and Robins (2000: 12) noted:

> Far from being the pose of a tiny minority in revolt against "square" life, by the 1990s cool has become the majority attitude among young people (and more to the point, among those who want to sell things to them). Given a complete loss of faith in radical political alternatives, cool is now primarily about consumption.

Scholars researching youth cultures have shown how the process of consumption of a style as self- and community-making is significant to young people. In his classic work on youth subcultures and style, Hebdige ([1979] 2002: 101) saw style as ensembles of "dress, dance, argot, music, etc." that confer identity to young members of a subculture. Like his University of Birmingham's Centre for Contemporary Cultural Studies colleagues, he was interested in studying how working-class (male) youth used style to construct spectacular subcultures as "intentional communication," and a way of resisting and coping with structural social oppression. Hebdige ([1979] 2002: 101) noted that:

> intentional communication . . . [is]—a visible construction, a loaded choice. It directs attention to itself; it gives itself to be read. This is what distinguishes the visual ensembles of spectacular subcultures from those favoured in the surrounding culture(s). They are obviously fabricated.

By contrast, middle-class Cool Christianity is about the opposite process. This is a minority culture endeavoring to become mainstream. Rather than resisting by being spectacular, Cool Christianity is about fitting in, becoming invisible among other secular youth so that they can engage with them. Their religious aesthetic style is then about invisibility but for a few items in the ensemble that are clearly marked as Christian—be they lyrics, tattoos, church-branded clothes and accessories that display a Christian slogan—as a way to assert identity or start a conversation with others about Christianity. As Sandler (2006: 86) notes, it is about "relatability." According to her (2006: 6, my italics):

> This Evangelical movement isn't just about internally held principles, it's a matter of *lifestyle*. Young Evangelicals look so similar to denizens of every other strain of youth culture that, aside from their religious tattoos, the difference between them and the unsaved is invisible.

More recently, scholars of youth studies and youth transitions have shown that consumption offers youth the raw materials to negotiate meaning and imaginings of a life that can be "otherwise" (Willis 1990; Allen et al. 2016; Hodkinson 2016). While most people choose clothing, accessories, and other forms of body decoration to construct their style, for young people such style "offers a means . . . to explore and perform identity within a transitory, insecure period of the life course" (Hodkinson 2016: 266).

In addition to creating style, brands have an important role in the work of self-making. Gauthier et al. (2013: 12) use Marcel Mauss's concept of "total social fact" to posit that brands "resonate throughout the social." They (2013: 13) write:

> As indicators of lifestyles (a certain pattern of values, aesthetics, ethics, ideals, and so on), brands are recognisable symbols around which social relations and communities coalesce. An important aspect of this type of identity production is that it must be expressed in order to be warranted and recognised by others, which the brand allows for.

Significantly, brands are not about the goods per se, but about creating a close association between goods and feelings, sensations, experiences, imagination, aspirations, and social relations. In this light, goods are dependent on the brands and not the other way around. Religious brands have the added task of "invoking and organizing access to the transcendental" (Meyer 2009: 14). In this light, we can think of "experiential religious brands" as sensational forms, as Wagner (2017: 263) suggested. In his study of Hillsong in London, Wagner (2020) has explored the role of branding in how the megachurch engages with the congregation. He (2020: 4, my italics) argues that "Hillsong is a *lifestyle brand* that is inseparable from the economic, social, and cultural value(s) that define both consumer culture and evangelical Christian culture." As a brand, it uses marketing techniques to connect with consumers through emotion. For Wagner (2020: 5, 51), the various ways in which the megachurch connects with its followers (through music, celebrity pastors and worship leaders, services, merchandise, logos, books, buildings, online, etc.) constitute an "ecosystem of branded media" that "adds value" to the experiences of its followers. Similar to Meyer's observation that sensational forms must become valid for religious communities, Wagner (2020: 92–93) notes that while the megachurch engages in branding, celebrity culture, and marketing, it seeks its authenticity in its religious power:

> The authenticity of Hillsong's worship leaders and songwriters is in their personal relationships with God. Their songs are understood as authentic expressions of this relationship and because the songwriters are also church members, are as such understood to be reflective of the church as a whole. The church, its values, its music, and its musicians are all parts of the gestalt of the Hillsong brand.

Two aspects of Wagner's analysis are significant for this book. First is the approach to Hillsong as a lifestyle brand that engages with all aspects of people's lives through an "ecosystem of branded media." In the following chapters we will see up close how these media—that draw on the larger sensational form of Cool Christianity—invoke young Brazilians' affect, imagination, and aspiration for a cosmopolitan life where they are interpellated as modern, autonomous subjects. Second, like Wagner, I also found that Hillsong faced a conundrum in its engagement with the business world's strategies of marketing, branding, and consumption, while striving to keep its spiritual authenticity. I now turn to another aspect of how Hillsong as a Cool Church blurs the boundaries between Christianity and the secular world of entertainment and spectacle to appeal to young people.

Celebrity Culture and Celebrity Pastors

Like other megachurches, Hillsong engages deeply with celebrity culture. Its pastors and worship leaders have become famous, both offline (through services, global conferences, books, jet-setting around the world to preach and play at Hillsong branches and other churches as well as concerts in large venues) and online (through virtual services, social media, the Hillsong TV channel, etc.). Celebrity culture comprises two processes which are deeply entangled with mediatization (traditionally through mass media but more recently through the Internet and social/interactive media). The first process, celebritization (Boykoff and Goodman 2009), has to do with the ways in which celebrity culture—in tandem with mediatization, self-reflexivity, individualization, commodification, and consumerism—has become an integral part of late modernity. The second process, celebrification (Gamson 1994; Turner 2006), addresses the transformation of individuals into celebrities. While in the twentieth century the film and TV industries built up and controlled their celebrity stars, in the twenty-first century, social media allows for ordinary people to become instant celebrities through self-commodification—curating their own style, their own branding, and promoting themselves. This is clear in the new generation of "influencers" and "YouTubers" who promote and market themselves.

Commodification is central in both processes of celebritization and celebrification: "stars are manufactured by the celebrity industry and produce and help to sell other commodities" (Driessens 2012: 643). Moseley (2005: 6) has investigated the ways in which fashion, celebrity cultures, and consumers are entangled. For her, commodities endorsed by celebrities work as connectors between celebrities and consumers:

> On the one hand [fashion] is separating and defining; fashion and dress, in relation to stars, can become the supreme marker of their identity—indeed the uniqueness of their persona. It can make them special, unreachable and untouchable. At the same time, however, dress and fashion are also part of the connective tissue of the social, allowing us to make judgments—even sartorial choices—based upon our ability to read their articulations in relation to that identity.

In other words, celebrities are at the same time ordinary like us and special and unreachable. It is through modeling us in them and consuming what they consume that we connect to them and create our style and identity. This is why the dress or a style worn by an English Royal or by an actor in a Netflix series may become high-street bestsellers.[4] Aware of this, as we saw earlier, the fashion industry often works closely with celebrities (including celebrity pastors), gifting them their goods hoping that, as they wear them, they will increase their sales.

This tension that celebrities navigate between being ordinary and extraordinary has increased with stars' adoption of social media as a way of promoting themselves and connecting with their fans. Valentinsson (2020: 5) has noted that, because celebrities post casual (though heavily curated) pictures of their everyday lives, fans on the "Instagram feed experience a heightened sense of closeness and familiarity with stars and their legitimately authentic 'voice.'" Authenticity then is associated with the performance of mundanity. The dot.com era concept of "prosumption" (an amalgamation of production and consumption) is helpful here. Dawson (2013: 137–138) uses this term to account for the double process of commodification of the self as consumption in late modernity. In prosumption, "commodity value is both extracted and generated at one and the same time . . . maximizing profit" (2013: 137). For Dawson, prosumption is illustrated by the ways in which people harness creative energy by producing and consuming content from social media such as Facebook, Instagram, and YouTube. It is in the collapsing of two processes that the new celebrity culture emerges.

This is the same double process by which megachurch pastors become celebrities through their intense use of (social) media. On any given day, one can find Hillsong pastors' posts on every social media platform. In addition to some preaching and words of encouragement, these posts show pastors on everyday pursuits: on vacations, in their swimming suits at the beach, at the gym, out and about with their families, having a cup of coffee in the local café, and hanging out with celebrities and fashion models. Hillsong pastors are "pastorpreneurs" (Jackson 2003; Twitchell 2007; Klaver 2021), in that they grow their church by employing "entrepreneurial strategies combining elements from consumer culture and popular culture in packaging and distributing their message" (Rakow 2015: 216). For instance, in her *The Preacher's Wife*, Bowler (2019: 184) has shown that celebrity wives of megachurch pastors hired "professional social media companies to take their content (bible studies, books, and blogs) to create a series of personalized social media posts (on Twitter, Instagram, Facebook) that allowed the woman to seem public without excessive exposure."

Pastors' fame works in tandem with the congregations' fandom. Johnson (2017: 174) has shown that "celebrity pastors' brands [are] dependent upon the people in the pews and at their laptops." Thus, congregants are not mere fans but "laborers incorporated into the marketing practices that promote [celebrity pastors]" (2017: 160). They may volunteer at the church; shop at the megachurch store for their pastor's books, the church's branded clothes and accessories, and the worship bands' music; and spread and consume celebrity pastors' message on social media. Indeed, Hillsong's young congregation members are deeply involved in the labor of celebrification of the church and themselves through prosumption. As we will see in the next chapter, young Brazilians relate to Hillsong worship band members and Hillsong pastors as fans and groupies ("stalking" them online, adopting their dress styles, creating online fan groups, translating worship bands' lyrics, etc.). They also emulate pastors' cool dress style and use their creativity to dress for church, making the experience of being at church fun and desirable.

In doing so, they are engaging in and contributing to the commodification and marketing of the church and its pastors. I suggest that for middle-class Pentecostal youth, these megachurches' Prosperity Theology is not so much about wealth per se, but about experiencing the world of celebrities and feeling close to them, as we will see in the following chapter. By modeling themselves on celebrity pastors and worship band members, as well as on secular celebrities who "endorse" these churches given that they are part of the congregation (e.g., until recently, Justin Bieber and Hailey Baldwin in the case of Hillsong), young middle-class Christians create their own "Cool Christian style." At the same time, they use this understanding of Prosperity Theology (i.e., participating in celebrity culture from the Global North) to belittle and thus differentiate themselves from the Prosperity Theology of the Black and poor, which is closely associated with desire for material possessions (money, employment, housing), as I show later in this chapter. This distinction could be somewhat mapped onto Bowler's (2013: 125–128) differentiation between "hard" and "soft" Prosperity Gospel in American megachurches. For her, hard prosperity was popular in the 1980s; it was openly transactional and offered immediate connection between faith and prosperity, emphasizing the negative impacts of not giving. Emerging a decade later, "soft prosperity" megachurches like Hillsong emphasized prosperity in a more roundabout way: "It was therapeutic and emotive, a way of speaking that shed its pentecostal accent for a sweeter and secular tone" (Bowler 2013: 125).[5]

Cool Christianity's strong affective relationship between celebrity culture and the daily life of the church can lead to abuse, as we saw in particular in the New York and other US Hillsong campuses, where consumer capitalism and celebrity culture are much more advanced than in Australia and other parts of the world. There, the megachurch's courting of secular celebrities—who were seated in VIP areas during services; shared a "green room" with the head pastor Carl Lentz and his entourage; and were wined and dined using Lentz's corporate credit cards in glitzy restaurants and clubs, where paparazzi took pictures of them for the secular magazines—attracted youth to the megachurch (Hardaker 2021; Hardy 2022). In their desire to get closer to pastors and serve in the church, young members of the congregation volunteered their time and were asked to serve long hours in the church and outside it, as the pastors' drivers, nannies, and cleaners. The excesses of celebrity culture and abuse of volunteers were coupled with the usual lack of oversight and accountability structure that is common in independent megachurches that rely on the pastor's charisma (Billings 2020; Rocha and McPhillips 2019). In Chapter 4, we will see how Brazilians studying at Hillsong College in Sydney thought the long hours of volunteering at church were reasonable because they were gaining valuable knowledge and skills for their future lives and churches at home. For now, I turn to how this aesthetic style has been received by other Christian peers.

Contesting Cool Christianity

As a relatively new sensational form, Cool Christianity has been challenged within global Christianity and thus has become "hyper-apparent" (Meyer 2011: 32). Conservative pastors, and even a self-identified "hipster pastor," Brett McCracken, have criticized it for being theologically facile and privileging form over content in order to attract young people.[6] In his 2010 book, *Hipster Christianity: When Church and Cool Collide*, McCracken criticized church leaders' obsession with the marketization of coolness at the expense of the content. McCracken noted (2010: 12):

> Hipster Christianity is a faith more concerned with its image and presentation and ancillary appeal. It assumes that mere Christianity isn't enough or isn't as important as how Christianity looks and is perceived by the outside world.

Hillsong pastors usually counter this criticism by noting that while the Bible's message is the same, they use new media and strive to maintain high production values, or "excellence," in all offerings because young people have access to high-quality media production and experiences outside church. In the BBC documentary *Hillsong Church: God Goes Viral*,[7] Brian Houston explained:

> Churches are usually old, boring, irrelevant, and empty. I always thought church should be enjoyed, not endured, with plenty of life and spontaneity in it. It's an exciting place to be, and it's full.

A Brazilian pastor at Hillsong São Paulo echoed this reasoning when he told me:

> We will always change the method because the world is changing. The lights, the big screen.... If we want to reach young people, there is no way we can use a method that is twenty years old. They go to a party, a concert, which has the best lighting, the best technology, and when they get to church, it is using an overhead projector?

Here he follows the modernist and Protestant separation of form and meaning. But, of course, they are intertwined. McCracken (2014) made this point from a traditional Christian perspective: the "medium of cool isn't just a neutral vehicle for the gospel but rather a form that changes and even subverts the gospel." For him, the medium and the message are intrinsically connected. As such, he points out that Cool Christianity conflicts with the gospel in several ways. The first problem is the ephemerality of cool—just like fashion, cool needs always to be moving to the next thing as soon as it becomes too popular. However, he asks, "How does this fit with a faith that isn't ephemeral, but eternal? How can we simultaneously embrace a sacred view of time, and a valuing of tradition, when we're so compelled by the ever-changing contours of cool and disposability of trendiness?" The second issue is that "cool is necessarily exclusivist; it is about in-the-know subculture." He queries: "How does this exclusivism square with a faith that is fundamentally inclusive and open-to-all?" Finally, he equates coolness with individualism and the desire for unique and edgy tastes and asks: "Can the Christian values of community, collectivism and humility be effectively enacted in a community where cool is a valued currency?" McCracken concludes that what people look for in the church is authenticity and an alternative to the image-obsessed and narcissistic world, not a confected coolness that pegs onto secular youth cultures.

Another point of contention is the morality of pastors' adoption of expensive high-end streetwear fashion (e.g., Saint Laurent clothes and Rolex watches), as we saw early in the chapter. Wishing to highlight this issue, Ben Kirby, a young Christian American, created the Instagram account *Preachers 'n' Sneakers* in 2019. Initially featuring social media photos of celebrity pastors next to screenshots of the shoes they wear, and their brand and price, the account has grown to include pastors' choice of designer clothes and their prices as well. It has quickly grown to over 300,000 followers, generating passionate comments from Christians and atheists alike criticizing celebrity pastors for their expensive clothes. The author also published a book and produces a podcast featuring discussions about consumerism, capitalism, and celebrity culture within Christianity. Paradoxically, both McCracken and Kirby have adopted the same strategies of fashion marketing and consumerism of Cool Christianity. While McCracken sells books, Kirby's account sells its own merchandise, including hoodies, caps, and T-shirts with its logo and Christian messages. At any rate, such rapid growth and level of emotional engagement show how central sensational forms are to religious communities, and how new aesthetic forms need to be negotiated before being authorized. As the account creator noted in an interview for BuzzFeed (Chen 2019):

> I'm a Christian and I started questioning myself, "What is OK as far as optics . . . as far as pastors wearing hype or designer clothing?" It is important that followers of the Christian faith in America have a discussion about what is appropriate. Is the money I'm giving the church going to the salary, or spending on sneakers?

Cool Christian churches' stance on sexuality also clashed with older authorized forms of Christianity. These Seeker churches focus on love and inclusivity and engage with secular youth cultures to attract non-Christians and creatives to their congregations. This has meant that many churches have LGBTQI+ congregants in their midst and this may clash head-on with traditional Pentecostal churches. In 2014, Hillsong faced a lot of criticism when a conservative pastor outed a gay couple who led Hillsong's New York church choir. In his damage-control response, Brian Houston had to walk a tightrope between asserting that he and his church did not affirm LGBTQI+ "lifestyle," as he put it, but that at the same time they were welcome in the church.

In an interview with the *New York Times* (Merritt 2014, my italics), Houston asserted:

> On the subject, I always feel like there's [sic] three things. There's the world we live in, there's the weight we live with, and there's the word we live by. The world we live in, whether we like it or not, is changing around and about us. Homosexual marriage is legal in NYC and will be probably in most Western world countries within a short time. *So the world's changing and we want to stay relevant as a church.* Then the weight we live with is the reality that in churches like ours and virtually any other church, there are young people who have serious questions about their sexuality . . . who are literally depressed, maybe even suicidal and, sadly, often times grow up to hate the church because they feel that the church rejected them. The word we live by is what the Bible says. And it would be much easier if you could feel like all of those three just easily lined up. But they don't necessarily. We feel at this point, it is an ongoing conversation, that the real issues in people's lives are too important for us to just reduce it down to a "yes" or "no" answer in a media outlet.

Here we can see how negotiations about new sensational forms are entangled with religious content and norms and are thus central to religious transformation. Houston's vision for the church and Christianity is that it engages with the world to stay relevant and attract youngsters, and this includes discussions on homosexuality (and, more recently, support for the Black Lives Matter movement). On the one hand, this vision aligns with Hillsong's sensational forms: its nightclub-style services, celebrity worship bands, pastors and congregants sporting tattoos and designer/streetwear attire, the sales of church-branded clothes and accessories, heavy use of social media, and preaching directly connected to people's everyday lives. On the other hand, in McCracken's and other conservative pastors' vision, the authentic church should offer a retreat from a world gone wrong. Their view aligns with their own sensational forms—a strong stance against LGBTQI+, less emphasis on form, and services in brightly lit churches. In both these positions, a vision of the world and the role of Christianity in it is at stake.

In a similar fashion, Cool Christianity clashes with the more common sensational forms of Brazilian Pentecostalism that are associated with the poor. As we will see in the next and final section of this chapter, middle-class

Brazilians praise the former as rational, sophisticated, modern, and ethical while rejecting the Brazilian Pentecostal sensational forms adopted by the poor.

Reteté, *Crentes*, and Social Distinction

For middle-class Brazilians, it is precisely Cool Christianity's sensational forms—coolness, exclusivism, focus on image and quality of presentation, and a light touch in regard to sexuality and social behavior—that appeal to them. This aesthetic style fits their class sensibilities and aspirations and is mobilized for social distinction. In *Distinction* (1984), Bourdieu has shown that social identity is asserted and maintained through difference, which in turn is visible in people's habitus. According to him, habitus is the system of classification (the structuring structure) and the principle through which objectively classifiable judgments are made (the structured structure). Through this means, social classes would be defined by their habitus, that is, by their internalized unconscious dispositions as well as their relational position in a structure of taste. In other words, a social group would be identifiable by having similar choices in taste derived from a particular habitus situated in this system of correlation and distinction. Importantly, this system is eminently hierarchical so that the tastes of the upper classes carry prestige while tastes of lower, disenfranchised classes are regarded as vulgar. Because tastes do not have an intrinsic value, the dominant classes who hold economic and/or cultural capital make theirs rare and unreachable (in either economic or cultural ways) so that they may successfully imbue them with prestige. Conversely, the tastes of the poorest fractions of society are regarded as common and identified with vulgarity, for they are easily accessible. This entails a constant effort by the upper classes to maintain social distance by always creating new, rarer tastes and imposing an artificial scarcity of products consumed by them.

As I noted in the Introduction, Pentecostalism has been historically a religion of the poor in Brazil. In her analysis of aesthetics of Pentecostalism in Latin America, Berenice Martin (2006) has focused on how intellectuals who study the movement judged its aesthetic expressions as "bad taste." Like Bourdieu, Martin (2006: 146–147) reminds us that judgment of taste has to do with status and power. For her, it is the deeply embodied and dramatic practices of Latin American Pentecostalism (spirit possession/exorcism, glossolalia, healing, prophecy, testimony, music, dance), its controlling of women's bodies and sexuality (through modest dress and strict behavioral codes), in addition to congregants' "poor" aesthetics (their cheap clothes, home furnishings, and church materials and decoration) that attract the "elite's disdain." As a consequence, Martin (2006: 152) found that:

> Pentecostals in the professional middle classes, some of them second or third generation Protestants with experience of higher education, are acutely aware of the class connotations of the typical Pentecostal dress code and tend to modify, if not wholly abandon it.

This is a similar finding to Köhrsen's (2016) study of middle-class Pentecostalism in Argentina. According to him, this sector of society was deeply embarrassed about the ecstatic practices and poor aesthetics of Pentecostals. He noted that (2016: 2):

> [They] are torn between the word of Pentecostalism and the world of the educated, "European" middle class. In order to decrease this tension, middle class Pentecostals tend toward specific tastes and style of Pentecostalism that draw boundaries in opposition to the "inappropriate" characteristics of Pentecostalism.

Similar to the middle-class discourse in Argentina (Köhrsen 2016: 37), middle-class Brazilians see themselves as white, Western, educated, and rational as opposed to the poor whom they regard as Black, backward, uneducated, and superstitious (O'Dougherty 2002). Middle-class Brazilians thus praise the Hillsong style and criticize Brazilian churches' aesthetics because of their association with the poor—their focus on money, conservative values, poor aesthetics, and lack of rationality and bodily control. Importantly, they do this through a moral critique that conflates racism and classism.

Take, for instance, Juliana, a 22-year-old Brazilian woman who studied at Hillsong College in Sydney for two years. As I interviewed her in a shopping mall food plaza, I noticed her long straight hair with blond highlights, the tiny gold pendant around her neck, the designer backpack, and her trendy activewear. They all attested to her comfortable upbringing. I was not surprised when she told me her father was a lawyer and her mother a physiotherapist. She was brought up in church and went to Australia right after graduating from High School in Brazil. In our conversation, she constantly differentiated the Hillsong style from that of Brazilian churches. She aligned herself with the former while denigrating the latter. She told me that besides theology, at Hillsong College she learned to be "more Christian and less *evangélica*" (evangelicals, as Protestants, including Pentecostals, are called in Brazil). She added that, in fact, she thought that Brazilians were not "real Christians." Juliana explained that Brazilian churches focused "more on judgement than grace, more on the devil than Jesus, more on *reteté* than the Word of God." These binaries (of inferiority/superiority) demonstrated how, for Juliana (and so many others), these different styles were in fact about class and race distinction.

The last binary is particularly telling. *Reteté* is a Brazilian onomatopoeic word commonly used in Pentecostal circles to mean ecstatic rituals found among the poor and mostly Black followers in small churches in the periphery of Brazilian large cities. These rituals are marked by visceral bodily practices—as congregants are filled by the Holy Spirit, they scream, jump, gyrate, run in circles, faint, and fall to the ground (Guerreiro 2018). It is a contentious term that is mobilized by historical Protestant churches and middle-class Pentecostals for boundary work purposes (Gonçalves Pereira 2019). Churches that practice *reteté* rituals are accused of not being serious in their faith and thus illegitimate, as opposed to those churches that are rational and theologically informed. Indeed, when I asked what she meant by *reteté*, Juliana laughed and immediately stood up, spread her arms sideways, and gyrated imitating an airplane. She told me that *reteté* was about "all sorts of craziness." She added that it was not "her style" and that "at Hillsong they speak in tongues, but they never lose control." Köhrsen (2016: 226) also found that Pentecostal middle-class Argentinians rejected strong emotional outbursts and that middle-class churches moved ecstatic practices such as glossolalia to the private sphere, a similar strategy to Hillsong's where glossolalia is never displayed on the platform. Significantly, she overlapped class and race prejudices when she concluded:

> I'm a Christian and a *racista* [racist] against *crentes* [believers, i.e., Pentecostals]. It's funny, my friends at my church, in our creative team, man, everyone is a racist. We keep repeating the [Brazilian Pentecostal] jargon like "burning for Jesus." *We all mock crentes*. I can't stand them! It's annoying that you won't ever meet a *cool* believer in your life; it's very rare. Because *crentes* are very religious, very crazy, they are always going, "Ahhhh, the devil."

Although *crente* literally means "believer," it has historically been used by the middle and upper classes as a derogatory term that identifies Pentecostals as poor and ignorant. Her visceral hatred of *crentes* using the word *racista* to express her disgust, her (and her friends') mocking them, and her lamenting that cool *crentes* are rare show that class distinction through religious style is not just a rational choice but it is embodied through affect. I was taken aback when she characterized herself as a racist against *crentes* (i.e., poor Pentecostals) but then recalled that this attitude is not that unusual among Brazilian elites. In a country with a history of slavery, classism, and racism, there is pervasive violence against the Black and poor (these categories frequently overlap).[8]

For instance, anthropologist Jairo Alves (2018) has given a poignant account of the genocide perpetrated by the Brazilian state on the poor and Black segregated in the *favelas* (slums) in the periphery of São Paulo.[9] For him (2018:3), Brazilian civil society is "a political community that replicates the colonial structure of power even when including some black and indigenous bodies. Although not homogenously white, civil society is essentially anti-black." He argues that this anti-Blackness is also present in the country's working class. We can see this in the ways in which Pentecostal pastors of churches established in *favelas* associate with evangelical drug traffickers in order to expel Afro-Brazilian religious communities from the area (Boaz 2020; Da Silva 2016; Pinezi and Chesnut 2019). Anthropologist Vagner Gonçalves da Silva (2016: 489) has argued that this is due to "competition for followers from the same socioeconomic group, and Neo-Pentecostal preaching of 'Spiritual Welfare.'" Following others (Boaz 2020; Hofbauer 2016; Pinezi and Chesnut 2019), I would also suggest that this violence is a continuation of historical discrimination against Afro-Brazilians and their religions by the Brazilian state and the Catholic Church, and the racism that permeates Brazilian society. As Pinezi and Chesnut (2019: n.p.) have argued, "it's in the realm of Afro-Brazilian religions that intolerance and racism become most virulent."

Importantly, in his *Racismo Estrutural* (*Structural Racism*) Silvio Almeida (2019: 99), a Black academic and presently Federal Minister for Human Rights and Citizenship, argued that "the logic of racism cannot be distinguished from the logic of the constitution of social classes in Brazil." Indeed, similar to what I heard from Juliana and others, in her research on the Brazilian middle class in São Paulo, O'Dougherty (2002: 168) found that "informants constructed their class identity in part on negative boundaries—'their' vulgar versus 'our' cultured consumption and educational pursuits. . . . For some, the most radically different 'other' was the poor and dark-skinned." O'Dougherty (2002: 171) noted, among other things, that they frequently criticized and ridiculed domestic workers. She (2002: 16) argued that class was constituted through informal language; that is, discourse and practices were integral to identity formation.

I argue that this identity formation is also constituted by affect. In my own work, I found middle-class disgust (and sometimes pity) toward *crentes*, who supposedly practice the wrong kind of Christianity and have the wrong body and clothes. *Crentes* then give a bad name to "real Christians." I will expand on the idea of ridiculing *crentes* as a way of enacting social distinction a little later. Here I want to continue following in the ways in which Hillsong gives a sense of belonging to (upper-) middle-class Pentecostals in Brazil. Another young Brazilian told me that the first time he went to a Hillsong United concert, he was pleasantly surprised:

> I was connecting with people *who were like me*, they dressed and spoke in a different way [from Brazilian Pentecostals]. There were just beautiful skinny people there. No fat sweaty pastors; no hairy women singing. You can be a *crente* and be normal.

Like Juliana, who lamented the lack of "cool *crentes*," this young man was clearly drawing a line between two camps—the usual Brazilian *crentes* (fat, sweaty, and hairy—in a nutshell, ugly) and people like him (Christian but beautiful, skinny, and "normal"). Hence, he pitched the aesthetics and the bodies of the poor against those of the middle classes and normalized the latter. Like many others, another young man who went to Hillsong United concerts and then to Hillsong conferences in Sydney told me that once he found Hillsong, he left his church:

> When I saw Hillsong, I saw that they're human in the way they talk, they don't go whirling. I wasn't going to be that Pentecostal who keeps screaming, spinning, exorcising the devil, screaming into the microphone. No! Hillsong showed me that [Pentecostalism] can be sensible.

This affinity between middle-class sensibilities—a focus on education, rationality, and controlling the body and emotions—and the Hillsong style came up again and again in interviews. Similarly, Köhrsen found that the congregation and pastors in middle-class churches in Argentina rejected "'uncontrolled' emotions and outbursts as inappropriate" (2016: 219).

We can now return to mocking as boundary work. On a Sunday after the evening service at Hillsong in Sydney, I chatting with young Brazilians at the coffee area where people usually congregate. Because we knew each other fairly well since we were all part of the same connect group, they were relaxed enough to use banter as a form of communication. What was remarkable in the conversation was how they were sending up the Brazilian Pentecostal style and its attention to behavior. A young man greeted a woman in the group saying in jest, "Hello, my *evangélica* sister." To which she replied, "Hi, my *crente* brother." Everyone laughed, and another woman added, pointing to one of the women in the circle, "Well, Patrícia is not a *crente* anymore. The other day she was wearing a miniskirt!" Patrícia laughed, and a third woman interjected, "Yes, *and* she was wearing red lipstick!" The first woman added, "And if she has a haircut, she is not a *crente* anymore," alluding to the fact that some conservative Brazilian churches do not allow women to have a haircut. By then everyone was laughing wholeheartedly and having a great time. At that point, they started getting a bit more serious. One of the women told the group that in her church it was just like that. "There was even a bench where the pastor would order you to sit if you did something wrong! It was by the wall across from the pews and everyone could see you. So embarrassing!" Another woman confirmed, "Yeah, 'Go to the bench!,' my pastor used to say!" The first man recalled that he had been a bit of a rebel, "I had long hair. I used to go to church with that long hair and wearing *havaianas* [flip-flop sandals]! It was the Assembly of God and it was a scandal!" Everyone laughed harder.

In his essays on laughter, the French philosopher Henri Bergson (1911: 6–7) has noted that laughter is always social:

> However spontaneous it seems, laughter always implies a kind of secret freemasonry, or even complicity, with other laughers, real or imaginary. . . . Many comic effects are incapable of translation from one language to another, because they refer to the customs and ideas of a particular social group!

Similar to Juliana and her creative team, this group's laughter indicated that they were all in on the joke. For all of them, the subject of their joke was the Brazilian Pentecostal style. By laughing at it, they were affirming that they were not part of it. Juliana and her friends all shared in the understanding that the beliefs, language, and visceral bodily practices of poor Pentecostals were "not normal" and thus were laughable—poor Pentecostals are excessively "religious," irrational ("crazy"), use repetitive expressions (and thus irrational/automatic) like "burning for Jesus," and are fixated on the devil. Bergson posited that humor ensues from one's absentmindness and automatism, a mechanical behavior, such as someone walking absent-mindedly and failing to avoid a hole in the ground. According to him (1911: 25):

> Automatism, inelasticity, habit that has been contracted and maintained . . . makes us laugh. But this effect gains in intensity when we are able to connect these characteristics with some deep-seated cause, a certain fundamental absent-mindedness, as though the soul had allowed itself to be fascinated and hypnotised by the materiality of a simple action.

Similarly, the group of Brazilians ridiculed the jargon used in Brazilian Pentecostalism and the pastors' illogical and thus automatic focus on behavior. For Bergson (1911: 21), "This rigidity is the comic, and laughter is its corrective." Thus, laughter is not only about affect; it has a disciplinary moral element. The group that makes fun of others does so from a position of power. Of course, these young people have little power vis-à-vis their pastors in their home churches in Brazil due to their age, gender, and marital status, as we will see in Chapter 6. However, they do possess symbolic power derived from their social class and the prestige or cultural capital associated with having lived in the Global North, where they learned the sensational forms of a rich and successful church. In a way, it is the lack of real power to change the Brazilian Pentecostal sensational forms and the awareness of the stigma associated with Pentecostalism in Brazil that make them side with secular members of their social class and ridicule Brazilian Pentecostals.

Others I spoke to tried to be more understanding of poor Pentecostals. Yet they still did so from a position of moral superiority and thus social distinction. They felt sorry for the poor, who were ignorant victims of church pastors who were greedy and manipulative. They had no agency. Whenever our conversations veered toward church and money, everyone I spoke with promptly mentioned the Universal Church of the Kingdom of God (UCKG), well-known for the pressure it exerts on followers to make large donations.[10] At the UCKG, Prosperity Gospel takes very material forms. Pastors assert that the more one gives to the church, the stronger is God's obligation to return one's donations ten-fold—through blessings such as jobs, houses, cars, healing from addiction and illnesses, and so on. The church's motto "stop suffering" and its services in which pastors use magical objects (oils, flowers, fabric) and exorcise African-Brazilian spirits also attract the poor (Almeida 2009; Openshaw 2018; Premawardhana 2012; van de Kamp 2016; van Wyk 2014).

One young man told me: "The Universal [church] relies on people's ignorance.... We know it's a gang. They are thieves! But there are people with sincere faith there. You can't disqualify the people because of the church." In the same breath, he went on to criticize UCKG followers as ignorant and easily duped: "Man, you are more of an *otário* [sucker] than the pastor who stole from you. You sat there for five years. You didn't read the Bible. People who read the Bible can't stay in these churches; they don't stay." For him, had they taken responsibility for their own relationship with God (by reading and interpreting the Bible), they would not have been duped. When 29% of the Brazilian population between 15 and 64 years old is practically illiterate and another 8% is fully illiterate (Oliveira 2021), such a statement clearly implies a moral criticism of the poor which works toward class distinction. It also shows a difference in church style. While in Brazilian churches pastors exert authority over the church and congregants, Brazilians told me that at Hillsong they are taught to interpret the Bible and think for themselves. Indeed, middle-class Brazilians constantly praised Hillsong's neoliberal approach that gave autonomy to the individual while contrasting it with the pressure they felt in Brazilian churches to acquiesce to pastors' inexplicable and illogical policies in regard to their behavior. As we will see throughout this book, Hillsong pastors frequently refute legalism and judgment. One Sunday evening, as I watched the service with other Brazilians in the Sydney city branch, the pastor reiterated this:

> Legalism, judgement, how we should be and behave ... We beat ourselves up because we are not perfect. But we don't need to be perfect because Jesus already died and saved us. God loves us as we are. He is a loving God, not judgmental, not angry. So the Ten Commandments is the law; it's not really a God who loves us, who accepts us with all our flaws. Jesus is a welcoming God. Our God welcomes the weak, drug addicts, people who do bad things because he loves us. My non-Christian friends worry and apologize when they swear or drink when I am around. But who said I can't drink? That I can't swear? That's legalism, not grace.

The focus on grace was ever present when Brazilians differentiated the Hillsong and Brazilian styles. Some young Brazilians tried to explain their differences as reflections of the societies in which they originated. One young man who studied at Hillsong College for three years told me:

> It's a big difference in culture, right? I feel that our evangelical culture in Brazil, they present a God who provides for people's needs. There [at Hillsong] they present relational God ... is a God who wants a relationship with you, regardless of your problems, regardless of the difficulties you have. So here [in Brazil] is a very much, "Don't worry because God will supply your needs. If you are sick, he will heal you. If you need money, he will bless you."

By contrast, he admired Hillsong:

> What I most admired about the preaching was that they are very rational. If you watch the preaching, you'll see that they use a lot of teaching. They give points of what the Bible is saying for *you* to find your own truth. So, you know, it is not [the pastor saying] "that's right, that's wrong." Hillsong is a church that doesn't impose any doctrine ... they give you total freedom.

For him, the poor and their churches engage with God in a pragmatic way because of their social condition. Being destitute, they needed God to give them things and pastors to tell them what is right or wrong. By contrast, Hillsong comes from an affluent society where congregants are educated, and thus God is about a relationship and the pastor engages with the congregation rationally as a teacher rather than an autocrat. Hillsong then allows for self-reflexivity and autonomy for the individual. People learn and are able to choose what is best for them. Brian Houston's stance on LGBTQI+ people mentioned earlier illustrates well this move away from judgment and toward tolerance (within limits).

Conclusion

In this chapter, we saw how Cool Christianity is enmeshed in consumer capitalism, and processes of branding, commodification, celebrity culture, and self-making. Choices in consumption are central to processes of identity-making and community formation. Brands are not so much about the selling of commodities but about generating an emotional engagement with consumers, and thus having their long-lasting loyalty. For young people transitioning into adulthood, and thus working out their own style and identity, the appeal of brands, celebrity culture, coolness, and community in their imagining of a future is significant.

As a shared aesthetic style, Cool Christianity is materialized in Hillsong's music, celebrity pastors, celebrity followers, fashion and branded objects and rituals, and media attention. It shapes people's senses, bodies, and identities to generate community. Importantly, these materialities also work as mediators of the presence of the Holy Spirit. Cool Christianity can also lead to abuse because of the interlacing of celebrity culture, charisma, and youth fandom. Furthermore, because it is a new sensational form, Cool Christianity has to be negotiated to become authorized as a medium that offers the experience of transcendence. Pentecostals have criticized Cool Christianity's heavy engagement with youth and celebrity culture and branding. Hillsong, in particular, has been criticized in Pentecostal circles for its tolerance of LGBTQI+ individuals in the congregation.

Middle-class Brazilians come from a socially conservative Pentecostal culture whose style is associated with the aesthetics of the poor and Black. For them, Hillsong's sensational form legitimizes Pentecostalism as suitably modern, sophisticated, cosmopolitan, and white. They adopt it as a way to distinguish themselves from the sensational forms of the poor, often Black, "uncool" *crentes*—their lack of bodily control through practices of *reteté*, exorcism, and their loud preaching; their fat, hairy, and sweaty bodies; their ignorance in the face of pastors' cunning. It is through language, practices, and affect that they constitute their middle classness. Some display a bodily revulsion toward poor, Black Pentecostals and their churches. Others have a paternalistic attitude toward the poor. All in all, it is clear that Cool Christianity is mobilized toward asserting moral superiority and establishing social distinction. In the next chapter, we will see how Hillsong's Cool Christianity generated a fan community connected by affect among Brazilians. Hillsong and Australia thus become "mattering maps" that orient them to a new life.

2
Fandom

> In Brazil there is an immense fascination with Hillsong. They idolize the church, the worship [bands], and even some pastors and singers. This idolization makes many Brazilians sell their car, borrow money from their father, uncle or grandfather to come here to enroll at the Hillsong College.
> —Strazzery (2011), former Hillsong College Brazilian student

A lightbulb moment. I went back to the Hillsong Sunday service shortly after a long period of fieldwork in Brazil. "Welcome Home" read the old banner at the entrance. As I stepped in the foyer, I suddenly felt excited, grateful, and privileged to be there. I had spent my time in Brazil among students who had returned home and pastors who had been to Hillsong conferences in Sydney. The stories of their lives in Sydney and experiences at Hillsong were full of nostalgia and longing. As we chatted, we sighed and laughed together at the little things they missed from Australia: the safe, fun life by the beach; the café culture; the avocado toast they started preparing at home to the dismay of their Brazilian families who only ate avocado for dessert. Nostalgia for them was embodied: "Next time you come back bring me some Tim Tams biscuits," asked a woman I was interviewing. Her husband pleaded: "Bring me some Messina ice cream!" They also longed to be back at Hillsong. They missed their group of friends from church, the way "everything was done with excellence," its large and successful structure, and the opportunities to do volunteer work where they had learned so much. Above all, they missed the atmosphere of excitement and the perfection they said they found *both* at Hillsong and Australia. In sum, they were longing for Hillsong's sensational forms. During my time in Brazil, I also met many young Brazilians who had never been to Australia but loved Hillsong music and heard these returnees' stories, and thus desired to travel there and join Hillsong. The twinkle in all these people's eyes during our conversations revealed how Hillsong created powerful imaginaries in Brazil.

As I felt equally excited, grateful, and privileged to be at Hillsong in Sydney, I was surprised by these emotions. After all, I had always been a bit ambivalent during fieldwork at the church services. For starters, the very loud music and the lights directed occasionally at the congregation sometimes gave me headaches. I was also annoyed when pastors acted as TV entertainers, eliciting responses from the audience to obvious questions such as "Who loves Jesus here?" just to rouse them. Yet here I was, having this warm sensation in my belly. As I thought of how I felt, I was amazed at how successful Hillsong was at generating affect. Through this affect, it seemed to me that I was embodying my participants' desires and imagination. I wrote in my notes: "It's like I am bringing them with me. I have embodied their longing for and excitement about this place. I am where they so desire to be."

* * *

In this chapter, I investigate the ways in which the Hillsong style of Cool Christianity arrived and spread in Brazil via the United States, and as such, it was imbued with the same prestige US culture has in the country. Here, I am interested in how this sensational form generated a fan community connected by affect. Massumi (2002: 28) differentiates affect from emotion. Affect is an intensity that is both embodied and impersonal; emotions are how we recognize these embodied experiences once the affect is gone. Emotions are the "subjective content, the sociolinguistic fixing of the quality of an experience which is from that point onward defined as personal." Although affect produces expressions of emotion, affect is not completely captured by these expressions. As Mazzarella (2009: 291) has argued:

> Affect points us toward a terrain that is presubjective without being presocial. As such it implies a way of apprehending social life that does not start with the bounded, intentional subject while at the same time foregrounding embodiment and sensuous life. Affect is not the unconscious—it is too corporeally rooted for that. Nor can it be aligned with any conventional conception of culture, since the whole point of affect ... is that unlike emotion it is not always already semiotically mediated.

Anthropologist Rutherford (2016: 286–287) has noted that "the concept [of affect] turns our attention to the forces that move people, forces that attract, repel, and provoke." This embodied intensity that propels people to action—particularly to become fans and desire to travel—is what interests me in this chapter. But how is affect connected to fandom? In his study of the "affective sensibility of fandom," Grossberg (1992) has defined "sensibility" as a particular form of engagement that binds cultural forms or texts and audiences. He posited that while the sensibility of consumers produces structures of pleasure, fans generate excess affective investment in cultural forms. Like Massumi and Mazzarella after him, Grossberg (1992: 56) perceives affect as the "feeling of life," but feeling here is "not a subjective experience. It is a socially constructed domain of cultural affects." According to him, "affect is what gives 'color,' 'tone' or 'texture' to our experiences." Importantly, affect produces *maps* that organize people's investments in the world. As people invest energy in places, events, and cultural texts, these become significant to them and assist in constructing their identity. They matter to them. Thus, Grossberg (1992: 57) calls these maps of affect "mattering maps." Notably, he (1992: 61) points out the circular nature of the affective sensibility of fandom: once fans invest affect excessively in a cultural form, this form becomes important to them, which makes them invest more affect and, in turn, it differentiates them from non-fans, thus creating a community. Grossberg makes two further important points for our understanding of how and why young Brazilians invest affect in Hillsong's sensational form. First, he (1992: 59) notes that "Fans actively constitute places and forms of authority (both for themselves and for others) through the mobilization and organization of affective investments." Second, "fandom is, at least potentially, the site of the optimism, invigoration and passion which are necessary conditions for any struggle to change the conditions of one's life" (1992: 65).

Wade and Hynes (2013: 174) have demonstrated that "Hillsong produces and mobilizes affect in order to attain the collective experience of the spectacle, which is so crucial to Hillsong's visibility." Similar to my findings, for them, affect and the church's success work as a recruitment tool and produce "particular kinds of subject, namely, subjects who are at once comfortable, enthusiastic and loyal." As we will see in this chapter, this affective dynamic starts much before people experience its spectacular services. Young Brazilian fans invest affective energy as they learn about Hillsong and Australia, sing/play/listen to Hillsong music, and dream of one day joining the church headquarters. Such excess investment functions as a mattering map which structures their lives—they spend time and interact with Hillsong star musicians and pastors on social media; they learn English; save money for their trip; and imagine their lives elsewhere and "otherwise," as we discussed in the previous chapter. As they do so, they create an affective community with other fans and thus build borders between them and others. I argue that Hillsong and Australia then become places and forms of authority—they exert power and offer hope and optimism as paths to change their lives. This is so because content (Hillsong as cultural form), form (Hillsong's sensational form), and context (its origins in the English-speaking Global North, a site of modernity) are deeply intertwined. Brazilian fans yearn to remake their local churches and their homeland in the image of Hillsong and Australia. For them, this is possible because of Australia's apparent similarities to Brazil. Like Brazil, Australia was once a settler-colonial society, is now a multicultural society with a beach culture and laidback lifestyle, and is located in the Southern Hemisphere. However, as part of the Global North, Australia is imagined as safe, technologically sophisticated, and lacking in stark class divisions, political corruption, and poverty, as I showed elsewhere (Rocha 2019).

In what follows, I first give a historical context for the arrival of Hillsong music and church in Brazil. I then explore the narrative of a Brazilian Hillsong fan as an exemplar of how young Brazilians overlap their love of and excitement for Hillsong and Australia. Finally, I analyze the tensions that arise when the megachurch invests in celebrity culture and congregants relate to them as fans.

Pentecostalism in Brazil

Following other scholars of Pentecostalism who endeavored to establish a taxonomy for the movement (Anderson 2010), Paul Freston (1995) divides Brazilian Pentecostalism into three waves. Freston (1995: 120) notes that "the concept of waves emphasizes Pentecostalism's versatility, but also the way each church carries the marks of the era in which it was born." The first wave starts in the 1910s with the arrival of Christian Congregation and the Assemblies of God via European missionaries who had converted in the United States. The second wave occurs from the 1950s and early 1960s onward in São Paulo, Brazil's largest and most industrialized city, as Brazilian society becomes more urbanized. It is brought about by American missionaries of the Foursquare church in 1951, who had "enterprising methods forged in the birthplace of mass media, interwar California" (Freston 1995: 120). Many Brazilian churches were established in this period, but the largest ones,

Brazil for Christ (1955) and God is Love (1962), make use of mass media and divine healing to expand their reach.

According to Freston (1995: 129), the third wave takes place in Rio de Janeiro in the late 1970s and grows considerably in the 1980s. At the time, two-thirds of the Brazilian population were living in urban centers; mass media reached the large majority of the population; the number of Catholics was decreasing; and the country faced an economic crisis. After the national capital moved to Brasília in the early 1960s, Rio became a poor and violent city, controlled by populist politics and gambling mafias. It is in this environment that the neo-Pentecostal churches such as the Universal Church of the Kingdom of God (UCKG, 1977) and the International Church of the Grace of God (1980) were established. Their planting pastors had previously been part of New Life, a church founded by a former Assemblies of God Canadian missionary in 1960, attesting to the influence of foreign missionaries at the origin of some earlier Brazilian churches, even as they went on to create their own style of Pentecostalism that responded to Brazil's cultural and social contexts.

Neo-Pentecostal churches are marked by a focus on spiritual battle, Prosperity Theology, and a departure from ascetism, legalism, and sectarism in favor of this-world engagement. These churches adopt a for-profit businesses model. They focus on entrepreneurship, use of mass media to attract more congregants, and expand their activities to influence politics. For instance, the powerful megachurch UCKG owns a large media conglomerate (a TV channel, radio stations, a publishing company, and newspapers) and even a bank, and since the 1990s has elected many federal, state, and municipal politicians. It is well-known for its focus on sacrifice, tithing, donations, healing through exorcism, and Prosperity Theology. Having a mostly urban poor congregation, UCKG preaches that members should make large offerings because God will return these ten-fold in the form of this-worldly material gifts (jobs, homes, cars, a better life). Freston notes that in Brazil's savage capitalism, where the poor see poverty as privation rather than a path to redemption, one of the reasons for the UCKG's success is its embrace of neoliberalism. It exhorts members not to accept poverty as fate and become small entrepreneurs (Freston 1995: 129–132). The UCKG is one of the largest churches in Brazil and has expanded to many parts of the world (Oro 2014b; van de Kamp 2016; van Wyk 2014). In Australia, its congregation is not comprised of Brazilians but of refugees and poor migrants from Sudan and the Pacific islands because Brazilians in Australia are mostly middle-class international students and skilled migrants (Rocha 2006b; Openshaw 2019, 2021). There have been schisms within the UCKG, and some of its pastors have founded other large churches adopting UCKG's successful practices.

Neo-Pentecostal churches have become so influential and successful in Brazil that some traditional Protestant churches have adopted Pentecostal theology, and depending on their pastors' inclinations, have also emphasized this-world engagement, and a much less sectarian, ascetic, and legalistic outlook to different degrees. "Pentecostalized" Protestant churches in Brazil are called *renovadas* (renewed). Many Brazilian Baptist churches have become *renovadas* and some of them have embraced the Hillsong style and often send their pastors and members to Hillsong conferences and Hillsong College, something that I explore in Chapter 5.

As we can see, the Pentecostal movement in Brazil is heterogeneous, complex, and dynamic. It has grown considerably in the past 40 years, influencing Brazilian politics and society. Rather than a history of the movement, here I am interested in its connections with Pentecostalism from the Global North. The cultural influence of the United States in Brazil is well documented and that includes religious culture. Indeed, Brazilian sociologist Ricardo Mariano (2014: 41) has noted "the growing influence and insertion of theological fashions and American institutions in Brazilian Pentecostalism." More recently, Barreto and Chaves (2023) have shown how these historical transnational Evangelical networks linking the United States and Brazil have led to the insurrection against the newly elected Brazilian President Luis Inácio Lula da Silva on January 8, 2023, which mirrored the one in the US Capitol two years prior. They argued that "A century of transnational evangelical cross-pollination has seeded shared theologies, social imaginations and strategies that help explain the right-wing authoritarian impulse in Brazilian and American politics."

Indeed, Brazilian churches may bring American pastors to teach courses and preach at services or conferences. They also invite American Christian singers and worship bands to play at their churches. The many Brazilian Pentecostal publishing houses have translated books by well-known American Christian authors and pastors, such as Kenneth Hagin (creator of Prosperity Theology), Benny Hinn (founder of the Orlando Christian Center, which adopts Prosperity Theology), Peter Wagner (theologian and Professor at Fuller Theological Seminar), and more recently, Brian Houston (the Hillsong founder). For their part, Brazilian pastors may train at American seminaries including Fuller, participate in American Christian conferences, follow their favorite American pastors on social media, and do internships at American churches. Many of the pastors whom I interviewed in Brazil and who had been to Hillsong conferences also participated in large American-based conferences such as Summit (of Willow Creek church) and Passion (Passion City Church) and received materials and resources from large American megachurches such as Saddle Back, Willow Creek, North Point, Passion, and Bethel.

Similar to my findings, in his *Boundless Faith*, Robert Wuthnow (2009) also noted that American churches are still influential in the Global South. Thus, he is critical of what has been called the "Global Christianity Paradigm" (Jenkins 2002), that is, the idea that the center of gravity of Christianity has moved from the Global North to the South due to a demographic shift and the alleged secularization of the North. Wuthnow argued that although the number of Christians may be higher and Indigenous churches are proliferating in the South, an asymmetry of wealth and resources makes American Christianity still influential in the Global South. He found that churches still sponsor missionaries and raise funds to support poverty and disaster relief, and about 25% of congregants traveled as missionaries to Global South churches for short periods of time. I would suggest that, in addition to resources and wealth, the fact that these churches are located in the United States also adds to their influence in the Global South, as I show in this book. Moreover, Wuthnow does not take into account that there are now also powerful flows of Christianity from the Global South to the North. Wealthy megachurches—such as the Brazilian Universal Church of the Kingdom of God and the Nigerian Christ Embassy and Redeemed Christian Church of God—have established several branches in the Global North, although they cater mainly to migrants rather than the white local population (Freston 2010; Openshaw 2021). Furthermore, Wuthnow's research was based solely on American churches and did not explore their influence in the South. As we will see in the next sections, it is through a habitus (Bourdieu 1984) of adopting new trends in music and church liturgy arriving from the United States forged over the twentieth century, that Hillsong arrives in Brazil. American Christianity functioned as a gateway for Brazilians to learn about Hillsong music and church, which were only later identified as Australian. What emerged from my study is a complex network of flows circulating among the United States, Brazil, and Australia.

Hillsong Music Lands

Hillsong first arrived in Brazil as music. This is understandable since music is key to the appeal and expansion of Pentecostalism (Ingalls and Yong 2015; Meyer 2009, 2010a; Thornton 2020). Music is both an affective and communicative medium, used for followers to feel the presence of God as well as to spread the word of God. Music is fundamental to Hillsong's branding and marketing (Wagner 2020), and it made the megachurch well-known globally.

The explosion of *música gospel*[1] (as Brazilians call the whole gamut of "praise and worship music" and "contemporary Christian music" [CCM]) in Brazil in the 1990s paved the way for the arrival of Hillsong music. Influenced by developments within Pentecostal culture in the United States, beginning with Renascer em Cristo (Reborn in Christ) church, other Brazilian churches started focusing on music and youth cultures in the late 1980s and the 1990s. According to Cunha (2007: 49), while Brazilian Independent/neo-Pentecostal and Renewed Baptist churches maintained practices of divine healing and this-worldly engagement via Prosperity Theology, they invested heavily in music and mass media to attract the middle classes and youth. New bands adopted international and national secular rhythms and styles (pop, rock, funk, punk, heavy metal, lambada, samba, forró, pagode).

In time, *música gospel* turned into what Cunha (2007) denominates *cultura gospel* (gospel culture) and Mariano (2014: 213) calls *indústria gospel* (gospel industry). While this Pentecostal culture was still conservative, it was packaged as modern via mediatization, entertainment, and consumer capitalism—a similar phenomenon to other parts of the world, as we have seen in Chapter 1. One way *música gospel* transcended Pentecostal churches and entered secular culture was through the media. Popular television and radio programs started featuring Brazilian gospel singers and worship bands. Following the American Grammy and Grammy Latino Awards for contemporary Christian music, local prizes were also created. CDs and DVDs were sold in secular bookstores, supermarkets, and other outlets. Cunha (2007: 55) notes the increase in Brazilian Christian record labels, TV producers, and shops for musical instruments, Christian sheet music, and CDs. This industry expanded to other goods: Christian clothing, beauty products, toys, and books sold at large supermarkets and shops. As the Pentecostal market grew, large secular labels also got on the bandwagon and started to contract gospel musicians and hold large concerts.

By the late 1990s, Brazil became the largest foreign market for American CCM, while many church bands translated lyrics of American CCM into Portuguese (Mariano 2014: 214). One of these foreign CCM bands was the Australian Hillsong United.[2] In an interview, the sole Brazilian distributor for Integrity Music (one of the largest CCM labels in the United States) told me that when he introduced Hillsong United to Brazil, the band was not well-known outside Australia. He was surprised how successful they became in Brazil. He explained that this success was "due to the American music influence [in Brazil]." When I asked how an Australian worship band could be successful because of American influence, he explained:

> Because [Hillsong United] came from the States. It didn't come via Australia; it came via Integrity distribution. So, it took time for people to realize it was an Australian band. Integrity distributed the best international music at that time: Ron Kenoly, Don Moen. It was praise and worship music. This had a great repercussion [in Brazil]. Everything that came to Brazil via Integrity Music people thought that it was American music [because] they sang in English. When I say, "influence of American music," let's say the influence of Integrity Music.

He went on to say that Hillsong's success was also due to one of the songs in the first CD they distributed in Brazil already having Portuguese versions. The now world-famous Shout to the Lord, composed and sung by Darlene Zschech, had been recorded by two Brazilian Baptist megachurches whose worship leaders/pastors had strong ties to the United States.[3] Edson Rebustini, the senior pastor of Igreja Batista Bíblica da Paz (São Paulo), frequently travels to the United States. Ana Paula Valadão, the worship leader of Diante do Trono band at the Igreja Batista da Lagoinha (Belo Horizonte), previously studied in an American seminary and has led the Boca Raton branch of Lagoinha church since 2018. By the time the Hillsong album arrived, Brazilians knew the song.

The distributor for Integrity Music argued that Igreja Batista da Lagoinha and its famed worship band Diante do Trono would not be as renowned in Brazil were it not for their first recordings of Hillsong music. That is a big call to make, since the Diante do Trono is now famous throughout Latin America and southern Europe, having toured the world to audiences of millions of fans, and sold around 15 million album copies by 2018. However, Cunha

(2007: 120–121) has also observed that Diante do Trono became well-known after partnering with Hillsong to record Shout to the Lord in Portuguese in 2000 and popularizing the praise and worship genre with its associated conferences, megaconcerts, and training courses in Brazil. Similarly, in her PhD thesis on Diante do Trono, Rosas (2015: 125) backs the Integrity Music distributor. She argued that the band's partnership with Hillsong and with the American Gateway church were strategies of legitimation and prestige for the band in Brazil. Certainly, this is the result of not only the appeal of Hillsong music but also the asymmetry of power between the Global North and South. Oro (2014b) found the same rationale in Brazilian Pentecostal churches' desire to establish branches in the Global North. Rather than just reverse mission, they were moved by a desire to strengthen their prestige and legitimacy within the very competitive Brazilian religious market. More importantly, Rosas (2015: 125) observes the strong influence of the Hillsong style on Diante do Trono (in terms of sound and production values of services and concerts), and how the band became a catalyst for the formation of other bands in the same style in local churches. This shows the reticular way the Hillsong style has spread in the country.

Hillsong United success resulted in Integrity Music distributing its CDs to Christian and secular bookstores and supermarkets and selling over half a million copies annually. As more young people became fans of the band, they created a fan club community on Orkut (a precursor to Facebook closed in 2014). Named *Eu Amo a Hillsong* (*I Love Hillsong*), it gathered over 50,000 young followers who behaved like fans of secular bands: they translated lyrics, exchanged gossip about the musicians and shared their biographies, and organized meet-ups at concerts. From 2006 onward, Hillsong celebrity singer Darlene Zschech and Hillsong United started actually touring in Brazil to perform in large concerts and in the annual March for Jesus.[4] In line with my own findings, the Integrity Music Brazilian distributor noted that the majority of the fans were middle class, and most sales occurred in the southeast region (in São Paulo, Rio de Janeiro, and Minas Gerais states), a more developed and wealthier region of Brazil. In these states, he told me,

> They consumed [international music] because they were closer to the releases. They also understood foreign languages, had more contact with the international [culture], and TV and radio stations played a lot of international music. To such an extent that Hillsong [United] performed in the

southeastern states of Brazil, not elsewhere. It was gratifying to see them singing in English with the band during concerts.

Significantly, he mentioned the role of illegal translations and piracy in the spread of the Hillsong United songs. Some churches and Brazilian singers would make their own translations and not use the official Portuguese translations that attracted copyright fees. Some singers would just add their own name to their translations as if they were their authors. He noted: "people would buy the song thinking that it was by that Brazilian singer or that group, when in fact the music was Hillsong's!" As CDs were phased out and music moved online, many young people would download their songs before they were launched by Integrity in the country. While piracy has helped in disseminating Hillsong music, it has also caused upset at Hillsong. An Australian pastor and musician who taught at Hillsong College told me in an interview that illegal translations have been a problem globally for large churches for a long while. He observed that in Brazil, Hillsong Publishing (the arm of the church in charge of music) had to meet with an unnamed megachurch and give them an ultimatum for them to pay royalties for the Hillsong United songs they had recorded. At any rate, illegal translations and downloads show the immense appeal the band has among Christian Brazilians.

Becoming a Fan

> Children watch Snow White, Cinderella, so their biggest dream is to go to Disneyland. For people who love the church, our biggest dream was to go to Hillsong.
> —Brazilian pastor couple who studied at Hillsong College

Many young Brazilians at Hillsong College and church had been to Hillsong United concerts as teenagers after listening to the band on tapes or CDs given to them by their friends and family. They told me of the strong impression it made on them, which in turn made traveling to Australia into a dream. Here I will share Paula's story in detail because it exemplifies so much of what I heard from young Brazilians. I interviewed her five years after her return to São Paulo from Hillsong Sydney. Her love of Hillsong and Australia had not abated in all that time she had been back. At times in our interview, nostalgia, and a sense that God had been present and supported her during her time alone in Australia as a 19-year-old, brought her to tears. This is how she described how she found out about Hillsong:

> One thing that influenced me a lot was Hillsong. I got to know Hillsong when I was ten, eleven years old. My cousin came home one day with a CD which she copied from the son of a pastor she met . . . that CD, *Shout to the Lord*. I remember it to this day. We heard the songs, and it was an amazing experience for me. I didn't understand the English lyrics, but I was captivated somehow, by the praise, by the worship. It was something like a call from the Holy Spirit . . . After that, I used to play Hillsong CDs all day long every day. And we recognized a few songs which we sang in church in Portuguese, which we didn't even know were translations! So we said, "Wow, so this band created the songs we sing [in church], so it must be really important and we didn't even know it!"

Here we see the role of affect as a force that moves and attracts Paula. It does not matter that she does not understand the lyrics; she is still "captivated" by the music and "the worship" because she feels the presence of the Holy Spirit. The intensity of feeling elicited in that particular moment becomes an "amazing experience" so vital that she "remembers it to this day." This makes her play the songs again and again to produce the same experience. After this, Paula and her cousin researched Hillsong on the Internet, and found out that it was in fact a church (not only a band) in Australia that "had influenced churches all over the world. Even the big Brazilian bands." She then realized that the worship band of Lagoinha Baptist church, Diante do Trono, which was exploding in the market at the time, had released a CD (*Aclame ao Senhor/Shout to the Lord*) only with Hillsong songs in Portuguese. Paula started looking for original Hillsong CDs, but she found it very hard to get them at that time because they were imported. Some months later, she finally found and bought a Hillsong DVD in a specialized Christian shop. The DVD explained the church, included preachings by Senior Pastor Brian Houston, and showed scenes of the services and youth events. Paula's parents were pastors and she started thinking that she could transform her family's church. She went on to say:

> I saw that it was the young people who composed and recorded the CDs, and I started to see that as a dream, God's dream, a dream for our own

church. I started to think that if this ministry were the best in the world, the most influential church, I want to study there because I want to give my best to God and the church.

The large majority of Brazilian churches are run by middle-aged pastors, so the fact that young people had agency and even positions of power at Hillsong made Paula imagine a world that could be "otherwise." She felt that she could be part of this change with God's blessing. The impact Hillsong had on her life was so great that she started studying English at 12 years old so that she could travel to Australia, study at Hillsong College, and bring what she learned back to her church. It is significant that Paula blurred her love of Hillsong and Australia, using the word "fan" to describe her relationship with both of them:

> I had all their CDs. And I kept researching about Australia on the internet. I had several photos, I studied the [Australian] culture, customs, curiosities, its exotic animals . . . I studied virtually everything about Australia, I became a fan! [laughs] Just like a teenage fan. Every teenager has an idol singer, right? Mine was Hillsong [United]; I was a fan. I already knew the names of the band members from the DVD, so my cousin and I researched everything else about Hillsong on the internet. At the time it was more Myspace [that was] the social network, so we would even check out their [United band members'] profiles on Myspace! We were following them online, finding out where they were going to give concerts, how old they were, their family; I found out that Joel [the band leader] was Pastor Brian's son!

For Paula, and so many others, Australia and Hillsong become blurred as "places and forms of authority . . . through the mobilization and organization of affective investments," as Grossberg (1992: 65) noted. When the band finally came to São Paulo in 2006, she went to the concert with her cousin: "We arrived early, so that we could be right by the stage . . . Just like a fan that goes to a concert to see the band they love." The following year, Darlene Zschech gave a concert in Rio, and Paula and a few friends took the five-hour bus ride from São Paulo to Rio on the day of the concert and returned home that very night. Significantly, social media played an important role in connecting them with other young Brazilians who also loved the band. Paula joined the "I Love Hillsong" fan club on the then social network site Orkut. She recalled:

On Orkut there was this Hillsong community, in which many Brazilians like me who had this dream, were exchanging conversations [about Hillsong and Australia]. In fact, after the concerts we used to organize a get-together with other people from the Hillsong Orkut community. So we were making more and more friends who also dreamed of going to Australia, who loved Hillsong.

We can see here how the online and offline worlds are deeply connected. While in her interview Paula frequently overlapped Australia and Hillsong as objects of her and her friends' dreams, they were also God's dream for herself and her church. She told me: "In their concerts we had experiences with God. He was speaking to me about this dream through the songs." In order to fulfil this dream, she started working to save money for the trip at fifteen. Finally, in 2009, when she turned 19, she left for Australia. As Grossberg (1992: 56) theorized, affect inflected her new fandom experiences with "color, tone and texture." As a fan, Paula invested excess energy in Hillsong and Australia and hence both became "mattering maps" that organized her life as a teenager. They gave her an identity as a fan and offered a community of like-minded youth with which she shared her passion for and dream of joining Hillsong in Australia. Her fandom was made more potent because it was not only her own dream but also God's.

All the people I interviewed used the word "dream" to explain how they imagined traveling to Australia and joining Hillsong. In addition, I heard those who were in Australia frequently telling each other that they were "living the dream," as we will see in Chapter 4. Dreams are about aspiration. They are about imagining a positive future. They also signify an almost unreal future that depends not only on one's agency but also luck or, in this case, a miracle to come true. Paula told me: "I was able to go to Australia and join Hillsong because it was God's dream [for me]; it was God's miracle." This understanding that God was in control of one's life and inspires one to go in a different direction or act a certain way was a constant in my interactions with these young Brazilians, as we will see in the next chapter. For Paula, as she believed that this was God's dream for her, it gave her the enthusiasm and confidence to invest considerable energy and time to change her life—working, saving money, and learning English. Eight years after she first listened to that Hillsong CD, she traveled to Australia and joined Hillsong. There, she was successful in an audition to join the choir. She then chose to sing in the choir on Saturday and Wednesday services and join the

Sunday evening services as part of the congregation because that was when the Brazilian community came to church.

Unfortunately, as was the case for others who traveled to Australia to join Hillsong, she was not able to change her church upon her return. She told me: "I wasn't able to contribute [to my church] because they didn't allow me. I talked to them [the pastors]. I wrote a letter where I shared all the things I learned at Hillsong, and gave it to the pastors, the leaders." She explained that the church had "a different culture" (what I call a sensational form), and as a single female she was not able to be in a leadership position. Paula is now married to a pastor's son and is helping out at a new church her father-in-law started.

As we concluded the interview and I asked her whether she missed her time at Hillsong in Australia, she got emotional again. While she patted her eyes, she said: "I miss it a lot. It was my church! Some Sundays I wake up wishing I could go to Hillsong service. I miss the way they conducted services, the atmosphere, the worship, participating in the choir, and their conferences which were fantastic. I have all these memories." As we can see, Paula still has a strong affective relationship with Hillsong. She misses its style of service and events and singing in the choir. For her, Hillsong's sensational form created a particular atmosphere that connected her to God and a different life. I can only speculate but perhaps the vignette at the beginning of the chapter, in which I describe my own emotions—feeling excited, privileged, and grateful—as I walked into a service in Sydney after I returned from Brazil, goes some way toward describing Paula's and other young Brazilians' affective relationship to Hillsong and Australia.

Constructing Dreamlike Places

The case of Western fans of Korean popular music (K-pop) boybands can help us understand how digital media structures Brazilians' imagination, dreams, and affective investment in Hillsong and Australia to the point that they become mattering maps. As I compare the two kinds of fandom, I am aware that, unlike K-pop idols, Hillsong pastors and worship leaders are also believed to be anointed by God—they speak and sing inspired by the Holy Spirit. Their charismatic appeal thus has a different quality to that of K-pop idols. Still, Rebecca King-O'Riain's work on Western K-pop fans is helpful in so far as she (2020: 2) investigated how K-pop fans' "loyalty is elicited through the emotional experiences of fandom online," and "how these emotions are validated as authentic." She argues that fans' experiences of "liveness," produced by online engagement with idols on a daily basis, allow them to feel emotionally close to their idols, creating loyalty. K-pop fans watch their bands perform online, follow band members on apps and social media, and post comments online to them during these interactions. For their part, Korean idols constantly post clips and pictures of allegedly their everyday lives, which are in fact heavily curated to produce a sensation of intimacy, and thus make fans feel that they have a close connection with them. King-O'Riain (2020: 2) found that participation in fan communities created a "corroborated authenticity" that validated fans' emotional investment.

Similarly, Hillsong celebrity pastors and musicians constantly post pictures and stories of their mundane pursuits on several social media platforms, as we saw in the previous chapter. This also imparts a sense of intimacy and authenticity among Brazilian fans, as we saw in Paula's case. In fact, young Brazilians' relentless engagement with Hillsong musicians on social media became a running joke among the latter for a while. A member of the Hillsong staff told me that musicians coined the expression "the come to Brazil effect" to account for the fact that as soon as any of them posted something on social media, Brazilian fans would write in the comments, "Please, come to Brazil!," even though the band often toured the country. As with K-pop fans, Paula's participation in the Hillsong fan community on Orkut also created a "corroborated authenticity" that validated her excess affective investment.

Importantly, King-O'Riain showed that the digital world is not "placeless" (2020: 3). The location of K-pop idols in Korea gave a sense of authenticity to fans' digital experiences and made them feel emotionally closer to their idols. She (2020: 16) writes, "some fans come to idolise Korean society . . . they loved everything about Korean culture, language, and Korean people without knowing much about Korea". Many fans started to learn Korean language and culture to feel closer to their idols and attributed their characteristics to Korean culture. This was brought home to me by my teenage niece who is part of the large K-pop fan community in Brazil. Through her I learned how they idolize the singers and desire to learn about Korean culture and language, flocking to K-pop bands' concerts in Brazil.

As we saw in Paula's story, a similar process of overlapping their love for Hillsong with its location in Australia took place among Brazilians. They start idolizing and learning about Australian culture and society to feel closer to the band and the church. Australia thus becomes an object of their dreams, just like Hillsong. They associate both with the idea of perfection. Australia, as part of the Global North, is idealized as "perfect" in the Brazilian media and in the minds of Brazilians. This idealization overlaps with the key feature of Hillsong's branding: excellence. Australia first entered the Brazilian imaginary after the 2000 Olympic Games in Sydney. Since then, Australia has featured more prominently in Brazil through an ever-increasing amount of (overwhelmingly positive) images circulating in the country. They are created as much by the increasing number of Brazilians in Australia (on social media and in conversations with their families and friends), the Brazilian media, and the Australian government. For instance, as early as 2002, *Folha de São Paulo*, a prominent Brazilian newspaper, ran a story on Brazilians in Australia. One of the sections was titled "Everything Works in Sydney, Even Street Traffic," and it described how there were no traffic jams in the largest city of Australia. Of course, this was a construction derived from a desire for what Brazil lacks: organization. Traffic jams are common occurrences in Sydney, and public transport is in some ways worse than in São Paulo (Sydney relies on a train rather than a subway system). In 2018, *Exame*, a weekly business magazine, reported on the best cities to live in the world—Sydney was ranked sixth, while Rio de Janeiro was ranked 118th, and São Paulo 122nd (Ruic 2018). This kind of news is always reported by Brazilian magazines, blogs, and on social media. This comment was posted as a response to this news on a blog called Brazil-Australia:

> I have a *dream*, that one day I'll be in this wonderful country. I pray to God that I am healthy and have money to go to Australia [one day]. I study everything about this fantastic country: its culture, way of life . . . everything makes me believe that Australia is a model to be followed by other countries. (http://www.brazilaustralia.com/os-paises-com-melhor-qualid ade-de-vida-em-2015/)

For its part, until the country closed its borders for two years in March 2020 due to the COVID-19 pandemic, the Australian government heavily marketed Australian education and tourism in Brazil. It organized annual education fairs around the country to sell Australia's "excellent" education system, illustrating its marketing pieces with images of its beaches, the outback, and glittering cities. It also organized an annual Australian Festival, in which prominent artistic groups (e.g., Sydney Dance Company, Circus Oz, and Indigenous groups) to perform in several capital cities. The Australian Embassy in Brazil entices Brazilians to travel by promoting a positive image of Australia on its Facebook site. There, it posts articles referring to Australia as one of the best places to live in the world, describing its laid-back lifestyle and places to visit in the country. This is understandable since both education and tourism play a significant role in Australia's economy. This increase in awareness of Australia comes hand in hand with a burgeoning number of Brazilian students, migrants, and tourists to Australia and the increase in the number of Brazilian companies selling educational packages to Australia.

When these two idealized perceptions meet, you have a very strong pull factor which allure Brazilians to Australia. Traveling to the country and being able to serve or study with celebrity singers in a fashionable church become infused with a dreamlike quality. The asymmetry of power between the Global South and North contribute to the dream of traveling to Australian and joining Hillsong. Indeed, celebrity culture is even more potent when it flows in English, the language of power of globalization, and from North to South. Peggy Levitt (1998: 927) has coined the term "social remittances" to describe "the ideas, behaviors, identities, and social capital that flow from receiving- to sending-country communities." Significantly, she (1998: 940) argues that "remittance impact is also a function of size and power differences between sending and receiving country. . . . Some recipients will be more receptive to remittances because they want to be more like those in the 'rich,' 'modern,' receiving community."

That is one of the reasons why, for many young Brazilians, going to Australia to visit or study at Hillsong College in Sydney becomes "a dream." Indeed, when I asked a young Brazilian in his second year of the Hillsong College what his Brazilian friends thought of him studying there, he replied: "They think is it fantastic! I have a friend [who] tells everyone that his friend is studying at Hillsong, [that] his friend is part of Hillsong and such." His young friend was obviously hoping that the sheen of celebrity, which he felt the student acquired by studying Hillsong, would rub off on him.

Similarly, many Brazilians become emotional on their first visit to the church. Pondering on that very moment, a young upper-middle-class Brazilian (his father is a judge and mother a lawyer) told me when I talked to him in Sydney:

I think ninety percent of Brazilians *cry* when they arrive at Hillsong church for the first time. Because I think it's kind of thrilling. It's not so much about

Christianity, in relation to God, but I think it has to do with [the structure of] Hillsong which you don't find at Brazilian churches.

Significantly, he does not associate young Brazilians' affect upon arriving at Hillsong Sydney with a spiritual experience of God but with the large structure and production values of Hillsong services which they associate with the Global North. Crying as embodied affect is understandable when we know that, as fans, they had made an excess of affective investment by directing their energies for this moment in which they would arrive at Hillsong. For many years they had imagined themselves at the church while they sang its songs, went to the bands' concerts on their global tours, followed the pastors, bands, and services on social media, and exchanged gossip about them in online fan clubs. As fans, they had spent time, money, and imagination preparing for the trip—by following the band online and going to their concerts in Brazil, singing their songs in their local churches, learning English, saving money, securing visas, and researching about Australia and Sydney. The fact that many Brazilians see their ability to travel to these dreamlike places as the work of God in their lives makes their fandom even more compelling.

The Trouble with Fandom

As megachurches use celebrity culture and spectacle to appeal to their congregation and the unchurched, they run into a problem. Are they still places of worship or have they succumbed to secular culture? As we saw in the previous chapter, as a more recent sensational form, Cool Christianity has become hypervisible, and it has its detractors. Many pastors accuse Hillsong of being light on theology. Hillsong's reliance on celebrity culture as a key part of its global branding causes tension since it blurs the secular and religious domains. According to Wagner (2020: 13):

> Hillsong's transnational structure dictates that it uses mass mediated, "celebritized" images of its musicians to communicate its values efficiently. However, it must do so in an evangelical Christian context in which only Jesus is the "Famous One" and celebrity is often viewed with suspicion. The "celebrity" of its musicians must therefore be carefully managed. To do this, Hillsong promotes its values and message through a group of well-known

worship leaders who are also part of the church's inner circle. Darlene Zschech, perhaps Hillsong's most well-known worship leader during its transition from a locally facing Australian congregation to a globally focused one, was during that time co-branded with Hillsong—she and the church were inextricably associated with each other.

Darlene Zschech has long left the band and Hillsong, but the church continues to create celebrity worship leaders, such as Joel Houston, Jonathon "JD" Douglass, and Taya Gaukrodger (née Smith). Lyrics are also employed to justify engaging with youth cultures and celebrity worship leaders. Hillsong's Young & Free song "Only Wanna Sing" (2015) seems to be written to make sure that congregants understand that music is not about spectacle, entertainment, and hype (despite the clubbing atmosphere of performances) but to worship God. Its lyrics state: "This is no performance; Lord I pray it's worship; Empty words I can't afford; I'm not chasing feelings; That's not why I'm singing; You're the reason for my song; I only want to sing, If I sing for You, my King; I can't imagine why; I would do this all for hype; Cause it's all to lift You high."

The full celebrification of Hillsong took place after it established branches in the United States from 2010 onward. Particularly in New York City, more and more celebrities such as Justin Bieber, Hailey Baldwin, Kendall Jenner, Selena Gomez, models, sport stars, and fashion editors were attracted to the church by the then charismatic lead pastor Carl Lentz. As they posted their experiences at the church on social media, they created a hype around the megachurch, which was then featured in American secular media, as we saw in the last chapter. After its increase in profile in the United States, Hillsong's celebrity status in Brazil strengthened. As with other people in the Global South, Brazilians are very much aware of and copy trends from the North (Rocha 2006a). Brazilian celebrities then joined the church services overseas and posted their experiences on social media. For instance, while playing for Chelsea, the Brazilian soccer player David Luiz converted at the Hillsong London branch and was baptized at the Paris branch after moving there to play for Paris Saint German. He then posted pictures of his baptism and other church activities on social media for his millions of fans. Another local celebrity, Bruna Marquezine—a soap opera star at Globo TV network and former girlfriend of soccer player Neymar—has been to Hillsong Los Angeles. While there, she posted short videos of her church visit on Instagram and reproduced the lyrics of the song "Alive" on a subsequent post to her fans.

These posts were widely shared on social media and ended up as stories in Christian online news sites (Chagas 2014). The fact that Brian and Bobby Houston's son Joel—the worship leader of Hillsong United and co-pastor of the church in NYC—is married to a Brazilian model has only strengthened this connection among music, fashion, celebrity culture, and Hillsong in the minds of Brazilians.

However, while the church stimulates engagement with youth via celebrity culture, once Brazilians arrive at Hillsong in Sydney, their fandom becomes a problem. Pastors and musicians with whom Brazilians engaged online are frequently present at the church's headquarters and branches in the city. They have real lives and do not expect people to approach them as groupies at church. Aware of how Brazilians relate to Hillsong through fandom and how this causes issues in Sydney, a Brazilian student in his second year of Hillsong College who is in charge of assisting new arrivals from Brazil devised a strategy. In his first meeting with new students, he always warns them not to treat those connected to Hillsong as celebrities. As I interviewed him at a café close to the Sydney branch near central station, he explained:

> I tell them, "Guys, please, this is their home, don't ask these famous Hillsong people to take pictures with you. I'd rather you have a chat, have a conversation [with them]." Because what is the photo for? To show someone who's not here that you had a moment of closeness (which you did not have!) with a person you never even met. For example, Taya Smith, the singer of United you just saw walk by... This girl has 300,000[5] followers on Insta! She's super famous, but here she feels at home.

The association of Hillsong with celebrity and youth cultures also poses a problem for Brazilian diasporic churches in Sydney. Scholars have demonstrated the ways in which religious institutions from the home country support their migrant congregation by creating a home away from home (Freston 2008; Levitt 2007; Vásquez and Marquardt 2003; Tweed 2002). Religious institutions in the diaspora function as social institutions. They help migrants cope with the pressures and anxieties of migration by offering them a meeting place where they can speak their language and eat food from the homeland, meet others in the same situation, make friends, find jobs, accommodation, and learn the culture of the host society.

However, for many Brazilians I spoke to this was not enough. Traveling to Australia by themselves and being young and middle class, they also wanted to learn English, meet Australians, and integrate in society to recover their middle-class status as soon as possible. Hillsong potentially offered these things plus the gloss of being part of a famous church. A Brazilian pastor told me that recently arrived Brazilians joined his church as soon as they arrived. Many had contacted him before departure to make sure they had a safe place in the new country. However, once they were more established, they left for Hillsong. He sighed when he concluded: "It is more fashionable to have a picture of themselves on Facebook by Hillsong than by my church. Brazilian churches do not give them the glamour that Hillsong gives." This revolving-doors situation resulted in his church not having a stable community of congregants and him not being able to plan the future of the church. This was a common complaint in other Brazilian churches. Even those churches that catered to older, working-class Brazilians who arrived in the second half of the twentieth century worried that the second generation born in Australia were leaving for Hillsong and other Australian megachurches. During my fieldwork at CJC (which I discuss in the next chapter), I spoke to many parents whose children begged them to be allowed to go to Hillsong services and activities. They acquiesced, reasoning that at least they were excited to go to church.

Conclusion

In this chapter, we saw how Hillsong arrived in Brazil and entered the imagination of young Brazilians as a church that offered a life that could be otherwise. Hillsong music traveled to Brazil using the same pathways as American Christian music and culture. This meant that Hillsong quickly acquired the prestige that American cultural products enjoy in the country. As Brazilian Christian singers, worship bands, and churches translated and recorded songs by Hillsong, these songs became well-known by congregations and joined a burgeoning Brazilian gospel industry. In time, young Brazilians created fan clubs on the emerging social media environment and Hillsong bands started touring the country. Hillsong uses celebrity culture to expand globally. Once it established branches in the United States and US celebrities joined the church, it became even more famous in Brazil with local celebrities posting their experiences in the Hillsong US branch on social media.

In this context, I analyzed how young Brazilians became fans of Hillsong, overlapping their love of the megachurch with an excitement for Australia, and turning them into sites of authority and optimism. For them, traveling to Australia to join Hillsong became a dream that propelled them to make excessive affective investments. However, different from other pop culture fans, their fandom was authoritative because, in their eyes, it was inspired by God. This fandom constituted a mattering map that structured their lives. Many started working, saving money, and learning English to be able to make their dream come true. In the next chapter, we will follow these young people's lives in Australia. We will see how God became even more central in their lives, as they faced loneliness, precarity, and downward mobility while transitioning to adulthood away from their families and homeland for the first time in their lives.

3
Resting in God

"Latino Night" was widely advertised on Hillsong social network sites as part of the church's "Diversity Month." During that month, other communities were highlighted in the Sunday evening services. Hillsong offers space for different ethnic groups to express their "cultures" within the church because of its location in Australia, where multiculturalism is such an integral part of society. Starting as a government policy in the 1970s, Australian multiculturalism is based on an essentialization of ethnicity which emphasizes cultural difference (Castles et al. 1990). Diversity Month, of course, also helps Hillsong to emphasize its global outlook.

As usual, I attended the evening service at the Sydney city campus, where most Brazilians congregate. The service was in English but emphasized Latin American culture: the band played popular secular Latin tunes (La Bamba, Macarena, etc.) while the pastor and members of the congregation danced on the stage. Groups of young people held up flags of the different countries they hailed from. The service ended with everyone doing a conga line starting on the platform and moving through the auditorium. After service, young Latin American volunteers were selling food from their countries at the café. Before I move on, I should note that the presence of secular music and dance on the platform marks an important difference from the Brazilian Pentecostal style, as we saw in the previous chapters.

The pastor who preached that night was Chris Mendez, an Australian-Argentinian pastor who later that year would move with his family to Buenos Aires to plant a new Hillsong campus. A year later, in 2016, together with his wife, he would also be appointed "Lead Pastor" of the São Paulo campus in Brazil. At 44 years old, he sported the usual Hillsong pastor dress style—skinny jeans, white T-shirt, black leather jacket, a silver necklace, sneakers, and an undercut hairstyle. As he preached, he addressed a common issue for this particular congregation: the discrimination many in the congregation had faced as foreigners in Australia. He started by telling us that his parents had come to Australia in 1974. When he turned 21 years old, he decided to visit his cousins in Argentina. At the time Argentina was a dictatorship.

He told his story as a dramatic but fun narrative, gesticulating emphatically and walking from side to side on stage. He said that one night when he was driving home from a party with his cousins, a police officer stopped them and dragged them out of the car. He felt the gun on his neck, at which point he produced his Australian passport and started speaking in English. Immediately, the policemen treated him differently and apologized. He enacted the scene by lying on the floor and then raising his own Australian passport on one hand high above his head. In the midst of several "wows" and "awesomes" from the congregation, he continued: "Because of my citizenship I had access to a set of rules which were not of this country. Rules which were from somewhere else."

Mendez then mentioned Philippians 3:20 ("For our citizenship is in heaven, from which we also eagerly wait for the Savior, the Lord Jesus Christ"), and the words "Our Citizenship is in Heaven" were beamed on the large screens on the back of the stage. He asserted that even if people were discriminated against in Australia, they belonged to a more important place than a nation on earth. He stressed: "because we are citizens of high heaven, we are safe, just like when we have an Australian passport in another country." Mendez then explained how he himself had been discriminated against as a migrant in Australia:

> I grew up in an area of Sydney where migrants were treated differently, where your fate was already set. You could only have certain jobs. But in God we have access to something higher; there is no limitation. On this Earth your ID, your citizenship will be tested, but not in heaven. In the dictionary, citizenship means that you are entitled to government protection. That tribulation you are going through is nothing because you are entitled to the protection of heaven. You lost your job, your promotion, you don't have a job. That's not the end of you. This month here we are having African Day, Latino Day, Asian Day. But what is important is Kingdom Culture. Multiculturalism is really important on Earth. Christianity transcends countries, cultures; it is supranational. Regardless of the place you were born, the color of your skin, the accent you have, in Christ we are one. What makes us one is Kingdom Culture, not Latino, Asian, African cultures. We are entitled to the protection of the Kingdom of God. The citizenship of heaven has a start date but not an expiry date. It's forever. The Bible is the passport to the citizenship of heaven. It states who we are, what we are, it

speaks to us what our rights are, and gives us access to Kingdom rights on this Earth. Remember, you are not a citizen of this world, but of heaven.

At this moment the band, which had returned to the stage a little earlier, started playing a classic Hillsong Worship tune "I Surrender": "Here I am down on my knees again, surrendering all ... Find me here Lord as You draw me near, Desperate for You, I surrender ... With arms stretched wide, I know You hear my cry."

The night's theme, Mendez's preaching, the worship songs that followed, and the food from their homeland served afterward all gave young Brazilians in the congregation a warm feeling of being at home and protected by God, in the context of the downward mobility, precarity, and structural racism they found in Australia.

In this chapter, I explore the role of Pentecostalism in the lives of the middle-class Brazilian students who have traveled to study in Australia and have joined Pentecostal churches. Brazilian students lead precarious lives. They are transitioning into adulthood and living away from the homeland and without their families for the first time. In addition, they experience downward mobility and are at the mercy of constant changes in Australian migration policy. Here, I open my focus of analysis to other two churches that adopt similar sensational form to Hillsong's—C3 and CJC, an Australian megachurch and a Brazilian church, respectively—as many Brazilians strategically circulate between these and Hillsong to find a home away from home. I argue that Pentecostalism offers them a framework to make sense of their student migration journey. Pentecostalism calls for a break with the past, belief in the supernatural, an unmediated individual relationship with God, and prosperity in this life. It offers the possibility of joining "a group of fictive brothers and sisters based on a shared moral ethos" (Martin 2002: 23) and acquiring supranational citizenship in heaven, as Pastor Mendez alluded to earlier. As I will show, their (for some, new) faith fashions God as a father and intimate friend, who loves and protects them, and works miracles in their lives (including becoming permanent residents in Australia and recovering their middle-class status through professional jobs). Furthermore, the church makes them visible when society renders them invisible (Vásquez 2014: 87–88), and gives them a sense of belonging, not only to the church congregation which becomes their family but also to a place above the nation state: the Kingdom of God.

Scholars researching religion and migration have pointed out that, by allowing transnational membership, religion presents itself as a map through which individuals, particularly transnational migrants and organizations, attempt to locate themselves amid fragmentation and dislocation generated by mobility (Vásquez and Marquardt 2003: 53). They have contended that religion is an important aspect in the insertion of migrants in the country of settlement as well in transnational processes (Levitt 2007; Vásquez and Marquardt 2003: 53–54). For instance, in their research with Brazilian migrants in Florida, Vásquez and Ribeiro (2007: 13) have shown that churches offer solace:

> Churches offer resources to help Brazilian immigrants create spaces of sociability, collective identity, and mutual aid. More importantly, beyond the institutional support, religion serves to render the process of migration meaningful, linking it with the deeply affective experience of the sacred in a hostile environment.

However, we know little about the role of religious affiliation for temporary migrants, such as the growing cohort of middle-class youth studying overseas. For them, the usual consequences of migration—isolation, loss of references, depression—are even more acute because of their young age, downward mobility, and the fact that they are not living with their immediate family. Wellman, Corcoran, and Stockly (2020: 152) use the concept of "total environment" to describe "a context that provides megachurch attendees with sufficient ministries, resources, and social ties such that attendees generally do not need to seek secular sources to have their fundamental emotional needs met. The megachurch and its activities provide a structure for their life." Here, I show that for these young people who are traveling alone, this "total environment" is supercharged: the church becomes even more important as a place of sociability, and emotional and financial support than for migrant families or local congregations. Many share accommodation with other congregants, go out with them after work and on weekends, and work together.

Significantly, I show that in their narratives of student migration to Australia, Brazilian students narrate the governance of mobility (visas, jobs, English language courses, sponsorships for permanent residency [PR]) in the language of religion. While in the past, governmentality was thought of as the power of the state to regulate and discipline its own citizens (Foucault 1997), it has now taken on global dimensions, with states policing their borders and regulating mobility and settlement (Glick Schiller and Salazar 2013: 188; Ong 1999). Significantly, the negotiations between the state as gatekeeper and the mobile individual are influenced by a global power geometry (Massey 1994: 149) in which some states and their citizens are ranked higher than others. As a result, white, wealthy, skilled citizens from the developed world are more mobile than citizens from the developing world, particularly if they are non-white, unskilled, and poor. This means that Brazilians in Australia are not eligible for working-holiday visas and other entitlements such as prompt recognition of their professional qualifications, which facilitate settlement. Leading such precarious lives, they see every obstacle and achievement as God's work in their lives. For them, God determines whether they can stay or must return to Brazil. Importantly, citizenship in God's Kingdom gives them a more significant sense of belonging than that of the Australian state. I suggest that the social context in which these young people find themselves is central to their choice of religion.

Brazilians in Australia

Brazil was traditionally a net immigrant nation, but the socioeconomic crises of the late twentieth century exacerbated social inequalities, crime, and violence, prompting many to emigrate. Although this situation improved in the early twenty-first century, presently, the country is experiencing renewed political and economic crises with alarming rates of crime and violence. According to the World Bank, in 2021, Brazil was the tenth most unequal nation in the world (just after Botswana), with a Gini coefficient of 52.9.[1] While the poor leave the country to find work elsewhere, young middle-class professionals and students leave to escape crime, violence, and stress in everyday life (Rocha 2014: 498–499; Rocha and Vásquez 2013: 7–8). For middle-class students, moving to the Global North is not always perceived as "migration" but as an *intercâmbio cultural* (cultural exchange)—a period of time living overseas to become fluent in a new language and culture. It is also perceived as an adventure and a rite of passage during which they learn to live alone and to support themselves without family and friends by their side. Like many other middle-class youths elsewhere, what propels their travel is a desire to see the world and to become independent adults and cosmopolitan. This is similar to what Robertson (2014: 1924) found for middle-class Australians, who travel abroad for what is called a "gap year" (a break between the end of high school and the start of university) seeking "self-actualization, professional development and leisure travel." However, for the Brazilian middle classes, international travel also "serves as genuine and irrefutable milestone for middle-class social identity. In public situations, the verbal display of international experience and knowledge is ... operative ... for claims to social distinction" (O'Dougherty 2002: 124). Furthermore, many also desire to accumulate "flexible citizenship" (Ong 1999) by settling permanently in the Global North to escape the high levels of crime and violence and the profound socioeconomic crisis in Brazil.

Since the beginning of the twenty-first century, Australia has become a favored destination for this sector of Brazilian society. The country's beach/surf culture, safe streets, English language, strong economy, and developed-world status are significant attractions (Rocha 2006b: 147; Rocha 2013: 68; Rocha 2014: 498–499; Rocha 2016: 166; Rocha 2017a: 127; Wulfhorst 2011: 42–44). Traditionally, the United States, which also boasts many of these features, has attracted a majority of Brazilian student migrants. However, Australia's visa system, which allows them to work and has the potential for future migration through a point system or an employer sponsorship scheme, makes the country more attractive. In addition, in the past decade, young Brazilians started increasingly referring to Hillsong to explain why they had come to Australia, rather than the usual, "I came to study English in a First World country that (thank goodness!) has a beach culture and laid-back lifestyle just like Brazil."

The precise number of Brazilians in Australia is hard to estimate, but it is clear that the community had been growing quickly until Australia closed its borders in March 2020 to contain the COVID-19 pandemic. Official statistics greatly understate the nation's Brazilian-born population, as most Brazilians are reluctant to complete census forms because of a generalized distrust of government (Hess and DaMatta 1995: 6–9) or they feel that as temporary international students they should not do so. In the latest census of 2021, there were 46,720 Brazilians in Australia (ABS 2022a). Of these, the majority was between 25 and 39 years old (28,234). This total can be broken down into three age groups: between 25 and 29 (7,303), between 30 and 34 (11,330), and between 35 and 39 (10,234). That less than half were citizens (14,785) indicates that the majority were international students or those in temporary working visas. We have to keep in mind that the census took place more than a year after the first extensive lockdowns and border closures. During this period, hundreds of thousands of international students returned home. They were living in destitution after losing their jobs while having to pay for tuition and high rents. The Prime Minister at the time explicitly told them to go home, and the government did not extend to them the financial support it was giving its citizens.

Many Brazilian students returned home, bringing their numbers down. While in 2019, there were 40,763 Brazilians students enrolled in Australia, this number decreased to 33,563 in 2020, and to 12,233 in 2022. Brazil was the fourth-largest supplier of students to Australia in 2019 and 2020, just behind China, India, and Nepal (Department of Education and Training 2020). But by May 2022, Brazil had fallen to seventh place (Department of Education 2022). Most of these Brazilian students either already have tertiary education or have deferred their university studies halfway through their degrees to study English in Australia. They see fluency in English as a way to become cosmopolitan, be able to stay in Australia, or, if returning to the homeland, convert the cultural capital acquired in Australia into economic capital (Bourdieu 1986: 53–55) as they find better jobs in Brazil. In their research on cosmopolitanism and the educational strategies of the Brazilian middle class, Windle and Maire (2019: 725–726) found a similar phenomenon:

> For both economic elites and middle-class Brazilians, cosmopolitan cultural capital has gained importance as a marker of group membership, particularly in the form "native-like" English fluency. . . . The prestige of English as the language of US economic hegemony is recognized across society. While English may be used in travel, it is in the domestic labour market and in national social circles that it has greatest currency.

Throughout my decade-long research, young Brazilians constantly referred to learning English as a goal that would give them a cosmopolitan outlook in life. That is why the large majority of Brazilians in Australia arrive as language students and subsequently move on to Vocational Education and Training (VET) courses, hoping to be sponsored by their employers in order to become Australian permanent residents and future citizens, which many of them are able to do. That they have been to university and are able to afford studying overseas attests to their upper- and middle-class status in Brazil.

Leading Precarious Lives

Australia has traditionally had a large migration intake. Results from the 2021 census show that out of a population of 25.5 million, 27.6% was born overseas and almost half (48.2%) has a parent born overseas (ABS 2022a). Like other Organization for Economic Cooperation and Development (OECD) countries, migration policy in Australia was moving away from permanent settlement to a flexible labor force. However, things are changing. Because of the border closures between March 2020 and 2021 due to the COVID-19 pandemic, and the number of people out of the workforce because they are ill, there has been a substantial labor shortage. To address this shortage, in September 2022, the new Labor government decided to engage in the biggest overhaul of the migration program since the end of World War II, shifting the focus to permanent rather than temporary residents (Galloway 2022). It announced an increase of skilled migrants' annual intake to 195,000 and increased the number of years international students can stay and work in the country after they graduate. Within the context of aging populations and skills shortages in the Global North, neoliberal governments have envisaged international students as a way of attracting highly skilled workers who are trained locally and at the same time bolstering their education industries (Robertson and Runganaikaloo 2014: 210).

Presently, the Australian government offers international students two pathways to PR and eventual citizenship. The points-system pathway awards points according to the characteristics of a "desirable" migrant. That includes age, language fluency, qualifications, area of work, and work experience. In the employer sponsorship pathway, employers have to make a case for the need to retain their foreign employees on a permanent basis. Both pathways rely on "in-demand occupations" lists that are constantly changing according to the economy's needs. Robertson and Runganaikaloo (2014: 210–214) found that the "student-migration nexus" has meant that the migration process has become long and drawn-out. Student migrants spend years as temporary residents, going through a series of student visas, bridging visas, and temporary graduate-work visas. Changing visa status also adds to the length of the process. According to Universities Australia, the peak body for the university sector, recent graduates were waiting up to ten months to shift visas in 2022 (Galloway 2022).

Since 2000, there have been several policy revisions regarding the points system and the list of in-demand occupations, and therefore, the student migration process is never guaranteed. Given the length of the process and the constant changes in migration policy, students experience long-term insecurity concerning their future. While they become socially settled over the years—making friends, studying and working, paying taxes, and acquiring an Australian habitus and worldview—they are not legally settled. Until their PR is awarded, there is always a chance that the time and money they have invested in their pathways to migration may not pay off. Leading such precarious lives, these students experience high levels of stress and anxiety.

Brazilian students face a similar situation in Australia. I interviewed a Brazilian travel agent in Sydney, who represents a Brazilian study-abroad company for Christians (to be discuss in more depth in Chapter 5). She explained how the situation of being *in* but not *of* Australia (i.e., socially but not legally settled) plays out for young Brazilians:

> Australia is paradise, but not for us. It's an illusion. There are people who have been here for five, six years and they feel they are Australian because they live here; they have documents—tax file number, driver's license; they get a tax return. They have the majority of the rights everyone has. And they start criticizing Brazil and they haven't even got their PR! They are not Australian; they are Brazilians on a student visa. Besides, they have only superficial relationships with Australians. They don't have Australian friends. That's why I say we are ghosts here.

When I enquired why she said they were "ghosts" here, she explained that they lived in a parallel world, which rendered them invisible. For instance, they were mostly studying in privately run vocational colleges designed for international students (a cheaper version of the government-run Technical and Further Education [TAFE], where Australians study). They also lacked language fluency, socialized within the Brazilian community, and held unskilled jobs in areas where there were few Australians. For her, the illusion of Australia also derived from the fact that, even if students planned their migration pathways well, there were no assurances they would be awarded PR. She gave me an example of a young Brazilian pastor at the Brazilian church CJC located in Sydney that adopts many of the features of the Hillsong style. He was studying theology at Alphacrucis College, the official college of the Australian Christian Churches (formerly known as Assemblies of God in Australia). He applied for PR through a migration lawyer as a church pastor when he graduated. The following week, the Australian immigration department changed the rules, but unfortunately the migration lawyer had not lodged the application before these changes. She explained:

> His occupation was not on the list anymore. It was down to one weekend! His lawyer could have applied up to Friday and he didn't. On the following Monday, his occupation had been dropped from the list. . . . There are lots of rules and laws; occupations are added or dropped all the time. People become very vulnerable. They are in this rush [to get PR], and sometimes they are not able to make it.

Although international students live in limbo and suffer high levels of anxiety, Robertson and Runganaikaloo (2014: 214–215, 221–222) found that they have a modicum of agency and develop coping strategies. The same can be said for Brazilian students. For instance, the pastor mentioned earlier moved to Canberra to fast-track his PR application, this time as a construction worker, the occupation he had held for many years to make ends meet. He then took the opportunity to open a Canberra branch of CJC. The Department of Home Affairs gives incentives for potential migrants to settle in rural and regional Australia, and the national capital is considered a regional center for immigration purposes. Accordingly, many Brazilians have moved there for migration purposes as it is only a three-hour drive from Sydney.

Another strategy to deal with the precarious situation in which students find themselves for years on end is to develop a fatalistic attitude: whatever is best will happen (Robertson and Runganaikaloo 2014: 222). Many Brazilians add to this fatalism a trust in a higher force. They place their worries in God's hands. For them, "God is in control."

Pentecostalism, Everyday Life, and the Governance of Mobility

Pentecostalism has helped those who suffer displacement. Miller and Yamamori (2007: 23) have argued that "Pentecostal churches often function like surrogate extended families. Within these churches, it is also possible to have a social role, an identity, as someone who is valued and needed." That is why Pentecostalism and (internal or international) migration are interconnected phenomena (Levitt 2007).

Young Brazilians suffer anomie when they arrive in Australia (Rocha 2006b: 156–157; 2013: 72–73; 2017b: 129). They may have had short holidays with their parents overseas, but for most, not only is this the first time they leave their family home and have to work to support themselves. They also have to do it overseas using a different language and in an unfamiliar culture. Middle-class Brazilians only leave their parents' home and start working after finishing university and finding full-time professional jobs. There are social and structural reasons for this. In Brazil, unskilled work—such as in the hospitality industry, which is usually taken up by students in the Global North—is performed by the large unskilled working-class sectors of society. In addition, service, be it in hospitality, supermarkets, and cleaning industries, is associated with the poor and thus something to be avoided. In her work on domestic workers and social class in Rio de Janeiro, Goldstein (2009: 158–159) has found that:

> It is simply anathema for the [Brazilian] middle classes to take an interest in the kinds of manual labor that are required or manage a household properly. Being middle class in this sense signifies that you are not the serving class. . . . [In Brazil] the middle classes are defined by their ability to pay somebody else to do the manual labor for them. . . . The members of the middle and upper classes who have domestic workers and have always had them don't really know how to do basic things for themselves—clean, cook, wash clothes, or take care of life's little nasty chores.

As they arrive in Australia without their families, they must learn to perform these chores for the first time. Most students told me how lost they were as they had no idea how to cook, clean, or manage a budget. They also feel lonely and anxious about their new adult lives in a foreign country. A young Brazilian, who left for Australia at the age of 17 right after finishing high school, emphasized how transformational his experience overseas was:

> The moment I left the family home and went to live the first time alone was very powerful. I left my family home with a backpack and a teddy bear under my arms, that's what I had. I had a wallet and a cell phone in my pocket. To look down and literally see everything I had at the time on the table . . . Sure, except for my family assets and all that, but at that moment that was what I was. That kind of experience changes your life.

As they are at the cusp of adulthood, many see their stay in Australia as a time to be free from the surveillance of their parents and community. Pastors and young Brazilians told me in interviews that many start drinking heavily, taking drugs, and/or fall into depression. Australia's binge-drinking culture aggravates the problem. Research in Brazil (Sanchez et al. 2013) has shown that binge drinking is more prevalent among wealthy students in private high schools than among poor students in public schools. It is also strongly associated with lack of parental monitoring and family structure, and time spent with friends at parties and bars at night. However, the same studies showed that teenagers who participated in prayer groups and attended church were less at risk of binge drinking. When upper and middle-class Brazilian youth move to Australia, this situation is exacerbated. They are far from their parents' supervision, but more often than not still receive money from their parents, and thus have a lot of time and freedom to go out and party with friends at night. Australia's own binge-drinking culture only aggravates the problem.

For instance, the Brazilian Senior Pastor at CJC told me that their social class and new freedoms in Australia create a lot of problems for Brazilians:

> One of the most frequent difficulties [we find] are people who are depressed because they arrived here and got disillusioned in some way. For instance, there is an image that they sell in Brazil which is not true. They say you are going to get here, learn English in six months, live by the beach, and earn $20 an hour. They arrive here, and it's hard to find a job, and it's hard to learn English, and they have to live in a shared three-bedroom house with another eighteen people. Reality bites and they are far away from their families. They can't go back to their mum and cry on her shoulder. And they are alone here, and they get pretty depressed. There is a lot of frustration. There are people who come here and have post-graduation degrees and are cleaning offices. It is very hard for them. They thought they were coming for something, and they end up in a worse situation than in Brazil.

Among the many reasons for their frustration and depression that the pastor identified is the downward mobility indicated by having to share a bedroom and work as cleaners when they have a postgraduate degree, a clear maker of being (upper) middle class in Brazil.

Many students told me how they either enjoyed this drinking and clubbing culture or avoided it for fear this would deviate them from their goals of learning English and integrating into Australian society. For instance, João is a 33-year-old Pentecostal IT worker from São Paulo who came to Sydney attracted by its surfing culture and the option to learn English. He joined C3 because it was closer to his home than Hillsong. He pointed out in an interview that this drinking and clubbing culture made him avoid other Brazilians: "I studied in two English schools here and 99.9% of Brazilians were in Australia to fool around. They were into drinking, clubbing, drugs and sex." When I pointed out that it was also easy to do these things in Brazil, he clarified:

> But there you have your family. No one knows you here. And you are here for a short period, so [you think] "let's enjoy the time that we are here." People come here to do what they haven't done [in life] yet. The issue is that most of them are really young, [they are] sixteen, seventeen, twenty. They were very much under their parents' control [in Brazil], and then they come here they are free, so [they think:] "let's have sex with everybody, let's drink" . . . And their parents are supporting them financially, they didn't have to work hard to come here anyway.

I then asked why he was not into that, and he explained it was because he was older and because he had "a relationship with God," who showed him to differentiate right from wrong. He used to have that kind of life but gave up after he started "walking with Jesus." He had so much faith that God would help him find a professional job that he asked a friend, who went to Brazil during the holidays, to drop by his home and pick up a suit for his future job. A suit is, of course, a marker of class distinction and hence its significance for him. He explained:

> Christ is with you every day, in natural things and spiritual things. Like, when I'm going to sell the car or change my visa. Today I have a student visa, [so] it's hard to get a job. But I have faith. I don't look at the natural things because that is discouraging. But I can see what is not here yet because I have faith.

He believed that God not only would find him a job, but also had supported him to come to Australia and would tell him when it was time to go home:

> My mother keeps asking me, "When are you going to come home?" I always say, "I don't know. My life is in Jesus' hands. If he tells me to go back, I'll go back right away." Because whatever he tells me to do is for the best. If I obey

Him, I'll be successful. He knows what I like, and I believe he likes to please me sometimes. He likes to see me happy, so he is telling me, "Yes, son, for now live in this beautiful country, enjoy surfing these fantastic waves with your friends." So that's what I am doing.

In this interview it is clear that João's beliefs and his everyday life, including his migration project and desire to be successful by recovering his middle-class status, are deeply enmeshed. João changed his life after he started "walking with Jesus" and believes God is a good father who will tell him how to live his life.

Other students had been Pentecostal in Brazil but rebelled against their church's strict rules and left their faith in their teenage years. However, after finding themselves in Australia's "party culture" for months on end and feeling they were losing control of their lives, they decided to find a church. Take, for instance, André, who deferred his last year of university in Brazil to go to Australia. He lived in Sydney for five years, first studying English and then business in a private vocational college. He also worked as a laborer in construction sites to support himself. I interviewed him in Brazil, some years after he had returned to help in his father's business. He told me:

You mature [in Australia]. You see the difference . . . things you don't appreciate here in Brazil . . . your father and mother. There, you have to work in construction, wake up at 5 am! You dig holes; you break walls. My goodness! In Australia the child cries, and the mother doesn't see. And you can't ask your dad for money every time.

André realized his privileged upbringing after he moved to Australia by himself and had to work in a blue-collar job for the first time. His parents were members of a Pentecostal church in Brazil, while he and his older brother had left the church. However, after he arrived in Australia, he soon joined CJC. He explained his decision with these words:

I asked God: "I want to find a Church and stay there." Because in Australia it's all too easy. I'm talking about falling off track. Many Brazilians are far from their parents. They didn't use to drink and begin drinking; they didn't use to take drugs and begin taking drugs. I was afraid that would happen to me.

He then explained that receiving money to renew his visa made him believe God wanted him to stay in the country:

> The first time I needed to renew my visa, a friend helped me and it was from that moment that I saw that was really God [who wanted me to stay longer]. I had no money to renew the visa. I was going to return to Brazil. I was not going to ask my dad for money. I thought: "God, it was difficult to come here; I don't want to go back now." [I had no idea that] My friend began to raise money in the Church. [One day] She said: "I got the money for your visa" and gave me an envelope. [She gave me] exactly the amount I needed. It was a pretty cool thing; [the church] was like my family. This was something that had never happened to me in Brazil . . . a person I met in church! It was a miracle! So I felt I was supposed to stay. I just started crying, believing.

We can see the church's role as family for André in contrast to his church in the homeland. This is so because Brazilians move to Australia by themselves, without their family or friends, at a time when they are vulnerable because of their transition to adulthood. Moreover, André left to God the big decision that would determine his future: Should he stay in Australia and continue on the treadmill of constantly paying to renew his visa and working in menial jobs in the hope of getting enough points or a sponsorship to apply for PR? Or should he give up "the dream" and return to Brazil to start "real life" in a country marred by crime, but where his family and friends were? Lacking control to have their dream choice, Andre, like many others I talked to, relied on God and saw each hurdle in their path to stay in the country, that is, the regime of governance (visas, school assessments, jobs, sponsorship) as sacred to their biography.

In all these stories, we see the church community playing the role of *locus parentis*—providing a moral compass in the absence of their parents—but also the common trope of God as a caring father. It is their going to church that supports them as born-again Christians and protects them from the dangers of being alone without their parents for the first time. Similarly, in her work on Brazilians in London, Olivia Sheringham (2013: 127) found that Brazilians perceived churches as providing "a moral framework to follow in an otherwise 'immoral' city of pleasures." Such a discourse echoes the notion of "before" and "after" expressed in many of the conversion narratives of evangelical interviewees. Suma Ikeuchi (2019), who studied Pentecostalism among Japanese Brazilians in Japan, proposed that migration and morality are intertwined. For her (2020: 6), "Morality of mobility refers to the fundamental interworking of migrant mobility and religious sensibility in the reformation of subjectivity among itinerants in diaspora." While migrants are far from their ethnic home, they are also yearning for a celestial home—the Kingdom of God. In this "double diasporic consciousness" they forge new moral subjectivities. As Robbins (2010: 160–166) has noted, Pentecostalism is preeminently a lived religion. When people convert, they endeavor to make a break with their past. They adopt new rituals and lifestyles which are deeply embodied and morally sanctioned, and they develop a relationship with God in everyday life.

In addition to dealing with the lack of parental supervision and the emotional toll of being alone for the first time in their lives, young Brazilians must deal with downward mobility in Australia. This is especially daunting for them, given that manual labor in such a significant indicator of social distinction in Brazil (O'Dougherty 2002; Goldstein 2009; Rocha 2006a: 75–78, 141; Rocha 2006b: 149–157). The two frequent jobs Brazilians have in Australia—cleaning for women and construction work for men—are thus a source of class anxiety. As Goldstein (2009: 159) noted, in Brazil "domestic workers are a good example of cultural capital (Bourdieu 1984) objectified as a kind of good or service.... You cannot belong to the elite classes without utilizing these services."

During fieldwork, I participated in many conversations that tangled people's downward mobility and God's will. For instance, during a three-day Easter church camp organized by CJC, I was chatting with two young women when they started sharing their predicament in Australia. Claudia, a marketing manager in Brazil, had just arrived in the country and was lamenting the fact that she might have to work as a cleaner. She said: "I had a maid at home! I can't possibly become a maid." Feeling a bit embarrassed by the other woman's likely interpretation of this as snobbery, she explained: "It is not that I find it bad, but I have allergies [to cleaning products]." Jessica, who had converted and joined CJC church three years prior to this chat, had no problem admitting that working as a cleaner was challenging for middle-class people. She replied encouragingly:

> If you are here, it is because God wants you to be here. He must have something planned for you. When I came here, I didn't go to church. I converted here. I had to work as a cleaner. It was an impossible situation for

me. I felt humiliated. I hated it! As a result, no one wanted to hire me. [After converting I understood] God was working on my humbleness, on my pride. Before He gave me what I wanted, He gave me what I needed. He is always working on us. This trip, your being here, is for Him to work on you, to transform you.

For Jessica, as for countless others I met, God orchestrated her migration project because He had a larger plan for her life, which had to do with a transformation of the self and a new life. This explained her hardship and humiliation. At the church and connect group meetings, these student migrants learned to reframe their physical journey in spiritual terms. The Bible offered narratives of trust and resting in God. Importantly rather than a harsh, judging God, this is a loving father who knows what is best for his children, which may mean working as cleaners and laborers and not getting PR in Australia. By putting their hopes in God's hands, they find an in-between space where they dwell in optimism and stave off anxiety about the future. This is also something emphasized by pastors. For instance, a young pastor at CJC, a Brazilian migrant himself, told the congregation: "God has a plan for your life. He did not promise everything you desire, but what you need. Don't miss the opportunities Jesus places in your life to live the Gospel in everyday life."

Marcelo's story is another good illustration of how upper middle-class Brazilians arrive in Australia, suffer downward mobility, and rely on God to support them to overcome difficulties and recover middle-class status. Marcelo owned a large eyewear shop in an upmarket suburb of São Paulo. He decided to go to Australia after his shop was robbed, and the insurance company used a loophole in the contract to pay just half of what they owed him. After years of working long hours to establish the shop, he was exhausted and disillusioned. So he decided to enjoy life for a change. At 28 years old, he sold his shop and enrolled in an English course in Australia. Like many other Brazilian students whom I interviewed, he chose Australia because of the similar climate, its surfing culture, and the possibility of working 20 hours a week. Upon arrival, he joined other international students in the unskilled labor force. In an interview he told me how he called on God's help when things became unbearable:

I was delivering milk one morning. It was four in the morning, it was raining cats and dogs, and I had to go up a steep street to deliver milk to the door of some house. I said: "God, I just can't do this anymore!" He replied clearly [in my heart]: "Get your CV ready to find work in your profession." I put together my CV in the same week and handed it out in shops. He was giving me directions, and I was doing it. The last store I left my CV was the one that called me, and that is where I am today.

He had been a Pentecostal in Brazil but had left the church behind some years prior to the trip. After he arrived, he sought a church where he could learn English and meet young Australians. He found this in C3, an Australian Pentecostal megachurch in Sydney's northern beaches, where he lived. There he learned that people's own efforts are not enough to be successful in life. They need to listen to God and follow His will. He told me:

I've always been a very confident guy. I've always believed in myself, and God closed the doors for me. When I said: "Enough, I quit," He said: "Now I can do my job." And He transformed [my life]. Today I know that I have to do my part, but if God does not open doors in your life, forget it. If I got where I am today, it is because of Him. God has transformed my life. I left Brazil feeling like a loser, but three years later *I'm living a dream* that is much bigger than I ever imagined in my life.

We see once more the trope of dream and its association with Australia and God's grace in contrast to the difficult life in Brazil, which we saw in the previous chapter. At the time of the interview, Marcelo was a sales manager for three shops and his boss was sponsoring him for PR. Countless other interviewees told me that God loved them and knew what was best for them, which was not always what they wanted (to stay in Australia). They just needed to listen to Him so that He could point them in the right direction for their lives.

On another occasion, the young Brazilian CJC pastor who missed his PR application deadline gave a sermon that I thought was very close to his own experience of migration to Australia. He pointed to a throne-like chair placed on the platform and told the congregation:

You don't have to worry with the immigration department, visa, or your boss. You just need to place your forehead on the floor and pray and rest in God's arms. Because when the [Australian] government rises against you, when it doesn't allow you to stay, He protects you. No other throne will take the place of God's. In Acts 12:23, Herod was killed when he didn't give praise to God. No earthly power can win against God. Rest in God. You don't have control of your life. What other evidence do you need that you will lose against God [if you fight him]? It is best if you give your life to God. Don't fight against Him. He created you. He is in control anyway.

He clearly pitched the power of the state against that of God and revoked the authority of former. For him, and so many others I spoke to, God ultimately controlled the governance of mobility. He could make the immigration department issue visas but also deny visas if the person was meant to go home. Through prayer, people were able to establish a relationship with God and ask for what they wanted. However, they also had to listen to what God wanted for their lives and follow His instructions. At any rate, they ultimately belonged to God's Kingdom, which was more important than becoming a citizen of Australia. Indeed, on another occasion, he quoted Isaiah 40:29–31 in his preaching: "He gives strength to the weary and increases the power of the weak. Even youths grow tired and weary, and young men stumble and fall; but those who hope in the Lord will renew their strength." He then affirmed:

> Since I came here, I have had only worries. We only think of visas, finding work and a place to live. But we have to remember that we are citizens of heaven. All this here is fleeting. Our homeland is elsewhere. Keep your eyes on Christ. Don't lose hope.

Because these churches emphasize an ethic of personal success in this world, it makes sense for student migrants to think that God will help them with their everyday problems and, if they follow His will, they will be successful in this life, even if that means they have to return home. Once I met a young Brazilian who, after living in Sydney for six years, had acquired PR and was graduating from the C3 College. In the last semester, one of his teachers prophesied that God had a plan for his life, which was return to Brazil to plant a C3 church. He told me, "Through the Holy Spirit, this teacher prophesied my life. I had goosebumps from head to toe, and I started to cry. I understood that it was exactly what I needed to hear." I then asked whether he was not upset that, having finally received PR after so many years of struggle, he had to go back to Brazil. His answer mirrored what others told me: "I learned never to prioritize my will. I like to prioritize God's will because I know He knows what is best for me." As people feel they hear God's will, they surrender to it because God has a plan for their lives. Their main job is to discern the voice of God among so many other voices, a similar process that Luhrmann (2012: 41) showed in her research of Vineyard Church in the United States:

> These evangelical Christians, then, not only have to accept the basic idea that they can experience God directly; they must develop the interpretive tools to do so in a way that they can authentically experience what feels like inner thought as God-generated. They have to pick out the thoughts that count as God's and learn to trust that they really are God's, not their own, and they have to do so in a way that does not violate the realistic demands of their everyday world.... To an observer, what is striking is how hard people work to feel confident that the God who speaks to them in their mind is also the real external God who led the Jews out from slavery and died upon the cross.

Likewise, in one of Hillsong services I heard a pastor tell the congregation: "The Bible is not a historical text; it is relevant for your everyday life." In the three churches where I conducted research (Hillsong, CJC, and C3), during prayer requests at the beginning of services, people were constantly asking for prayers for visas, jobs, and accommodation in addition to the more usual prayers for healing. In this sense, we can see the ways in which Pentecostalism is a lived religion and how these young people develop a relationship with God and experience His presence in their daily lives.

"It Is the Season to Rest in God"

As we have seen in the many stories in this volume, all students traveled alone to Australia and the church became their family. While the pastors played the role of parents, congregants became siblings to each other. The way Brazilians participated at Hillsong connect groups gives us a good understanding of how they build a sense of family. Megachurches are many times impersonal, so they have "connect groups"—small groups from the congregation who meet outside church weekly or fortnightly to study the Bible, share a meal, and support each other. Many Brazilians at Hillsong prefer to join Brazilian connect groups since they are able to speak Portuguese and share their concerns with others from the homeland. As part of my fieldwork, I participated in a Hillsong connect group for Brazilians for two years. Typically, the group would meet fortnightly on a weeknight at a flat that one of the group leaders and two other participants shared. We all would bring food to share—usually a mix of Brazilian food such as packaged *farofa* (toasted cassava flour) and *pão de queijo* (baked cheese balls) and ready-made food such as roast chicken and dips and crackers. Normally, they bought food in the large supermarket on the ground floor of the building before going up to the flat. They had little time or money to prepare something more elaborate. Because I was older and not precarious, I always made an effort to bring a homemade dish that would nurture them as a way of giving back.

After eating together and socializing for an hour, we would move from the dining table to the living room. The actual meeting would start with one of the leaders asking: "How was your week? Would you like to share something?" One evening, no one volunteered a reply to these questions, so the leader added: "We are your family here. Our families are far away in Brazil, so we are family. That's how we survive here. We support each other." Thus prompted, people started opening up. A young woman told us she was happy that she had found a place to live. A man said he had just arrived in Australia the previous week. He explained that he had lived in the country in 2008 studying English for six months. He had returned to Brazil but always wanted to come back. He then told us: "The doors were closed. I did everything I could to return, but nothing worked." He interpreted this as God telling him that it was not the time yet. Now that it had finally happened, he decided to be baptized again, this time at Hillsong, so that it would mark his new life. Excitedly, he told us that the pastor had set his baptism date for Easter Sunday, and therefore he felt that God had been preparing this special occasion for him. After others had shared their fears, difficulties, and accomplishments as temporary migrants in Australia, the leader summed up their stories with these words:

> You pray and you think God is not listening because nothing is happening. But He is preparing things. Your time is not His time. God has wonderful things for you. He is madly in love with you. He looks down and sees Jesus in us. He loves us so much that He gave up His own son, His best thing, for us.

The co-leader took this cue to add:

> I have a message for you today. God told me, "My daughter, be still and know that I am God." There are two seasons in life: in one you fight for what

you want, and you pray for God to do it for you. It's struggle. The other season is about surrendering your life to God and letting Him do things in your life. God's timing is not your timing. When things are not working out, stop struggling. It's not the right time. It is the season to rest in God. God has our best interests in mind. At the right time, God opens the door and things happen. He's a good father; He is a loving father. We are His children, and He wants to be our best friend. We should ask God what He wants for us; we should ask Him: "What do I have to do to be the person you want me to be?" If God is not giving you something, it is because you are not ready yet. You have to make changes in yourself before He can help you. God answers if you ask, and you should keep your silence after your question. Give space for God to answer you.

Thus, the connect group leaders' speech affirms that God had a plan for each of them, and it depended on them to listen, transform themselves, and then "rest in God," that is, have faith that He was working in their best interests. As we wound down the meeting after discussing a passage of the Bible (which we all read on our phones app), the leaders asked us whether we wanted prayers for ourselves and others. As usual, people mostly asked for prayers for jobs and PR visas, and some asked for prayers for family members in Brazil. Then, we all stood up in a circle, held hands, closed our eyes, and took turns praying for others. After the prayers, we opened our eyes and hugged each other. We then started clearing up, doing the dishes, and organizing lifts for people to return home. I routinely gave lifts to people as most of them did not have a car. In the car, we continued sharing about our lives and their dreams for the future in Australia. These fortnightly rituals generated a strong sense of community through commensality, socializing, quasi-group therapy, prayer, hugs, caring, and cleaning. Through these rituals participants were able to feel the presence of God, be part of its Christian community, and be co-present in Brazil and Australia. They were also engaging in transnational family caregiving through prayer. In addition to these meetings, students established strong friendship ties by living together, engaging in other activities at Hillsong such as volunteering, and participating in Bible classes, barbecues, parties, dinners, day trips, and church camps. Consequently, most people remained in the congregation while they lived in Australia and stayed friends through social media with those they met in church, even after they had returned to Brazil.

Conclusion

In this chapter, I explored the role of Pentecostalism in the lives of Brazilian students in Australia. I showed how Pentecostalism supported them in their student migration pathways. For them, God was a loving father and intimate friend who was there in times of need and knew what was best. These churches provided a caring community akin to family. These characteristics were particularly significant to young people who led precarious and uncertain lives. They were in transition into adulthood and living away from their homeland and without their families for the first time. They also suffered anxiety because of downward mobility and being at the mercy of constant and sudden changes in Australian migration policy. In this highly stressful situation, a caring God and congregation, and the belief in a personal relationship with God are significant for their welfare.

In their narratives of student migration to Australia, young Brazilians intertwine the governance of mobility and their religious beliefs and practices. As citizens of the Global South, they have little control over whether they are able to settle in Australia. Thus, they pray for visas, jobs, and sponsorships and see every obstacle and achievement as God's work in their lives. For them, His power is superior to that of the Australian government, and He determines whether they are able to stay or must return home. Importantly, citizenship in the Kingdom of God gives them a more significant sense of belonging than that of the Australian state.

Since they are middle class, these young Brazilians had resources available to them in the homeland and coped well if they were not able to stay in Australia. Many had professional jobs they had left behind to study in Australia and were happy to leave their construction and cleaning jobs and a life of strife trying to make ends meet to return to their parents' home where they had reasonably comfortable lives. Some students were also hopeful that they would go back to Australia as tourists to visit their friends, which some of them did indeed do.

4
Living the Dream

The Hillsong College Story: For over 30 years, Hillsong College has experienced *global impact, influence, and growth*! You may have heard *stories* or even roamed the hallways of Hillsong College for yourself, but now you can get a glimpse of the *whole adventure*. Learn where and how it all started, what we've walked through and where we're headed.

—https://hillsong.com/college/history/ (my italics)

"Do you want to come to Chapel?" the Vice Principal of Hillsong International Leadership College city campus asked me at the end of our interview. She explained that Chapel was a one-hour service run by and for all the college students on Wednesday mornings. It was like a practice service before they go into the world. She was going to preach that morning and was happy to have me there among the students. I gladly accepted the offer and walked with her from the café, where the interview took place, to the warehouse-like building that houses the church and college in downtown Sydney. While we walked, students passed by us in droves coming from all directions and converging in the church. Most international and out-of-town students live in shared flats near the church sublet by Hillsong[1] and were arriving back to college after their morning break.

As we went through the large doors, we found ourselves in a reception area flooded with light. There, three young people were working behind a round-shaped reception desk. They welcomed us with a smile. Four long, rough-timber tables were placed in diagonal lines departing from the desk, and some students were working on their laptops; others were chatting with each other. I looked up and realized that the lovely morning light bathing us was coming from a huge skylight in the shape of a spire or pyramid in the ceiling. Everyone was in their early twenties and looked fresh and healthy; they actually glowed. We entered the church auditorium and the Vice Principal left me to go to the stage. It was pitch dark inside, and for a moment I was not able to see where I was. But soon enough the lights flashed on stage, the countdown started, and then the band began to play. And it was mayhem! Many of the students moved closer to the stage and started screaming, jumping up and down, clapping, dancing, their hands in the air. A few opened both arms in the shape of the cross in an attitude of openness to receiving the Holy Spirit. A young man with long hair raised his plastic chair over his head and swung it around as if he was about to throw it. I saw others stand on their chairs and raise their index fingers in the air, meaning Jesus is the one.

After the worship songs, students took turns on the stage/platform to perform different parts of the service. At one point, the MC called a girl to do the "Out-of-the-Boat"[2] session—a three-minute preaching practice. Under a thunder of clapping and whistling, the Asian-American student came to the stage. Rapidly pacing up and down, she told us of the time she had been invited to go bungee jumping but almost gave up when she was about to jump. She likened that to the moment you give your life to God: "It's scary but you have to do it," she concluded. All the while her face was beamed onto the large stage screens behind. When she finished, more clapping and screams followed. She was a celebrity for three minutes (time has speeded up since Warhol told us that, in the future, everyone would be famous for fifteen minutes). Cool Christianity is about being part of celebrity culture not only because one hobnobs with celebrity pastors and worship leaders, as I showed in Chapter 1, but also because one may become a celebrity for a fleeting moment.

When the service ended, everyone was smiling, hugging, and chatting with each other. There was a lot of love there. I know these students have moments in which they feel lost and homesick and worry about being able to pay their college fees. The students and the Vice Principal told me this much in interviews and our conversations. Yet the whole morning looked to me like an advertisement for youth culture. If we were in the eighties, it would be one for Benneton. There were people of all nationalities and colors, many sported tattoos, mostly were smartly dressed in hipster style—ripped skinny jeans, buttoned-up tight shirts, thick, black-framed glasses, boots, boho hats, and long or undercut hairstyles. As in a Benneton commercial, they were beautiful, joyful, well-fed, diverse, and cool.

Fittingly, the quote at the start of this chapter and the pictures on the Hillsong College website[3] are also an advertisement for young people. It likens studying at the College to an "adventure" in which students will join others who have come before them—while they "may have heard their stories," now they "can get a glimpse of the whole adventure." They will be able to be part of an institution that makes a "global impact." The college marketing material then has all the hallmarks of the Hillsong branding: excitement, enthusiasm, and global growth, impact, and influence. It is a brand that will be associated with new students' own life stories, as brands are.

* * *

In this chapter, I discuss young Brazilians' experiences at Hillsong College, something they frequently equated to "living the dream." Scholars have explored how megachurches mobilize the congregation's affective labor in order to grow (Johnson 2017; Thumma and Bird 2015; Twitchell 2004; Wade and Hynes 2013). Here I consider the powerful affective and transformational experiences of youth enrolled and housed at Hillsong College and who arrive alone in Sydney. I am interested in how they affectively embed their subjectivity within the church and come to think of their experience of studying and serving full time (thus donating substantial time and energy to the church) as "living the dream." What makes them feel this way? In previous chapters, we saw how affect created fandom and mattering maps for young Brazilians to join Hillsong in Australia. We also saw how difficult their lives become after they arrive in Australia and experience downward mobility. In this chapter, I consider a cohort who is more deeply immersed at the church than those Brazilians who join the church services and serve when and if they choose. I argue that there are many reasons for them to feel so enthusiastic about the college, although it means that their time is consumed by classes and serving/volunteering.

Hillsong College's focus on leadership rather than straight theology, coupled with mandatory volunteering, offers young Brazilians tools to transform their subjectivities while transitioning into adulthood. Seeker churches, like Hillsong, are well known for embracing neoliberalism and consumer capitalism. They employ business strategies from corporations, focusing on marketing, branding, growth, and management to become relevant for the unchurched. Hillsong College is no different. Formerly known as Hillsong International Leadership College, it teaches students how to become exemplary Christian leaders in whatever future field of work they choose. But students learned much more than leadership strategies. They were taught punctuality, reliability, and excellence in work practices, and learned that they were on an equal footing with pastors and worship leaders when it came to serving in the church. They praised what they learned there as fundamental for their future adult lives once they found jobs and settled.

In this context, they learn to become not only adults but also modern subjects (Beck 1992; Giddens 1991). In a classic article, Thompson (1967) demonstrated how clock time (as opposed to nature's time), punctuality, reliability, and discipline became significant from the outset of industrial capitalism. They were necessary for the synchronization and exploitation of labor. As they gain these skills, young Brazilians feel positively supported to enter the labor market. Such transformation of subjectivity also takes place within the church environment. According to Giddens (1991), while in traditional societies individuals defer to an external authority and their own choices are limited by traditions and customs, in late modernity there are fewer traditional constraints on behavior, and society becomes more reflexive, as individuals "work" on their identity rather than inherit it. Because social roles are not given, individuals need to reflect and choose a "lifestyle" in order to create a narrative of the self (1991: 81).

In Brazilian churches, where the pastor holds authority over the churchgoers' lifestyle, it is very difficult for these young people to become autonomous and take responsibility for the course of their lives, a similar dynamic that occurs in their families. However, once they are alone in Australia and join a church and college that has a more inclusive and tolerant culture to attract the unchurched, they are taught that they have autonomy to interpret the Bible and behave as they choose (within the biblical teachings) for the first time in their lives. Most told me how they felt they were treated as adults in church for the first time in their lives. They were also shocked and pleased to see that the celebrity pastors and worship leaders were not entitled. They were, in fact, equal to them in the church's everyday work. That was a stark contrast to the way Brazilian pastors and celebrity worship leaders exerted power and privilege over less powerful others, as we will see here and in the following chapters as well.

Brazilian students also expressed a passionate desire to make a difference in the world. For them, joining the college of a church that had such a global impact, and learning how to "do church" the Hillsong style, was a way to do it. I also suggest that they perceived their lives at Hillsong College as living a dream because of its cosmopolitanism. There, they were able to learn English, study, share accommodation, and make friends with other students from all over the world. The fact that the college also focusses on the creative industries (students can choose from dance, worship music, TV and media, pastoral leadership, and production streams) made it fun and relevant to this cohort. Finally, learning the Hillsong style at the college allowed them to feel they were part of the church (and brand) they loved, which in turn became associated with their own subjectivity, as is often the case with brands. As Wade and Hynes (2013: 176) have noted, Hillsong churchgoers are "affective labourers enrolled into the production of [their own] subjectivity." This made the demanding hours an investment in their own future and the future of their home churches in Brazil, which they hoped to transform.

Overall, the Hillsong College elicited deeply affective responses from Brazilian students. Here, I consider how these emotional experiences are produced and their significance in the lives of these young people.

Volunteering

Thumma and Bird (2015: 2338) have noted that while megachurches have "strong personality authoritative senior pastors," they "must generate a very high level of both lay involvement in the functioning of the church and lay ownership of the vision and a strong sense of commitment." This is done through adopting a "team-leadership model" from the corporate world. For them, this model "empowers volunteers to function as small group or ministry leaders. This dynamic, in turn, trains them and gives them opportunities for gaining leadership experience that can also be applied to their lives outside the church." Other scholars do not have such a rosy picture of lay involvement through service. In her study of Mars Hill in the United States, Johnson (2017: 160) shows how volunteers donate their emotional, physical, and spiritual labor and time to turn their pastors into celebrities and to give the megachurch its "distinctive experience." She points to the considerable costs to volunteers' lives because their work goes unrecognized and they are ignored. This can also lead to (sexual, emotional, spiritual, and physical) abuse, such as those perpetrated by Mark Driscoll from Mars Hill, Bill Hybels from Willow Creek, James MacDonald from Harvest Bible Chapel, and Carl Lentz, Brian Houston, and others at Hillsong.

Indeed, at Hillsong Church, volunteers and their affective labor are an integral part of the branding and massive growth of the church. According to Wade and Hynes (2013: 176), "To the extent that Hillsong is both a theological and capitalist enterprise, the congregation of believers effectively serve as affective labourers for the church." Always sporting easy smiles, they will be in the car park directing you to an empty spot, driving the shuttle bus between the train station and church before and after services, at the gates welcoming you to church, at the reception desk, making coffee at the café, selling merchandise at the shop, inside the church directing you to your seat, behind the cameras and the audio-mixing console during service, and translating the service into several languages for those who do not speak English, among a myriad of other activities.

The excessive amount of volunteering demanded from the congregation in the United States and United Kingdom came to the fore with the firing of celebrity pastor Carl Lentz and its fallout on the New York City branch in late 2020. One media story at the *The Post* (Frishberg 2020) noted:

> "It's like you work for a major company—only worse," Nicole Herman, who helped found Hillsong LA in 2013, told *The Post*. Herman alleges the "abuse of volunteers and real, amazing people" by Hillsong leadership to fulfill their "petty needs" (a practice called "honoring") reminded her of instant Cup Noodles: Leaders think they can just add water, no emotional investment necessary, and get a flock of loyal, unpaid laborers.

A former Hillsong UK pastor (Jobes 2022) equated serving to slavery on his blog:

> Volunteers do massive weeks; I was often doing over 20 hours of volunteering a week, on top of a full-time job, and it was never enough. There was always another ask. And the free labour isn't just used to put on church services, interns were regularly used to clean our pastor's house, do the garden, and any number of other tasks.

For Hillsong College students, volunteering is mandatory. Supposedly, it is when they put what they learned at college to practice. Miller (2015: 244) has observed that "Attending Hillsong College . . . requires a considerable sacrifice of time and money without the guarantee of employment at the end." From talking to Brazilian students, it was clear that the serving/volunteering portion of the college involves an inordinate amount of time and energy. For instance, students are expected to follow up with new church members by giving them calls to check on their welfare and invite them back to church. They also must work on weekend services and at Sisterhood and Hillsong Men (weekly events for women and men), Easter and Christmas spectacles, and other internal events. They also serve at external large events like the annual women's Colour Conference and the Hillsong Conference. The latter is particularly grueling for college students. A bus takes them from Central Station or the headquarters in Baulkham Hills to Olympic Park, where the conference takes place, in the early hours of the morning and returns them there late at night. At conference they are divided into teams, and many never get to watch the conference because they are working in other areas such as shops and kitchens. Attendance in all these "practicum" activities is recorded, and students who miss them need to make up their missed hours.[4]

In 2021, while Hillsong was engulfed in many of sexual abuse and money scandals, the media also reported an incidence of sexual assault at Hillsong College of an American girl by a Hillsong worship leader.[5] On the college alumni Facebook page, students also made complaints. For instance, upon enrolment, students have to sign a nondisclosure agreement and are interviewed about their sexual lives. Hillsong uses information from interviews to place students into a system of stop lights to allow them to work with children. In order to address these issues, Hillsong ordered a confidential review of college policies by a large law firm. The review was leaked to the Australian media outlet *Crikey*, which reported (Hardaker 2021):

> A key finding goes to the exploitation of students as free labour for other Hillsong activities, such as providing the staff to run conferences. As Crikey has reported before, Hillsong's business model relies enormously on free labour—some 5790 volunteers staff various businesses and activities such as conferences and services. Its music productions—which provide the trademark razzamatazz of a Hillsong gathering—are almost entirely run by volunteers, with more than 1800 unpaid workers. The review, which reported three weeks ago, says "a number of former students" raised concerns about "an expectation to volunteer" over and above their college academic and "practicum" commitments—the practical components of their course work.

After the review became public, Hillsong put out a media statement asserting that it was responding by establishing "a student representative council, with elected and appointed student representatives to facilitate ongoing communication of key areas of concern for the student body" (https://hillsong.com/newsroom/blog/2021/08/hillsong-college-looks-to-the-future/#.YSh2CY77Sbg). The megachurch also started to run an advertising campaign on social media featuring college students and alumni extolling their experiences there.

Of over 20 Brazilian college students I spoke to, just a single one mentioned that serving at Hillsong College was excessive. In her late twenties, she had served at Hillsong for two years but decided to study at Alphacrucis (the official College of the Australian Christian Churches, formerly Assemblies of God Australia) rather than the Hillsong College because of the amount of mandatory serving involved in the latter. She remarked:

> I think the college [workload] is too heavy; you can't work [and earn a salary]. Actually, I think it's crazy. But the [college students] are so happy, aren't they? Sometimes I think they're a little naive, you know? I once worked at the conference and almost died. I stood by the doors, helping out. I thought that [the number of hours] was absurd; it's a lot of work. I don't think anyone can take it but they're young, I think that's the difference. And I think that when you are older, you start to be more critical of things, more selective.

Thus, for her it was students' young age that meant that they had more energy and were not critical of the situation they were put in. All the students I interviewed were in their late teens and early twenties when they traveled to Australia, so she has a point. Yet I suggest that there is more to it. It was their young age that turned the experience at Hillsong College into a key moment in their transition to adulthood, as we will see in the following sections. In addition, by serving they felt they were learning how to do church in the Hillsong style, which would be valuable on their return to their home churches, and they dreamed of transforming them. Indeed, in his study of megachurches as educational institutions, Cartledge (2020: 184) has argued that:

> It is not just about what people know and what skills they gain, but also *what kinds of people they become*. Megachurches provide service opportunities that help shape individuals and communities. This learning dimension is often lost in the analysis of megachurches but it is hugely important for them and for us in our assessment of their contribution.

In the following sections, we will see how their time at Hillsong College transformed them and what they gained from it.

Becoming an Adult

While there are costs associated with volunteering, for young people it may have benefits. Australian researchers found that more often than not young people's motivations for volunteering were as follows: helping others, personal growth, recognition of one's skills, and improving their employment prospects (Mason et al. 2010). These are the same reasons Brazilian students gave when asked why they were happy to volunteer at Hillsong College. As we saw in the previous chapter, for all of the people I interviewed, this was the first time they were away from their parents' home and their country. Middle-class Brazilians only leave their parents' home after finishing university and finding full-time professional jobs. Low-skilled jobs—such as those in hospitality which youth in the Global North usually take up during their studies—are filled by working-class workers, and thus there are very few opportunities for work for this cohort. In addition, while at the parents' home, they never learn to cook, clean, or shop for groceries, as this is done either by their maids or their mothers.

Brazilian students usually enroll at Hillsong College after completing high school or halfway through their university studies. They are in the cusp of adulthood, and for most of them their time in Australia and at college functions as a "gap year," a middle-class rite of passage in which they learn English and become independent adults and cosmopolitan. As we saw in Chapter 1, Hillsong, like other Seeker churches, offers a place for self-improvement for the neoliberal age. Its services are geared to using the Bible to solve people's everyday problems. The church also functions as a brand and stimulates consumption through its sales of merchandise from pastors' books to recordings of preaching to specialized Bibles to mugs and clothes. The college's focus on leadership, a characteristic of megachurches that adopts features of the corporate world, is also part of this engagement with neoliberalism. Carlos, a student in his second year, noted:

> The name says [it all], it is Hillsong International Leadership College. It's a Bible-based leadership school. The leadership classes that we have don't apply specifically to the church, so much so that we use leadership material that's not from church. I don't know if you know John Maxwell.[6] He's a leadership author ... For example, in the first year of college we have a subject that is Personal Leadership. We have to make a five-year development plan for life. Five years from now, I want to lose 10 kilos and run 10 miles. What's

your goal in a year, three months? What are you going to do tomorrow to get it done? This applies in any area of life, not necessarily within the church.

Carlos's secular examples (losing weight and running) exemplify how students are encouraged to reflect on their future lives, something that would not be taught to a middle-aged student cohort. Carlos went on to say:

> I think the reason why Brazilians are coming here is because Hillsong College not only gives you the theory but gives you the *practice*. It is not only concerned with theology, but to use what you learn in your day to day, in your life. I believe that Hillsong College can be for anyone because it gives you an understanding of *personal leadership*, how to organize your day, how to prepare your goals and everything else.

For this student, the college is attractive to other Brazilians not because of the study of theology but because it focuses on leadership and helps young people manage their lives as they transition to adulthood. A similar explanation was given by another student:

> I think it's because they don't just have the mentality of creating Christians, in the sense of, "Oh, I want everyone to be a missionary." They have a mentality of creating skilled people. So much so that the [College] motto is . . . "for all spheres of life," not just church. Business, law, medicine . . . if you have more leadership skills, you can read people more easily, you can solve situations more easily. So I think they're not just thinking about the church, but they think about the person's life in general.

In its course guide, Hillsong also places the transformational aspect of learning how to lead one's life ahead of its teaching of Christianity. In a sense, the college pitches itself as a modernized "finishing school" that teaches life skills to young people after they graduate high school. It is there that young people learn how to make an impact in the world:

> Hillsong College offers you a *transformational education and leadership training* experience. At the heart of Hillsong Church, *you'll learn about life, leadership, and ministry* alongside *influential leaders who are changing the world*. Within a proven mix of classroom learning, hands-on ministry experience and a vibrant College community, you are ideally positioned to

develop a life of purpose and impact. Around the world our graduates are making a difference in many *spheres including, ministry, business, education, health and many creative endeavours.* Come and join in the *adventure*! (Hillsong College Course Guide 2022–2023: 11, my italics)

Claudia is a good example of how the college helps students in their transition into adulthood and how it shapes their subjectivities through volunteering. She was 28 years old when I interviewed her back in Brazil. She went to Hillsong College at 19 and studied there for three years. After her first year of university, as it is usual in Brazilian upper-middle-class families, her mother suggested that she take a gap year overseas to improve her English skills and learn another culture. Her mother and herself were fans of Hillsong United, so when Claudia suggested the college, her parents were happy to oblige. Her upper-middle-class background is clear by the family's focus on education, the aspiration for Claudia to live overseas, and the fact that her father covered all costs of her time in Australia so she did not have to work. She reflected on her college experience with these words:

> *I learned everything there.* Hillsong as a church really shaped me as a person in all aspects. It's not just in Christianity. I had a very small life in Brazil. So the experience at Hillsong shaped me as a person, as a leader, as family member, as a future mother, as a daughter. It was all shaped by Hillsong and Australia.

By saying that she had a "small life in Brazil," Claudia implies that her time at the College broadened her horizons and offered her a life that could be different from the one she had before. This new "bigger" live gave her a new subjectivity at a crucial time when she was becoming an adult. When I asked what exactly she learned at Hillsong, she painted a picture of a shy girl whose parents cocooned her. As we saw before, this cocooning is typical of (upper-) middle-class families in Brazil. She explained:

> I thought I was antisocial. Today I know I'm an introvert, which is a feature of my personality, and yet I have something to offer people. Hillsong opened my mind. I learned so much! I didn't think I had anything to contribute, but today I know I have. I'm a service person; I love to serve. I learned how serving works. There I learned to have my boundaries, to know how far

I can let people suck [my energy]; when I must say: "Oh, that's not cool in our relationship." So I learned boundaries. There I learn everything, the Christian life. . . . I didn't have a fully-formed identity. My mum spoiled me; she used to do everything for me. I had zero discipline. Brazilians don't leave home till they are thirty. Essentially, parents don't prepare us to leave home. My mother didn't prepare me.

It is significant that at Hillsong she realized that she loved serving, that is, volunteering, and that by learning how to serve she realized her self-worth. Moreover, she cited Christian life at the end of the list of things she learned at Hillsong College, demonstrating that more than learning theology, the college experience gave her tools to become an adult. She went on to explain that in contrast to her life at church and at home in Brazil, at college she was treated as a responsible adult for the first time. She told me:

Here in Brazil you learn more what not to do as a Christian: you can't drink; you can't sin; you can't go out with your friends; you can't go to the street corner with your friends who are drinking, smoking; you can't dance; you can't listen to [secular] music. There is a lot of "you can't." It depends, from church to church. [For instance] at the AOG [Assemblies of God] I was bad just because I had a haircut! As a Christian, there were lots of things that I couldn't do because my pastor said so, not God, my pastor! And at Hillsong I started to see what God says and interpret that. At Hillsong you sort of can do everything, but you have to know what is good for you and what isn't. [I felt] that *for the first time I started to be treated as an adult.*

By contrast, she praised the volunteering jobs she did during college and at the Hillsong conference as a way to learn the church culture and how to be "a real Christian."

The first team that most students work [as volunteers] at the [Hillsong] conference is called "the excellence team." But why is the team that cleans bathrooms called the excellence team? Because everything is excellence. Everything has to be done with greatness, with love. [Hillsong's] motto is "Love God, love people." [People think:] "I came here to learn to be a preacher." "No, you came here to learn how to serve the people. That is your goal for the rest of your life. Serve the people." And how do we serve them? With excellence. Always.

Here we can see how Claudia learned to be a responsible individual who had a modicum of power vis-à-vis her pastor and the church. Rather than submitting to the pastor's whims, she was able to interpret the Bible and decide for herself what would be appropriate for her. She also associates serving with excellence and love for others. These are all part of the Hillsong branding, as we will see in the next section. Claudia summarized her thoughts with these words, "One thing you learn at Hillsong and Australia is that you are in charge of your own happiness, your own life, the things that happen in your life." Claudia was transformed by her time in Australia and at the college. Away from her church and family, where she was treated as a child, she was able to become an adult and a late modern subject. She stopped following tradition and an external authority such as the pastor, to reflect on her life and choose her own lifestyle and system of beliefs. Her subjectivity is inflected by neoliberalism as she perceives herself as an autonomous individual who is responsible for her own life and happiness. Society's structures and constrains do not seem to be visible to her.

Another student stressed the same point of becoming an autonomous individual at the college when he remarked:

When I went to Australia, I was a follower of Christ but I came back as a disciple.... It's because when you follow, you follow regardless of what you believe, but when you become a disciple, you understand the teachings.

Like all other students, he praised Hillsong's exhortation for students to think for themselves:

If you watch their preaching, you'll see that they give key points of what the Bible is saying so that you can find your own truth. [They don't say:] "that's right that's wrong." It is a church that does not force any doctrine on you. "Oh, that's what we believe, that's what you have to follow." No. They give you total freedom.

I heard this kind of assessment from Brazilian students very frequently. Although it is a Seeker church and hence more inclusive, it is still a Pentecostal church. As I mention before, when students first enroll, they have to sign nondisclosure agreements and contracts asserting that they will not drink, smoke, take drugs, or have tattoos. If they do, they may be expelled. This has been met with uneasiness on Hillsong College's Facebook page, as mentioned earlier. When I asked Brazilian students whether they felt constrained by this, they explained that it was understandable that the college had asked them to sign such contracts because the college had a duty of care to students and their families. One former student justified it with these words, "Why does Hillsong do that? Because the parents trust that they will return their children as they arrived. Imagine if they arrive home drunk, tattooed, with a piercing, taking drugs?" Another told me:

> A lot of people have tattoos. Brian [Houston] doesn't like it and said so to us. A guy got a tattoo and [Brian] came in and said, "Do you want to get a tattoo? All right, it's okay to get the tattoo but this is my platform, and I don't want you to be showing it off. Cover up!" Not that it's a sin. He did not say that it is a sin. He doesn't say that drinking is a sin . . . but Brian is a traditional guy. If he lets [people do whatever they want] . . . Imagine? It will be a mess!

I suggest that because Brazilian students come from a much more conservative Pentecostal culture, they find the rules imposed by Hillsong acceptable. Indeed, I spoke to scholars from Alphacrucis College who taught many Brazilians over the years. (Hillsong has partnered with Alphacrucis College for many years and recommends its bachelor of theology degree program after three years at Hillsong College.) They told me that it was difficult for these students to accept the more critical (and liberal) approach used by Alphacrucis. This included progressive views of homosexuality, abortion, and the science of evolution. Brazilian students' discomfort generated tensions in the classroom. Academics had to balance between teaching critical thinking as the bachelor of theology required, and not wanting to create a problem for students when they returned to their home churches. One scholar noted: "The Brazilian conservative theology got challenged with our academic freedom in the Degree . . . and they couldn't handle it." Another said:

> Some of the feedback that we hear is that they're very thankful that they've been able to be exposed to this. It's really challenged them but they feel like

they've been able to grow.... At the same time, some students resist and then they think, "Oh well this [Alphacrucis] College isn't the place for me," and so they leave.

Thus, although students praised the Hillsong College for teaching them how to think for themselves, the move from the Brazilian conservative Christian culture to a more liberal one is not without conflict.

Learning Excellence and Ditching *Jeitinho*

All Brazilians associated with Hillsong—from pastors to students to visitors—praised its emphasis on excellence. Riches (2010) has noted that excellence is a key feature of Hillsong's branding. From the high production values of its services to its corporate headquarters with the latest IT features to "the brands of media technology used (Apple only), down to the brands of the water bottles in the baby room," as Klaver observed (2021: 55), all denote Hillsong's preoccupation to exude "excellence" in every detail. As we saw in Chapter 1, the focus on excellence is about being relevant to young people who are used to the secular world's high technology. But it also pertains to Prosperity Gospel, as it is associated with success and affluence. In an interview, the Vice Principal of Hillsong College gave a theological justification for the focus on excellence:

> It comes down to... me bringing my excellence to this meeting is actually just placing value on you and placing value on the time that we have. Excellence is not a formula... Excellence is bringing your best... God gave his best for us. Like He gave His son, he didn't hold back anything, and He did that so that we could be in a relationship with Him and so at the heart of all of it is that. God didn't hold back His best, so why should we hold back our best?

Brazilians admire excellence because they associate it with modernity and the Global North, which is imagined as perfect. Once, a young Brazilian man I was talking with in church said in jest but also admiringly: "Even the toilet paper is excellent at Hillsong." When you come from a society where every single detail—from hair (curly or straight, black/brown or blond) to shoes to food choices to body shape to the car one drives—is a marker of class (and race, as they largely overlap), his joke on the use of top-quality toilet paper at Hillsong makes total sense. Moreover, excellence goes against the so-called *jeitinho*. Meaning literally "a little way," *jeitinho* is a "clever dodge" (DaMatta 1979: 184), an informal system of mutual favors where people bend the rules and bypass laws for others. Brazilian society is burdened by bureaucracy, regulations, and inequality on the application of the law. In order to counter this situation, Brazilians usually use *jeitinho* as a recourse to power (DaMatta 1979; Duarte 2006). Many Brazilians wish to leave this attitude behind since they perceive it as a root cause of their country's backwardness. They eagerly aspire to excellence as a sign of modernity and development. That Hillsong uses it in all its day-to-day practices only enhances its status in their eyes, as I noted in Chapter 2.

Gustavo, who studied three years at the college, noted that it had not been easy to learn excellence because he came from a *jeitinho* culture:

> Because we come from our culture of *jeitinho*. It's a process. Because you feel a little lazy [to do things fully]. It was one of the things I had to learn at the church and that I brought into to my lifestyle. For example, when you fill the freezer ice tray. I lived with other people; there were four of us, I was the only Brazilian. I used to use it and not fill it up with water again. Can you see? I was too lazy to take ten seconds of my time and be excellent. Did I just use it? I fill it up in ten seconds and put it back. It's ten seconds that it takes. That's how it works. *These little church things have affected my life*. Take two minutes and do the job once and for all. You've finished doing something, ask: "Is this excellent?"

While Hillsong does teach excellence, and all students mention how impressed they were by it, they assumed it held an important place in Australian culture. However, Australian culture is often perceived as "laid back," "easygoing," and one in which people tell each other, "She'll be right, mate." The latter expression meaning that something is not perfect but good enough, and things will sort themselves in time.[7] Thus, the overlapping of Hillsong and Australia as if both extol excellence tells us more about Brazilians' imaginary of the Global North and their aspirations than about Australian culture. For instance, Patrícia, who studied at Hillsong College for a year, contrasted Brazilian culture with Global North societies. As we discussed the upcoming establishment of Hillsong in São Paulo, she was sure that Brazilians' lack of responsibility and *jeitinho* would pose obstacles for the church there. While she learned commitment, following rules, and giving her best at Hillsong College in Sydney, these were not things that Brazilians knew.

> They [at Hillsong] just have a mentality that is *gringa* [of foreigners from the Global North], a mindset of excellence in service, commitment, a mindset that if you say you will do something, you have to do it right, and you will be held accountable. *This is a culture that they have overseas*, and it is very strong there [at Hillsong]. They teach students that. I learned it there and tried to bring it here a little, but Brazilians are not like that. If they want to go to a movie on Sunday night [the usual service time], they won't call their [ministry] leader and say "today I can't go because of this and that. I've asked a guy to replace me." No, they just don't show up, and then there's nobody there at the right time. Hillsong is very punctilious about these things. So [when they open in Brazil], there will be a lot of people without training and it's not going to work the way they want. I think they are taking a long time to open here because of that.

Given that punctually, commitment, and dependability are not part of Brazilian culture, they need to be taught to first-year Brazilian college students (and to volunteers in Brazil when the church established a branch there, as we will see in Chapter 7). Once I spoke with a second-year Brazilian college student who was put in charge of assisting his recently enrolled compatriots. He said he had a ten-point advice to them:

> We had a session about [Australian] culture, kind of what we need to change [in ourselves] here. It was really cool because I presented it to them in a funny way as the "Ten Commandments" for Brazilians in the college. I said: "number one: the alarm clock is your friend; no Brazilian time here. If the class is at 2:30 pm, be there at 2:25 pm, five minutes before the class. Don't be late because this is not part of the Australian culture. It is socially acceptable to be five or ten minutes late in Brazil, not here; it is disrespectful, so don't be late."

Two aspects are significant here. First, like Patrícia from earlier (and many others we referred to in Chapter 2), this student overlapped Australian and Hillsong cultures (both call for punctuality and responsibility) and contrasted it with Brazilian culture (which lacks these traits). Second, his appointment to assist newly arrived Brazilians shows that, although the church is hierarchical, its base is flexible and led by volunteers. It is through these small (serving) posts that Brazilian students felt they were taken seriously, acquired leadership skills, and learned punctuality, reliability, and excellence. In brief, they felt they were being prepared for their future lives as successful adults and modern subjects.

Changing the World

In their research on young Christians in Scotland, Vincett et al. (2012) found that secularism, pluralization, relativization, and pervading consumer capitalism of the past 40 years has meant a change in the way young Christians engaged with religion. Rather than a focus on a set of beliefs, they were more interested in performing Christianity in everyday life and engaging with the secular world. They may volunteer to undertake charity work, and "speak up for social justice and accept others without prejudice or reservation" (2012: 282). The authors posit that for these youth, belief has become embodied. Believing is a practical process in which they work out their authentic selves. Rather than "Sunday Christians," for them authentic Christianity is about performing good deeds outside the traditional church.

This is very much what I found among young Brazilians at Hillsong College. Many Brazilian students told me of how they wanted to make a difference in the world. They explained that serving at Hillsong, a church that they believed had such an impact on the world, was a way to do it. On a weekday, in between his classes, I had lunch with Paulo at a hipster café decorated with many indoor plants just across from the Sydney Hillsong city campus. As we talked, he told me that he was fifteen when he found out about the college through the flyers he was given at a Hillsong United concert in São Paulo. Later on, someone prophesied he was going to be a pastor, and he took a theology course associated with his church. After a while he became frustrated with it because most teachers were retired and not active in church. He felt they did not have much to offer. He said he used to leave class with lots of doubts thinking:

I don't want that for me. *I want to change the world.* I want to leave the world a better place than I found it. I want to inspire people. I want people to have a better life because I helped them. I wanted to have a relevant life, and not follow the script: go to university, date, get married, have children, grow old.

He then smiled and said:

I've always been a dreamer. And I said "God, I want to study in a place that I'm going to be inspired, that get out of the classroom with my heart burning." That's when God reminded me of that flyer I got at the Hillsong United concert in 2006.

At the time, he was studying graphic design at university. So in order to save money to go college, he started to make and sell T-shirts emblazoned with Hillsong's Easter message "cross equals love" (†=♥) and other biblical messages in English. He also created a blog where he wrote about his life and dream to study at Hillsong and used it as a platform to sell the T-shirts online. It is a testament to the fame of Hillsong, that soon he was selling these T-shirts faster than he could produce them. That he did not translate the Christian messages on the T-shirts into Portuguese also demonstrates the importance of English as a sign of aspiration to lifestyles of the Global North. He was so successful that after a couple of years he had enough money to enroll at Hillsong College. When I interviewed him, he was in his second year of college and had just joined the Hillsong graphic design team as an intern. Needless to say, he was very excited about his new life. He said:

Look, to be honest, I still wake up and think: "I can't believe I'm living in Sydney." I still wake up and think: "I can't believe I'm working for Hillsong." As a graphic designer, *I always followed the Hillsong style. Hillsong is a reference in graphic design to Brazilian Christian churches.* You see their envelopes, flyers, video—"excellence" is their hallmark; everything is beautiful. They were an inspiration for me.

Once more, we see the praising of Hillsong because of its focus on excellence, a quality associated with the Global North. Attesting to how Cool Christianity spreads reticularly and materially (through T-shirts, envelopes, flyers, videos, etc.), he notes that Hillsong's graphic design aesthetics is a reference for Brazilian churches, and that he followed this style in his own work after graduating from university. As we continued our conversation, he told me, "At college, we have this saying: 'We are living the dream.'" For him, his new life was indeed a dream come true:

> I think this is the simplest way for me to explain [how I am feeling] is "this is a dream." I always wanted to be here; always wanted to live overseas. I never thought one day I would be fluent in another language. I preached twice [in the "Out-of-the-Boat"] three-minute session at Chapel in English! I have the video and I can send it to you later. While I was doing that I thought: "Wow, I never imagined that I could be living this." Because it is so far from the Brazilian reality! I tell my *gringo* [foreign] friends here: "If you want to see a miracle, just find a Latino and talk to them, because it's a *miracle* that Latinos are here. Just to get the visa, we have to prove that we have AUD $18,000 in a bank account. This is a miracle in itself."

As we can see, although the idea of "living the dream" is common for Hillsong College students because of the association of the church with celebrity pastors and worship bands, it is even more so for Brazilians. While for some of them, like Paulo, funding is a problem, that is not the case for many of those I spoke to. The more significant issue all of them alluded to was that they had to overcome language difficulties. For them, learning to speak English fluently was a doorway into a life that would be otherwise, a common assumption among the economic elites and the middle class in Brazil (O'Dougherty 2002; Windle and Maire 2019). Hence, Paulo felt that preaching in English was a significant rite of passage into a new cosmopolitan life. As we saw in the previous chapter, "living the dream" is also associated with having fun and joy at college and church:

> In one of the Chapels, the College Director turned to me and said: "Paulo, I see you're going to be very influential. You're going back to Brazil and will transform that nation. I see that you will bring to Brazil some of that fun element that the churches don't have there. Theirs is a very heavy, very serious religiosity."

Most probably other Brazilian students had also conveyed to the director that pleasure and fun were not present at churches in Brazil, and this was something they learned at Hillsong. Paulo was not really sure he wanted to return to Brazil. In the years that followed our lunch together, he graduated from Hillsong College and completed a bachelor of theology degree at Alphacrucis College. He is now employed by Hillsong and still lives in Sydney.

Becoming Cosmopolitan

Hillsong, like other megachurches, continually "performs the mega" (Goh 2008). That is, it uses every opportunity to demonstrate that it is successful and has global impact, and thus is favored by God. We saw in Chapter 3 how the church in Sydney holds special multicultural services inspired by the Australian government policy of multiculturalism. On these occasions, services are dedicated to different ethnic groups, and college students from those groups prepare their country's typical food to be sold after the service. At Hillsong College the fact that its student cohort comes from all over the world is often emphasized. The prospect of having foreign friends addresses Brazilian (upper-) middle-class desire to become "global citizens" and erase their location in the Global South. In her study of Brazilians in Australia, Wulfhorst (2011: 113) found that upper-middle-class Brazilians in Australia usually described themselves as "cosmopolitan" or "citizens of the world." She argued that this is so because they "aim to recover their [social] position as white," freeing themselves "from the stigmas of 'exotic' and 'ethnic.' They use the ideology of multiculturalism to refer to Australia as a place to live out a cosmopolitan life and identity, so that they can feel they fit in." Similarly, Robins (2019) found that middle-class Brazilians who migrated to London for its lifestyle (as opposed to economic reasons) "frame their migration in cosmopolitan, 'anational' terms, as an exercise in 'world citizenship.'" Windle and Maire (2019) have shown the importance of living overseas for a period of time and acquiring language skills for middle-class Brazilians. They (2019: 727) argue that middle-class Brazilians seek cosmopolitan cultural capital with "the aim of distinguishing themselves within Brazilian hierarchies." It is also an aspiration to cosmopolitanism and fluency in English and consequently social distinction that moves Christian Brazilians to enroll in Hillsong College and their parents to fund their time abroad, as exemplified in Claudia's story earlier. For these Christian parents, Hillsong offered also a safe Christian place for their children to experience life in the Global North.

Students frequently associated cosmopolitanism with adventure and excitement of living overseas and meeting foreigners. A student told me that in one of the first days of college, the church takes everyone enrolled in the downtown location to the headquarters on the outskirts of Sydney on buses (a 42 km ride).[8] At the time, they traveled there for (the then Senior Global

Pastor) Brian Houston's welcome to new students. She could not hide her enthusiasm when she explained the event:

> At first, right, they always talk about how many people we have from each country. It's super cool. That's when Brian welcomes us, and everyone goes to the Hills Campus. And then in the massive auditorium he begins [asking]: "Brazil! Do we have anyone from Brazil?," then everyone goes: "Yeah!" And all Brazilians stand up. It is like barracking for a soccer team. It is so much fun [*muito gostoso*]!

Making friends from all over the world is one of the key aspects that made Brazilians enjoy their time at Hillsong College. A student commented:

> It was easy to make friends at college. People are very open and since most students are foreigners—less than half are Australian—it gets a lot easier because everyone is a bit lost. No one has friends to start with. Everyone is open to friendship. We then do what normal groups of friends do. We go to the movies, go for a walk, get together at home, have a barbecue, go to the beach.

The frequent parties at the college and their shared accommodation also stimulates friendships among different nationalities. Another student was deeply nostalgic when I interviewed her a couple of years after she had returned to Brazil:

> They always prepare reception parties. Students usually arrive two weeks ahead of the start of classes. So, during the week the second- and third-year students organize reception parties and there is food. They always play songs just for the gang, you know. Talking and meeting people is super cool. Everyone always ends up dancing and then everyone becomes friends with everyone. We exchange ideas; we go around circles in the party talking to each other. It's beautiful. Oh gosh, I miss it so much! I was so young! I'm still young but I had just turned eighteen. I finished high school and left [for Australia]!

A student told me that his apartment was famous for its parties where foreigners mingled with Brazilians:

I used to go out with everyone. I had several foreign and Brazilian friends. We threw a lot of parties in our place. Our apartment was known as "The 537." Everybody used to go there. We had several parties and barbecues. But there was no hanky-panky, no drinking, people behaved. We just had fun; we played video games. We used to go out at night to the arcades, to the movies.

Sharing homes, provided by the college, with other students is also another way Brazilians say they learn about other cultures, and open their minds, while making foreign friends. A female pastor of a Brazilian church in her mid-twenties, who had studied at Hillsong College, told me:

We shared a house with some Germans. Brazilian culture is quite different from German culture. It doesn't mean that [living together] was difficult, but it was an exciting challenge, you know? You learn to respect other people; you learn your own limits; you learn to behave better. So I think everything there in Australia, for those who are going on a student exchange [*intercâmbio*], is about growth.

Her pastor husband added:

What I've noticed a lot is that foreigners are very open-minded. In Brazil, if I'm going to move to a different neighborhood, we make a big thing out of it. As if it is something from another world; it seems that my life will end. There, they move country as they change clothes. So their minds are very open. It's very *open to the world*. I think our Brazilian minds are more limited in this way, and I think that's why it also gets in the way of how we do church. That's why we mirror ourselves in foreign churches.

In his assessment, he felt that Brazilians were quite insular and led traditional lives and this was reflected in their conservative churches. By contrast, his foreign friends were "open to the world," flexible, and highly mobile. My interlocutors never mentioned the structural reasons why Brazilians are less mobile: the lack of English language skills, carrying weak currency, and the difficulty in getting visas to travel. They were more interested in how this "closed mind" was connected with Brazilian churches' conservativism. To counter that, they sought foreign church styles such as Hillsong's. When I asked how Brazilian churches were different from Hillsong, she explained that they enrolled in the college not to learn theology but a new style of church:

> Our senior pastor [sent us there] to learn more than the Bible because we can learn about that anywhere. But when we go to Hillsong [we learn] the way to do the church. And it's the light way; it's a way of always pointing to Jesus. It's the way we accept people the way they are. What we see in the Brazilian church unfortunately sometimes is just many rules and doctrines. Sometimes people do things, and they don't have any idea why they're doing it. So what we learned most in Hillsong was how to apply the culture of the Kingdom of God to the local church, how we be more like what Jesus taught us in the local church.

Her husband added: "And it really is a *culture change*; it's a change of mentality."

Many students referred to how their lives had changed in similar terms. As Delanty (2006: 41) has argued, "It is in the interplay of self, other and world that cosmopolitan processes come into play. Thus, cosmopolitanism is a process of self-transformation grounded in everyday life. Indeed, Glick Schiller et al. (2011: 403), noted that "cosmopolitan sociability . . . do[es] not exist in the abstract but . . . [is] enacted and embedded within social relations and practice-based identities." For these Brazilians, it was not only their identity as Brazilians that was challenged and transformed when faced with other ways of living and understanding the world. It was also their deeper identity as Christians that was interrogated and reflected on. While self-reflexivity is part and parcel of modernity, as Giddens (1991) has argued, for these Brazilians, who were thrown into a different society overnight alone at a tender age, this process of self-transformation was much more radical and had a long-lasting impact in their lives, as we will see in Chapter 6.

Conclusion

The literature on affective labor in megachurches understandably points to the exploitation of congregants. Wealthy megachurches demand the congregation's free labor in order to grow. For their part, followers are willing to offer their time because the church community is key in their lives, and they wish to contribute to evangelizing. In this chapter, I focused on young

Brazilians enrolled at the Hillsong College in order to understand why they are so enthusiastic about it despite the enormous amount of time they must dedicate to serving. The many stories I heard on the field were of transformation and excitement for their future lives as cosmopolitan, autonomous adults. While their subjectivities were transformed as they gained skills that could be applied in their adult lives and made friends from all over the world, they envisioned their home churches transformed by their learning a new style of doing church. Their *mattering map* had finally led them to Australia, and they were now "living the dream." They were inhabiting the world of their beloved church. For them, their life stories had become entangled with the Hillsong brand, and thus turned out to be larger than the "small" lives they previously led.

5

Transnational Infrastructures of Circulation

In this chapter I turn my focus to the infrastructures that allow Hillsong to expand in Brazil. I analyze how Hillsong's transnational connections between Australia and Brazil are supported by particular materialities and infrastructures—its smart church buildings and their hip soundscapes, digital media, network programs, and teaching resources, and a Study Abroad Christian agency. I show that these infrastructures comprise an architecture through which Hillsong's "Cool Christianity" circulates. I argue that these infrastructures communicate success, sophistication, excitement, modernity, and cosmopolitanism to an (upper) middle-class Brazilian audience that aspires to break with Pentecostal traditions that cater to the poor and become global citizens. Indeed, as Klaver (2018: 228) has noted, megachurches like Hillsong "foster a cosmopolitan, consumerist lifestyle and predominantly attract upward mobile young professionals, creative, fashionable youngsters who share a postmodern urban subculture."

Importantly, such infrastructures, as mediators of the presence of the Holy Spirit, generate a global community by giving people a sense of "co-presence" (Madianou 2016: 1) with other congregants elsewhere. This is so because Hillsong is a global church and thus has highly standardized aesthetics, services, use of media, teaching programs, and soundscapes (Klaver 2018: 231–232). According to van de Kamp (2017: 3):

> Pentecostals extend the borders of their own cities by making themselves part of developments and practices elsewhere, which is facilitated by the borderless power of the Holy Spirit. One is transposed from a particular place into a much larger space that consists of flow, mobility and opportunities.

The sensation of co-presence afforded by these infrastructures has been intensified of late. Because of the COVID-19 pandemic and supported by its previously established global infrastructures, Hillsong moved all services, events, and activities online in mid-March 2020. (Even as I write in late 2022, when the pandemic is not so acute, it has kept some online services in branches around the world.) Accordingly, Hillsong has expanded in an even more reticular manner: people located outside global cities (where the megachurch's branches are located) are able to participate in live church services and church activities in ways that were not possible before. Indeed, Brazilian youth living outside of São Paulo City commented on Facebook how delighted they were that they could participate in Hillsong activities (in Brazil and in Australia) while living far away from these sites.

In what follows, I start by exploring the ways in which attention to infrastructures in mobility studies and the material study of religion have brought about a new understanding of how religion is lived and moves around the world. I then focus on infrastructures utilized by the megachurch to demonstrate how these transnational networks are established and the (virtual and physical) mobility it affords to those who move and those who stay behind.

Religious Infrastructures and Materiality

Since the mid-1980s, the "material turn"—with its focus on place and other tangible things such as the body, the sensual, the lived experience, practices, and material culture—has been at the forefront of the social sciences. At the time, scholars were reacting to constructivism and its emphasis on discourse, symbols, signs, and ideologies that may lead to understanding social phenomena as not real (Meyer and Houtman 2012: 5). As archaeologists, we had been excavating the genealogy of ideas and ideologies, and as semioticians, we had been analyzing how ideas were mobilized for different interests, but not exploring how things, practices, bodies, senses, and technologies mediated and created ideas and systems of thought.

Following the material turn, scholars of mobility have considered the scholarship on infrastructures to make sense of how people are able to or impeded from moving, and how moments of mobility/immobility are structured, organized, and given meaning (Lin et al. 2017). They have noted that infrastructures of mobility (roads, transport systems, telecommunications including the internet, airports, passports, visas, travel agencies, border checks) are not only physical/material architectures of movement, but they are also political in that they organize movement. For instance, global and nation-state regimes of mobility and labor migration policies screen, rank, and regulate who is allowed to move and how they are integrated in the host society (Glick Schiller and Salazar 2013; Robertson and Runganaikaloo 2014). In this light, Lin et al. (2017: 169) have called for scholars of mobility to focus on "human and nonhuman actors that move migrants within specific infrastructural frames," rather than solely focusing on those who move.

I respond to this call by investigating religious infrastructures that facilitate the circulation of people and religious ideas, practices, beliefs, and materialities between Australia and Brazil. Thus, I explore infrastructures as an architecture or a system rather than investigating each technology or materiality as a separate entity. Indeed, as Larkin (2013: 330) has noted, "Placing the system at the center of analysis decenters a focus on technology and offers a more synthetic perspective." Importantly, as mentioned in previous chapters, this system is embedded in a historically constructed global power geometry (Massey 1994), in which countries in the Global North and their culture hold more power in relation to flows and movement than those in the Global South. As I showed elsewhere, Brazilians are much more susceptible to adopt trends when they come from the Global North and flow in English, the language of power and globalization (Rocha 2017b, 2020a, 2020b).

Moreover, infrastructures have a form and a technical function, and these two elements can be autonomous. Form, or the aesthetics of infrastructures, also connects with people through affect. Importantly, while most of the research on infrastructures refers to those created by the state to bring about modernity (roads, buildings, monuments, bridges) and ways in which these are affective (they may inspire, and elicit pride, awe, or frustration), I suggest that we can also think of *religious* infrastructures in this way. This is particularly so when they are transferred from the Global North to the South, as is the case of Hillsong in Brazil. In this sense, just like Larkin (2013: 333) has noted in regard to state infrastructures, religious infrastructures also "hold sway over the imagination ... [and] come to represent the possibility of being modern, of having a future."

As I have noted in Chapter 1, here I am following scholars of material religion who understand religion as mediation, and thus see religious infrastructures (e.g., architecture, technologies of media and mobility), and the senses, the body, affect, aesthetics, and objects as integral to religion (Bräunlein 2016; Hazard 2013; Meyer 2009, 2011; Meyer and Moors 2006;

Meyer and Houtman 2012; Stolow 2005; Van de Kamp 2017). As Stolow (2005: 125) pointed out:

> "[R]eligion" can only be manifested through some process of mediation [be it through] written texts, ritual gestures, images and icons, architecture, music, incense, special garments, saintly relics and other objects of veneration, markings upon flesh, wagging tongues and other body parts.

It is through these media, or "authorized religious material forms," that scholars can investigate "the making of religious subjects and communities" (Meyer 2009: 2). I now turn to the infrastructures that allow this process of binding to the alternative network of Cool Christianity embodied by Hillsong.

Sounds and Sites

As we saw in Chapter 2, music is a significant element of Pentecostalism. It plays a strong role in the ways in which it expands globally, including in Brazil, and creates community (Ingalls and Yong 2015). Worship music mediates the connection between the Holy Spirit and congregants and makes God present for followers. Bowler and Reagan (2014: 208) noted that:

> Worship music produced by and for prosperity megachurches did not simply provide a religious mirror of secular paradigms. It had its own theological justification for cultivating a totalizing worship environment: the movement wanted to unleash the power of positive confession. Within the setting of congregational worship, music served as a vehicle for the cultivation and transmission of the power of faith. This understanding of faith elevated the spoken word—in speech and in song—to new heights as the primary tool of unleashing God's divine blessing.

Hillsong is well-known worldwide for its music. Music is so important to the church that in 2001 it changed its name from Hills Christian Life Centre to "Hillsong," after its worship band Hillsong United became famous worldwide.[1] Many scholars have investigated the Hillsong sound, analyzing the ways in which it is associated with prosperity gospel and celebrity culture; how it has helped the church's branding, marketing, and its growth worldwide;

and how it elicits followers' affective labor and a sensation of transcendence (Bowler and Reagan 2014; Connell 2005; Evans 2015, 2017; McIntyre 2007; Riches 2010; Riches and Wagner 2012, 2017; Wade and Hynes 2013; Wagner 2020). We saw in Chapter 2 how music made the church famous in Brazil and how Brazilians relate to its worship bands as fans—going to concerts; "stalking" musicians online and asking for their autographs; and buying, downloading, translating, and playing songs. This affective connection with the band is translated into a desire to travel to Australia to "experience" the Hillsong services, become church musicians, and study at its college.

For instance, a young upper-middle-class Brazilian told me when I interviewed him in Sydney, that, like many of his young Brazilian friends, he first came to Australia hoping to play at Hillsong services and to study music at Hillsong College. He had already passed the test to be a drummer at the church but was disappointed because he said, "at the time there were more than twenty drummers waiting for a call [to play at the church services]." When I asked why so many Brazilians liked Hillsong, he replied:

> I think the word "cool" sums up more or less this situation. I think Brazilians began to see that there was something cool, something modern *out there*. Hillsong is a church and it is cool. It is a modern church, a cool church.

According to him, the Hillsong sound was a novelty in Brazil at the time he decided to travel to Australia. He explained that most churches in Brazil adopted "a more American style of rock and roll," while Hillsong music brought something fresh: "it has an English quality to it, something like U2, with electronic keyboard, singing oohooo, you know; that's not part of Brazilian culture."

It is clear from this interview that Hillsong and its sound offer excitement, modernity, and coolness to upper-middle classes in Brazil. All this is found "out there" (overseas) because Brazilian churches do not have the large structure, fame, exciting worship music, and world-touring, award-winning band. By singing Hillsong songs and joining the church services in São Paulo or branches in global cities overseas (as some of them do when they travel to the United States or Europe, in addition to Australia), they feel they are part of a transnational soundscape that is shared by people in the Global North countries.

While there has been a large body of work on the importance of sound in the creation of a deterritorialized and transnational Hillsong experience, there has been very little research on the sites the church occupies but for Connell (2005) and Goh (2008), whose works focus on the corporate-like church's headquarters in the outskirts of Sydney. Here I am interested in how the hired sites of overseas branches, particularly in Brazil, elicit feelings of belonging to transnational urbanscapes that produce an alternative, "modern" belonging to its followers.

Hillsong São Paulo holds its Sunday services at Villagio JK, a nightclub frequented by the city's upper-middle-class youth and professionals. Located in Vila Olímpia, an upmarket neighborhood close to the financial center of this global city, the nightclub is in the vicinity of restaurants, hotels, banks, corporations, and a shopping mall. On nights other than Sundays, Villagio JK hosts bands as well as private functions for multinational corporations, banks, and exclusive private schools. The venue's architecture reflects its discerning audience: it boasts a retractable roof over the theater seating area; a rooftop garden; well-designed hallways, rooms, and furniture; and a smart black façade. On Sundays, before each of the church's five services, the crowded carpark and the queues of eager youth winding around the block are not so different from secular event nights. Congregants and their pastors also dress in similar attire to secular patrons of the venue: branded jeans, polo and designer shirts, T-shirts, and fashionable tank tops and dresses.

This site choice—a hired music venue in an upmarket area—is similar to Hillsong churches in other global cities. For instance, Hillsong London congregates at the Dominion Theatre, located on the corner of Tottenham Court Road and Oxford Street; in Paris, it congregates at the Théâtre Le 13ème Art inside a shopping center on the Left Bank; and in New York, it holds its services at the Sony Hall, near Times Square, in the heart of Manhattan. In calling for scholars to pay attention to religious buildings as a way to understand the role of materiality in social life, Brenneman and Miller (2016: 83) have noted that:

> The physical structure constructed by a congregation communicates particular values and meanings to those who congregate there as well as to the many who never enter the structure but who nevertheless draw conclusions about its members based on the building's shape, design, and size.

I suggest that this choice of venues and locations convey a sense of prosperity, success, excitement, and of being at the center of global cities to those in and out of the congregation. The fact that Hillsong branches overseas are not built for purpose but hired urban entertainment venues conveys another important value of most megachurches, especially Hillsong: they blur the boundaries between secular and sacred spaces, proclaiming that the Holy Spirit moves in both of them. Seeker churches (Sargeant 2000) such as Hillsong emphasize their openness and relatability to the secular world in order to attract newcomers. Their services resemble nightclubs with contemporary Christian music, professional lighting, and special effects. That is why nightclubs and theaters lend themselves easily to sites of worship and transcendence for Hillsong. These venues also reaffirm Hillsong's global branding identity and establish a network of sites through which Cool Christianity circulates in the form of highly mobile Hillsong pastors, who preach in many of Hillsong branches all over the world, and followers (including Brazilians who worship at other Hillsong branches whenever they are overseas).

Coleman and Chattoo (2020) have argued that megachurches grow through a double process of encroaching and enclaving. They encroach into the secular realm, particularly in popular culture, and also leisure activities, economics, and politics, seeking to find new converts. However, the secular is also a place of danger, where the faithful can lose themselves. As such, megachurches work on enclaving and domesticating these newfound areas within the church itself. This double strategy of encroaching and enclaving is materialized not only in the choice of venue but in the slight makeover these venues undergo every Sunday morning before services start. At that time, a team of Hillsong volunteers turn these buildings into churches by placing Hillsong banners on their façade, setting up stands at the reception area for congregants' prayer requests, to welcome first-timers, and to sell the church merchandise (books by pastors, CDs, T-shirts, etc.). During one of my visits to Hillsong London, the Hillsong banner over the Dominion Theatre front doors half-covered the sign for the musical "Elf, The Smash Musical." Likewise, at the Qudos Bank Arena where the annual Hillsong conference takes place in Sydney, large signs for the Hillsong Conference pinned to the building are juxtaposed with secular acts that are to take place after the conference.

The contrast with other megachurches in Brazil is stark. Most Brazilian megachurches cater to the poor or the aspiring lower middle classes. The social class of its congregants is reflected on their buildings—usually repurposed warehouses or supermarkets, or poorly built, cement-block churches located in outer suburbs of urban centers. Inside, they are brightly lit with fluorescent lights and furnished with white plastic chairs and tiled floors. As Martin (2006: 48) observed in her analysis of the aesthetics of Latin American Pentecostalism:

> In church architecture the priority is to get the maximum seating for the minimum cost, since what goes on within the building matters more than the architectural or design features or even the sacred character of the building itself.... The result tends to be utilitarian and [in many cases] positively a-aesthetic.

In the last two decades, following the American megachurch model, some Brazilian Pentecostal churches have chosen to build large headquarters to demonstrate their success and legitimacy in a country where they have long been stigmatized (Oro 2012: 89). Gonçalo (2020) studied a church that built a large headquarters in an upmarket suburb of Curitiba, the capital of Paraná state, in 2014. In contrast to Hillsong's rented hip nightclub setting in São Paulo, the church's main feature is stained-glass windows depicting Bible scenes and a theater-like modernist interior, in which the upper-middle-class congregation is seated in comfortable chairs. This choice of aesthetics that is reminiscent of modernist Catholic churches in Brazil, such as the Brasília cathedral, certainly suggests the desire for legitimacy in a country where Catholicism has been historically part of the establishment.

More spectacularly, the Universal Church for the Kingdom of God (UCKG) opened its multi-million-dollar headquarters, with capacity for ten thousand congregants, in a working-class suburb of São Paulo city in 2014. Called the "Temple of Solomon," it aspires to be a copy of Solomon's temple as described in the Bible, and thus bring prestige to the megachurch. It also reflects its poor congregation's imaginings of wealth. Its sheer size, taking over most of the plot of land, its gaudy façade of marble and kitsch entrance and interiors decorated with gold and velvet, and its location in the outskirts of the city all convey aspiration to wealth in an ostentatious, nouveau-rich style. Accordingly, middle-class media commentators have criticized the aesthetics of this monumental headquarters (Capriglione 2014).

Likewise, when Pentecostal churches cater for the lower-middle classes, their buildings are not as slick or corporate-like as the Hillsong headquarters in Sydney or the Villagio JK in São Paulo city. For instance, the headquarters of Lagoinha megachurch in Belo Horizonte is a circular concrete building decorated with tiles, whose interior is so awkwardly narrow that the long retractable arms of TV cameras hover very close over people's heads as they broadcast services. Another middle-class church in São Paulo, Renascer, had its headquarters' roof collapse due to the lack of maintenance in 2009. The accident killed nine people and injured 117 followers.

Church sites like those of the lower socioeconomic churches are rejected by upper-middle-class Pentecostals. When I interviewed a young Brazilian pastor, who had participated in several Hillsong conferences in Sydney and subsequently started his own Hillsong-inspired church, he observed: "[Many Brazilian] churches look like bathrooms. Those white tiles! And what about the plastic chairs?" Following the example of Hillsong, his own church congregates in a shopping mall cinema on Sunday mornings. A Brazilian student at Hillsong College in Sydney told me as he compared Hillsong with Brazilian churches: "I was very impressed by the church structure in general. You know, all that money invested [in the church], so much time invested in the bands and in the church team!" (Sydney, April 17, 2016). Clearly, these statements have to do with class and taste as well as a desire to break with the way and the buildings where Pentecostalism has been performed in Brazil and to connect with centers of Pentecostalism in the Global North.

Some churches such as Baptist Church of Água Branca in São Paulo, Lagoinha in Niteroi/Rio de Janeiro, Igreja da Capital in Brasília, and Brasa Church in Porto Alegre have built new headquarters adopting Hillsong's building aesthetics. They now operate from large purposely built warehouses that resemble concert venues: they have a large platform where pastors can move freely, dark walls, large screens, and professional stage lighting. I will analyze these churches' embrace of the Hillsong style in Chapter 7. For now, I will continue to explore the infrastructures within which Cool Christianity circulates and which offer a sense of co-presence with the Global North to Brazilians.

The Online Church

On Monday, March 16, 2020, the Australian government banned gatherings of more than 500 people to curb the spread of COVID-19. Hillsong in Australia and its overseas campuses had no issues moving the church swiftly online. For many years, the megachurch had made intense use of technology—developing its own apps; having a heavy presence of social media, blogs, and webpages; making videos for the "church news" section of its services; linking up campuses all over Australia and overseas in real time during services; and producing content for its own TV channel. Klaver (2021) has researched how this intense use of media technology across the Hillsong global network synchronizes and regulates time, offering congregants a sense of living in a continuous present with others elsewhere. Klaver (2021: 75) argued that, at the megachurch, "temporalities of modernity have become entwined with religiously infused imaginaries of time and the kind of theologies that stem from it, captured by a 'theology of immediacy.'" Technology, thus, is not neutral. It has an impact on the message and sermons and the experience of time and space. In this context, Klaver (2021: 95) coined the concept of "sermonic events" for video-recorded (and -edited) sermons shared across the Hillsong campuses. Similar to my findings, she contended that:

> Although the preacher is not physically present at all locations, a coherence of time and mediated presence is preserved. The shared real-time experience across multiple sites fosters a sense of belonging and being part of one church community.

This globally networked high-tech infrastructure became even more prominent after the government orders. Not only services started to be streamed online but also all of its activities (kids', youth, and women's programs) as well as a new weekly Mega Prayer night which features Hillsong pastors based in different global cities praying for doctors, vaccines, followers' requests, and the end of the pandemic.[2] While its overseas campuses streamed their own services in their own languages in different time zones, they also mixed the content produced by the headquarters in Australia. In non-English-speaking countries, English content was captioned in the local language. In the space of one week, the long-standing church motto, "One house, Many rooms" that had been used to explain the global church structure, turned into "One house, Many (living) rooms" to account for the fact that followers from all over the world were participating in the church from their living rooms due to COVID-19.

An important consequence of this switching to online streaming is that it created a much more visible and intensely personal and interactive global infrastructure within which Hillsong-branded content circulated. It enabled Brazilians and others outside Australia to watch services in real time at the Australian church headquarters, in addition to their own local services. They were also able to watch services in every country the church has a campus by clicking on the list of countries on the church website. Moreover, it also meant that Brazilians who lived away from São Paulo city (where the church is located) could participate in its services. Many of them expressed their happiness in joining the services for the first time on the church's Brazilian Facebook account. A heightened sense of co-presence was afforded by the chat function on the social media platforms where the services and activities are streamed (e.g., YouTube and Instagram) which enabled followers to participate by writing comments in real time. Particularly in the Australian services, people from all over the world wrote comments (sometimes in their own language) and received replies from the Hillsong team (at times, in those foreign languages).

In other words, moving the church fully online gave followers the sensation they were participating in a "global church family" (an expression dear to Hillsong) since it afforded co-presence with people from all over the world. An apt example of how the online church activity engenders a feeling of belonging to a global, affluent, and cosmopolitan church was the streaming of Hillsong's Easter spectacle in April 2020. Created by Hillsong London, *King of Heaven* was performed and filmed at the O2 Arena in London during Easter 2019. The O2 Arena is a London landmark and the second-largest entertainment complex in the United Kingdom with seating capacity of 20,000. It hosts global music acts and sports, as well as the annual Hillsong London Conference. By choosing this venue, Hillsong was again making a statement of being a part of secular popular culture and being global and affluent. Indeed, when Bobby Houston announced it on the previous weekend service, she stated that it was "brilliant and on par with anything produced by the West End or Broadway." The Easter spectacle was a one-hour-long super production. *King of Heaven* was a cutting-edge, dystopian take of the Passion of Christ. It included electronic music, powerful lightening, hip hop dancing, Roman soldiers in contemporary riot gear, Black men playing Jesus and the apostles, and the faces of Pontius Pilate and the Pharisees projected on large black screens.

King of Heaven was streamed on the church's YouTube channel on the evening of Easter Sunday in Australia and at church campuses all over the world, where it was captioned in local languages. As in the live services, followers were able to participate in the spectacle by posting messages on the chat function to which Hillsong replied in real time. The church also posted announcements regarding its events, offering links for people to talk to a pastor and connect to the church. Viewers were also able to see other people's comments being streamed and respond to them. For instance, whenever someone wrote the country they were based, others from the same country would greet them. Other times, participants requested prayers and others would write that they were praying for them. That created a community of affect, where they felt part of the global church and emotionally close.

Time differences still matter in a connected world, however. Many followers from other countries logged on to the Australian streaming because it happened before everywhere else in the world and they were eager to watch it. For instance, a Brazilian man from a country town in São Paulo state had a conversation in English with the church while he watched the spectacle:

Paulo Marins: Watching from Pindamonhangaba, São Paulo, Brazil. May the Risen Lord bless you all!
Hillsong Church: @Paulo Marins Happy Resurrection Sunday and welcome to church!
Paulo Marins: @Hillsongchurch thank you Hillsong Church! You are incredible because of the Christ living in you!

When Hillsong Brazil streamed *King of Heaven* with captions in Portuguese the next day, all messages were positive with followers astounded by the "excellence" of the spectacle and the modern take on the story. Followers commented on the chat function mostly in Portuguese, but some used English language to show their cosmopolitanism:

What an incredible production!
My God, how beautiful!
Is Bruna Marquezine watching?[3]
How creative!
Feeling so proud!
Super production! Wow!
It has a Game of Thrones vibe.
Amazing!
I'm watching for the second time.[4]
Goosebumps all over!
Unbelievable!
Our God always deserves the best!
So much excellence, my God!
I've never seen anything like this.

I can't stop crying!
No words.
We are all crying at home.

Another follower lamented Brazilian churches did not make use of the Hillsong sensational forms: "If only Brazilian churches understood how important art is to church!" Another wrote: "I had blessed experiences at Hillsong London and Hillsong France," indicating her upper-middle-class status and that by watching the play she had similar emotions to her experiences in the Global North. Similarly, a woman wrote in English: "This accent though . . . ," and followed in Portuguese: "I love our church's diversity of languages and accents." She was thus making two points. First, by writing in English and noting the use of British accent, she was asserting that she knew English well enough to differentiate accents. As I have shown, knowledge of English language works as a marker of class in Brazil. Second, Hillsong's global reach made her feel cosmopolitan.

These powerful emotions (astonishment, goosebumps, crying, and pride) were not only elicited by the content of the story but also by the aesthetics used to tell this story and where it was filmed. Hillsong's super production, akin to the award-winning HBO series *Game of Thrones* as a man wrote, took the Passion of Christ out of the church and into popular culture using secular entertainment aesthetics and venue. As such, it moved middle-class Brazilians away from their position in the periphery of Christianity and mitigated their shame in being associated with Pentecostalism in Brazil. By belonging to Hillsong they felt validated in their choice of religion and were proud to belong to an international church that creates state-of-the-art productions as good as anything produced by the American secular entertainment industry.

The Hillsong Network, Family, and College

Creating networks and partnerships, and selling resources and training are strategies megachurches use to grow and increase revenue (Ellingson 2013: 70–71). According to Goh (2008: 296), they do this to "perform the mega," that is, "to use their own body—[their] size, dynamism, rapid growth and ambitions—as [their] chief proof of [their] embodiment of God's power and presence." Hillsong has created its own network system that facilitates the circulation, for a fee, of its preaching, teaching materials, and techniques to loosely associated smaller churches around the world. Smaller churches can connect with Hillsong in two ways: through the Hillsong Leadership Network and the Hillsong Family. The former denotes a looser association of churches and maybe a first step before Hillsong invites the church to become part of its Family, a group of churches that have a closer connection and share the same sensational forms as Hillsong's. Churches that belong to the Network and Family are also able to invite Hillsong pastors to preach in their churches. Furthermore, as we have seen, Hillsong runs a three-year college for students from all over the world. Many students at the college (including Brazilians) are sponsored by their own home churches with a view to bringing Hillsong knowhow back with them. Brazilian pastors engaged with these infrastructures much before Hillsong established its campus in São Paulo in 2016. This has contributed to the expansion of the Hillsong's fame and influence in the country, and the constitution of an alternative religious geography of belonging for Brazilian pastors who want to link their churches to a successful, modern, and rich church as well as learn its methods to grow their own churches.

A good example of how a Brazilian church that is part of the Hillsong Leadership Network brings Hillsong's sensational forms to Brazil is a Baptist church located in Brasília, the nation's capital. In an interview, the senior pastor told me that he went to a Hillsong conference for the first time in 2006. He was astonished by the number of volunteers and their drive, as well as the general atmosphere and energy of the conference. The fact that there were people from many denominations and from different parts of the world made him think that Hillsong was more than a religious movement; it was a "cultural" movement. He was so impressed that he returned the following year, and then every year after that, to learn and take this new knowledge back to his church. Every time he went to the conference, he took junior pastors and members of his congregation with him. One of these junior pastors was enthusiastic about his church being part of the network, when I interviewed him in Brasília:

> We still pay to join the conference [like everyone else], but we have privileged access [to Hillsong pastors]. When I was there, there was a lunch event only for the members of the network. Each table had a Hillsong pastor as host, and we sat with pastors from all over the world. Pastor Brian

Houston was there too! People were chatting and exchanging ideas; it was very rich like that.

The exclusive access and the opportunity to meet Hillsong's founder and Global Senior Pastor, Brian Houston, other Hillsong pastors as well as pastors from all over the world played an import role in his excitement about the network. It gave him a feeling of participating in a global church and being cosmopolitan. In addition, privilege and exclusivity are cherished by Brazilians because this gives them a sense of being part of the upper classes. This is something I will discuss in more depth in the next chapter. For now, suffice it to say that those in the upper echelons of society are usually given privileges and exclusive access to places and power not given to those at the bottom.

The senior pastor, in turn, told me that Hillsong inspired him to make changes in his church. He focused on making the church attractive to the young "because traditional churches are losing them," and to seek excellence and simplicity in everything the church does. He contrasted these qualities with the way he felt things are done in Brazil: by halves and bureaucratically. Moreover, he learned from Hillsong how to increase the number and engagement of volunteers in his church by showing them that they make a difference in the church and society and giving them more autonomy. The reader may remember that young Brazilians often complained about the lack of autonomy in Brazilian churches. He also regularly sponsors young people in the congregation to study at Hillsong College and invites Hillsong pastors to preach at his church. At the time of the interview, the church had sent their Communications Ministry leader to study at the college for three years. While studying in the film and television stream (so that he would work in these areas upon his return), he was also employed by the church to produce all of its visual communication material (banners, flyers, website) which he sent back via Dropbox. Needless to say, the material was very similar to Hillsong's cool graphic design. Nevertheless, the senior pastor was aware that not all of Hillsong's sensational forms were appropriate for his church:

> My goal is not to recreate Hillsong here but to learn the good things Hillsong does that suit us, because it's not 100 percent of what is good for them that will be appropriate for us here in Brasília. [For instance,] we have around 400 elderly people in our congregation and maybe 1,500 between

40 and 50 years old. I can't dress or have a haircut like Chris Mendez' because he is cool, you know? I need common sense because there is a fine line between the modern and the ludicrous.

As we saw in Chapter 3, Chris Mendez is the Hillsong Lead Pastor for the Buenos Aires and São Paulo campuses and dresses in the hipster style of Hillsong pastors. The senior pastor's worry about Hillsong's coolness and modernity being too foreign bordering the ludicrous to his older congregation was echoed in other interviews with other Brazilian pastors. They admired Hillsong but had to juggle the local conservative Pentecostal culture and their desire to change this culture.

Another church that is facing this dilemma is the only church in Brazil that is part of the Hillsong Family. This church was invited to join the Hillsong Family in 2015, after being a member of the Leadership Network for six years. As a member of the Hillsong Family, its senior pastor couple goes to the conference every year, where they used to have meetings and meals with Brian and Bobby Houston (and since early 2022, Phil and Lucinda Dooley), and training workshops with other Hillsong pastors. They also participate in Hillsong camps with Hillsong senior staff. The church sends and funds around five students per year to Hillsong College so that, as they return, they help establish Hillsong culture at their church. It also receives resources and teaching materials, and hosts Hillsong pastors to preach at the church. Significantly, being part of the Family helps alleviate the pastors' doubts about the way they "do church" since other Brazilian churches are so different to theirs. The pastors told me in an interview that many other churches in town started demonizing them because their walls were painted black, they played secular music in the foyer as it is done in Australia, and their pastors did not wear suit and tie but ripped jeans. Thus, they had to compromise and go slowly with the changes. They noted:

> In Brazil, we don't have many parameters so it is good to have Hillsong [to guide us]. If we are going to equate our church with a higher level church [like Hillsong], we are going to have to raise the level of our church. I'm going to have to do things differently [to Brazilian churches] and this can open a lot of pastors' minds of how to do Church. Hillsong brings us freedom that other Brazilian churches don't have. Brazilian churches love to preach about right and wrong. At Hillsong, as here, we preach the Word, we say "the choice is yours [to decide what is right or wrong]."

They stressed that Hillsong's success as a global church gives them certainty that they are on the right path, even if they are "literally going on the opposite direction of other churches in Brazil." Here again we can see these pastors' desire to align their churches with what they see as a superior church as compared to Brazilian ones. For them, this superiority is also about rational, individual choices. By doing that, they detach themselves from the conservative Pentecostal culture of the country. Success, of course, is also a mark of God's grace, as we have seen. Klaver (2021: 21) observed a similar process in relation to a Dutch church that was part of the Hillsong Family:

> A significant return of being part of the Hillsong Family is that it enhances the identity of aligned churches as it adds value and prestige to their church. But perhaps more importantly, in being under the spiritual authority of "anointed spiritual leaders" like Brian Houston, God's favor toward and blessing of Hillsong Church is expected to trickle down to the pastors and churches in the network.

A Study-Abroad Christian Company

In addition to Hillsong's own infrastructures discussed earlier, there are also those created in Brazil to cater for young Brazilians who desire to join Hillsong in Australia. The study-abroad company "Christians Abroad"[5] works in conjunction with Hillsong's infrastructures to sustain the flow of peoples, ideas, aesthetics, and materialities between Hillsong and Brazil. I first heard of Christians Abroad from Brazilian students at Hillsong College and others who belonged to the Brazilian migrant church CJC. They explained that Christians Abroad is a Brazilian agency that organized their trip to Australia just like any other secular agency that sells trips to Brazilian middle-class youth who want to learn English overseas. The difference was that Christians Abroad placed clients in Christian families, or in particular churches and Christian colleges. Like Hillsong, the company also follows the "Cool Christianity" style. Its website is slick, displaying pictures of white, middle-class Brazilians at landmarks in several countries in the Global North, including Australia. On Instagram, its posts consist mainly of their young clients giving testimonials of the presence of God supporting them during their adventures overseas; for most, this is their first trip alone. These narratives are usually illustrated with travel pictures or short TikTok videos.

Visually, the posts are no different to those of secular young people posting their travels online. In one of the research periods I spent in Brazil, I visited the headquarters of Christians Abroad in an upmarket area of Curitiba, the capital of Paraná state. The company's hipster décor matched the dress style of the workers at their desks. There were several indoor plants, sofas with plenty of cushions, the framed advertising material of their global partners, and a world map with pictures of their clients pinned in the different countries hung on a white brick wall. Elsewhere there were posters of cool young people in their travels featuring the company logo. The travel agency interior, like its website and social media accounts, exuded excitement, success, modernity, and cosmopolitanism—hallmarks of the Hillsong style.

Paulo, the company owner, was in his early thirties and sported a long beard and undercut hairstyle. He welcomed me with a machine-made expresso and an attentive demeanor. An International Relations graduate, Paulo established the agency with two other partners whom he met at university in 2007. They decided to open the agency to professionalize a service that until then had been informal—exchanges of volunteers between churches were common and usually organized by pastors. Paulo told me that the company was committed to "excellence" in all its dealings echoing one of Hillsong's key values. He saw Christians Abroad as a "ministry" since he followed the concept of "business as mission" that he learned in America. He explained:

> That's the ministry. Anyone can organize a study abroad by themselves. They buy flights on the internet and enroll online at the Hillsong College. However, what about preparing the student for the trip? We developed educational material for the students within a biblical view about what it is to be foreigner. How did God prepare his people to leave their land? What are the things that you should be attentive to in a new culture? How do you influence a new culture by having Christianity rooted in your heart?

In Chapter 3, we saw that many Brazilians turned to churches when they were in Australia as a way of leaving behind the international students' party and drug scene. Paulo worried about this party scene and saw his company's pretravel preparation of its clients as key to keeping them on the Christian path. He went on to say:

> I don't really agree with this idea that you learn from the world. I had many church friends who went traveling through other agencies and got lost overseas. We never heard from them in church again; they abandoned their

ministries. [Overseas] It's all very easy to access . . . when you don't have your parents or the church around. We say to the students: "Over there you will understand if your conversion was really true."

He told me his clients came from all over Brazil though a system of franchising, and that 70% of them were between 18 and 24 years old, and the other 30% were either younger or older than that. Women made up 70% of his clients, and the vast majority were middle-class university students. They either travelled during their holidays or deferred their studies to travel. In 2015, Christians Abroad became an official representative of Hillsong College for Brazil, after sending many Brazilians to Hillsong conferences and Hillsong College over the years and peaking at half of the Brazilian cohort at the college in 2014.

Paulo described young Brazilians' desire to go to Hillsong conferences and enroll at its college in similar ways I heard during almost a decade in the field. Hillsong worked as a brand, in that it connected with followers through affect and then emotion (love, desire, excitement). Astutely, in his explanation, Paulo compared Hillsong with an iPhone, an object that inspires strong emotional attachment in users:

> Brazilians idolize Hillsong. It's very automatic. We do not even have the opportunity to discuss other educational institutions. They arrive saying: "I want to go to Hillsong College, I love that ministry." If you offer something else, and it's literally . . . imagine yourself in a store: "I came to buy an iPhone." "We have this Samsung here that is . . ." "No, I came to buy an iPhone." "But this one does the same thing . . ." There's nothing that will change their minds.

When I asked why that Hillsong is so idolized in Brazil, Paulo replied:

> I understand this as a *status* issue . . . and I'm going to be very open with you . . . When we post a picture on our Facebook of a student who is at Hillsong, and then we post a picture of a student who is in Africa surrounded by children, the Hillsong photo gets 600 likes the photo of Africa about 150, 200. The image people have of Hillsong here is of an *elite church*. It's like, "Wow, the guy went to that church [whose music] we play at our church!"

Here we see again that Brazilians use Hillsong for social distinction purposes. By associating themselves with the megachurch through affect, young

Brazilians attain the status of being connected with a church of the elite, a church with a celebrity band that sings in English. As they do that, they are able to leave behind their positioning in the Global South and feel they belong to the modern North. Christians Abroad functions as a safe bridge that takes them there.

Conclusion

In this chapter, I investigated the infrastructures that support the expansion of the Hillsong style among middle-class Brazilians. I analyzed significant infrastructures—Hillsong music and buildings, its online presence, its network and teaching resources, and finally a Christian study abroad company that sends Brazilian students to Hillsong College and conferences. I argued that these infrastructures communicate success, excitement, modernity, and cosmopolitanism in a country where, as we have seen, Pentecostalism is associated with the poor, corruption, and marginality. I demonstrated how Brazilians make use of these infrastructures to distinguish themselves from the Pentecostalism of the poor, to move (physically and virtually) away from their position of marginality in Christianity, and to find a central position of power that they feel Hillsong occupies.

Importantly, these religious infrastructures do not work separately, as single technologies, but as an architecture or a system through which people, religious ideas, practices, beliefs, and materialities circulate. I showed that these religious infrastructures evoke pride and excitement as they offer Brazilians the possibility to become modern and cosmopolitan, in a similar way that the secular state infrastructures built to bring about modernity elicit affect. As sensational forms themselves, these infrastructures convey a shared aesthetics that create a global community. They afford Brazilians the sensation of being co-present with like-minded others in other parts of the world, particularly in the Global North. Overall, this chapter called for a focus on human and nonhuman actors and infrastructures that move religion across borders, and a special attention to how imagination and power differentials shape mobility and immobility. In the next chapter, we will follow young Brazilians on their return to the homeland and their local churches after living in Australia, and the conflicts that arise there over church styles.

6
The Return

I interviewed Thiago in São Paulo three years after he had returned to Brazil. We spoke in Portuguese, but he frequently used English expressions, demonstrating how formative his years in Australia had been. Thiago was 18 years old and just out of high school when he left for Australia to study at Hillsong College. He had been so keen to go that he did not sit for his university exams despite his outstanding marks throughout high school. His parents were upset about that but, given that his father was a pastor and had his own church, they supported him. After three years of study and upon graduation, he followed other Hillsong College students and enrolled in a bachelor of theology program at Alphacrucis College. Yet, before the new school year had started, his mother asked him to return. His father was unwell and she needed him home. As he arrived in his hometown in central Brazil, it was clear that the church was suffering from his father's absence. Internal bickering had led to a split that left the church with a fifth of its congregation. The church needed healing, and he offered to work with it to implement what he had learned at Hillsong. At first, people were grateful, but soon attrition started. Thiago attributed this to the different styles and social contexts of Brazilian churches and Hillsong. He explained that in his third year at Hillsong College he had a class called "Global Ministering and Culture" where he studied "a bit of anthropology." That made him think deeply about the reasons that Brazilian Pentecostal churches operated the way they did.

As we sat in a café in the groovy Vila Madalena district that sunny morning, Thiago diagnosed the malaises of Brazilian society—a pervasive desire for power and money and its associated privileges, such as being above the law. He observed how they played out in churches and turned them into discredited institutions. As he told his story of struggle to transform his father's church, he reflected on the problems he had handled there from the time he was a young man to the conflicts that led him to leave it the previous year. He started by saying that the governance of churches was too centralized in the hands of pastors. He credited this to a model used by the Catholic Church, where the priest holds a lot of power. As many of those who turn to Pentecostalism in Brazil come from the Catholic Church, this could be a possible explanation. I would also suggest that this is due to the charisma of religious specialists and the prominence of authoritarianism and patriarchy in Brazilian society.

Like others I spoke to, Thiago criticized the Universal Church for the Kingdom of God (UCKG). For him, the UCKG's success due to an aggressive Prosperity Gospel that privileged material things meant that other churches copied its style. As the reader may remember, for many middle-class Brazilian Pentecostals, Cool Christianity's Prosperity is about joining the Global North (with its celebrities, English language, cool clothes, famous worship music, glossy churches, and a focus on grace and service), not a promise that once you make donations to the church, God will reward you ten-fold with material possessions. This, of course, has to do with their class position—they or/and their parents already have a house, cars, and jobs, and thus they aspire to a more cosmopolitan lifestyle. Their church tithing and donations are to support Hillsong's mission efforts and charity work in the Global South. Indeed, Thiago went on to explain:

> I started noticing that a lot of what happens at Brazilian churches is influenced by Universal church. I saw the decisions my father made. He was making decisions to fill the church and not to fill people['s spirit]. It's the tension you have when you're leading the church. "Gee, the guy's church is full . . . What's he doing?" He's doing exorcism. He's promising a new car. He's promising prosperity. . . . It's tempting. Because if the church isn't full, people start questioning your vision, questioning where you're going.

When Thiago mentions the need for churches to show growth, he is referring to the idea in Christian circles that a successful church is a sign of God's favor. In turn, people will join large churches because they want to be as successful as the pastor, and like him (most times it is a man), receive God's favor. He proceeded to criticize Brazilian pastors' greed and disregard for the poor:

> Few churches here invest in social justice. The churches that are more focused on offering [donations] have the richest pastors. Valdemiro[1] has so many farms! The pastor of Renascer was caught with American dollars hidden in his clothes.[2] I know some pastors who don't declare income. They declare that they have no income. They have offerings. "What offering did

you get this month? A car valued R$ 17,000. What about the other month? An apartment valued R$ 50,000." And they don't pay tax! This is lack of ethics. They want to be above law; *they want to take advantage*. It's not exemplary. That's why people feel hurt by the church.

Most Brazilians would recognize Thiago's expression, "they want to take advantage" as a reference to opportunism, corruption, and lack of ethics and care for others in Brazilian public life. The so-called *Lei de Gérson* (Gerson's Law) was coined in the 1970s after Gérson, a well-known Brazilian footballer, did a TV commercial in which he said, "We have to take advantage in everything, right?" The TV ad and Gérson were heavily criticized, and since then the expression has been used to point to these negative traits in society.

Thiago became more upbeat when he told me that Hillsong College had prepared students to return home, warning them not to point a finger at what they thought was wrong. "People are going to get defensive and you are going to be perceived as arrogant," his teachers warned. He drove this point home by citing John Maxwell, an American pastor and author of leadership books, whose work is used at the college, as we saw in Chapter 4. "People don't care what you know until they know what you care." Thiago then commented that the "reverse culture shock"[3] was hard on him. He had been very excited with what he had learned at college because it worked so well for the growth of Hillsong Church. He sighed: "But what happens there is not normal. What we lived there was *fora da curva* [out of the ordinary]. When we return, we are thrown back into the real world." Here again we see how young Brazilians associate Hillsong and Australia with perfection, excellence, and the extraordinary. For them, Hillsong and Australia are dreamlike places where they led exciting, cosmopolitan, moral, and miraculous lives. Significantly, Thiago and so many others associated these places and traits with modernity, located in the Global North. Once they return, real life happens: they need to return to university, find a job, deal with a church that is not as successful, rich, "perfect," moral, and exciting as Hillsong.

Thiago noted that everyone at his father's church wanted change, but no one wanted to be subjected to the new rules and systems that the church was adopting. "People in the leadership wanted to be treated not as examples [of proper behavior] but as exceptions." He gave me a few instances of this, starting with a small one. He recalled that people had to queue up to buy lunch at the church cafeteria. However, "The pastor would go in through the side door directly to the kitchen, get his lunch, and leave. Even my father would do that!" He noted how problematic this attitude became when he tried to professionalize the church:

> I had a problem with a worship pastor, for example. When I hired him, I gave him [a document with] the job description: "These are the areas we're going to ask of you." He looked at it and said, "This I don't want to do; that I can't do; and this I won't do." I thought it was weird. For example, I wanted a list of songs of the month in advance. And he said, "No, God speaks to me as I sing." I said, "In our church God speaks to you a month before. God is omniscient. He knows the songs he wants to play in the church for the rest of your life. And I want you to train new people to lead worship." "Oh, I don't feel comfortable doing that." "And another thing, and I want you to give music lessons to people who are interested in joining us. You are the worship pastor of the church after all." He became upset, rose from his chair, and said, "I am not a worship pastor! I'm a sheep herder!" I couldn't take it anymore; it made my blood boil! I replied, "And the people who play music are what? Goats?" He left the church then and there.

He linked the problems that he faced at his father's church to those of the Brazilian society:

> I can make an analogy between [attitudes in the] the national political scene today and churches. People desire power for power. Not to be able to make a difference in society, in the community. This is part of our culture; it's not something that happens only in churches. It's like, "I'm a judge. I'm above the rules."

Thiago's assessment is accurate. Brazilian anthropologist Roberto DaMatta (1979) has argued in a classic study that because Brazilian society is authoritarian and hierarchical, laws are not imposed equally across the board. Those with more power will impose their privilege by asking those trying to enforce the law, "Do you know who you are talking to?" They will then follow up with their (or a family member's) rank/profession, which is closely associated with social class. Examples include "I'm a senator," "I'm in the military," or "My father is a judge." Even the judicial system differentiates those who have higher education, typically the middle classes, from those who do not, the poor. The former is given special privileges, such as private cells and home detention, while the latter is placed in overcrowded cells. The Brazilian philosopher Marilena Chaui (2012: 158–161) attributes the origins of authoritarianism in Brazil to its colonial society based on slavery, where the private prevailed over the public domain. At its center, she argues, it is the family hierarchy (with the father on top) where social relations are between superiors, who give orders, and inferiors, who obey these orders. In the past as in the present, the role of the law is to keep the privileges of those on the top while suppressing those at the bottom. She also identifies a fascination for the signs of power and prestige such as the use of titles by those who have not earned them but use them to indicate their superiority. It is common in Brazil for males with a university degree to expect to be called "doctor" by those serving them.

I suggest that such a hierarchical, premodern authoritarian system based on the power of males over the family and society can be easily mapped onto the power of pastors over their flock. As I will show in the next chapter, one of the things Hillsong pastors had to counter, as they planted the church in Brazil, was the hierarchical relations of dependency between pastors and congregants. By contrast, at Hillsong and other Western megachurches, a lot of the church management is done by trained volunteers who are expected to act with a degree of autonomy. Thiago's grievances then reflect the conflicts that are generated when Hillsong brings a neoliberal and late modern system of power relations based on individual responsibility and the autonomy of the individual to Brazilian Pentecostalism.

As expected, Thiago segued his analysis of power inequity in Brazilian society with a positive take of Hillsong and Australian society:

> That's what I admire most about our church in Australia. Pastor Brian submits to the structure he created. He created the structure of the church and inserted himself into it. He reports to the board, to the other pastors, to the elders.[4] There is a circle of accountability. And that does not exist here. Here, the pastor is a dictator; he is above everything. The work ethic in Australia is very different to the one in Brazil.

As Thiago compares both societies, he follows the usual Brazilian imaginary of Australia as a classless and thus perfect country because it is part of the "First World," the expression Brazilians usually employ for the industrialized Global North.[5] While Australia is certainly more equal than Brazilian society, class differentiation exists and it has been increasing for the last 30 years (Connell and Irving 1980; McGregor 2001; Sheppard and

Biddle 2017; Threadgold and Gerrard 2022). Cases of privileged people trying to disregard the law are reported in newspapers (Robertson 2015; Scheikowski 2008). This imaginary becomes more powerful because it is spiritualized and embodied in the Australian megachurch. Some years after this interview, when the scandals at Hillsong broke and Brian Houston was forced to resign, it is this imaginary of perfection and accountability that Brazilians praised as they continued to support the church. In their view, the fact that the Houstons lost their position at the church they founded showed the strength of Hillsong ethics, where no one is above its code of conduct. This would not have happened in Brazil, where churches were riddled with scandals but those in power kept their jobs, they reasoned.

Throughout the difficult year and a half that Thiago spent trying to change his father's church, he received mentorship from his college teachers and particularly its dean. He would message or speak with them on FaceTime. After he returned, he also followed Hillsong Australia online, watching services on the church's YouTube channel and reading its blog. Significantly, he had organized face-to-face meetings with other Brazilians who had returned home after studying at the college and were a bit lost. In these meetings they connected online with the principal, the dean, and the teachers from Hillsong College. The affordances of the Internet allowed them to be back in Australia at the college while in Brazil, and thus continue to feel part of Hillsong and the global Christian community.

After a year and a half, he felt he could not do much more for his father's church. He said he "was feeling uncomfortable at the church." This is a significant choice of words when we know that Hillsong produces "comfortable, enthusiastic and loyal subjects" (Wade and Hynes 2013), as we discussed in Chapters 1 and 2. When Hillsong announced it would establish a branch in Brazil, he decided to move to São Paulo to assist in the process. He was placed in charge of training volunteers. His own job was done on a volunteer basis: "It is not the church policy to hire people," he told me.[6] He became an Uber driver to make ends meet. However, he was once hired by Hillsong to support the Los Angeles and New York City conferences due to his language and leadership skills, which I will show later in this chapter. When I asked him why he left his family and life in central Brazil behind, he replied: "I always loved Hillsong. I left [my father's church] because I knew Hillsong was my church." As we saw in Chapter 2, Hillsong generated such strong affect that it worked as a "mattering map" (Grossberg 1992: 57) for Brazilians as they turned into fans. Affect, as an embodied intensity, propelled people to action. His love for the church made him leave his family, friends, and city behind and move to São Paulo. It also inspired him to plan to return to Australia to resume his studies and join "his church" there. Unfortunately, the Brazilian currency had nose-dived while he was in Brazil, and he did not have enough funds for the trip. "But my heart still burns to return to Australia. God knows what is in my heart, and he is faithful." Thiago was finally able to return to Sydney in 2018 to finish his bachelor of theology degree. He still lives in Sydney and is part of the Hillsong congregation. As we can see, his joining Hillsong College in Australia at such a young age changed his life, and he gained a cosmopolitan outlook. It enabled him to make the familiar homeland strange so that he was able to analyze it as a foreigner, as anthropologists and migrants often do.

* * *

In this chapter, I follow young Brazilians as they return from Australia. I presented this extended narrative of Thiago's frustrations and his own understanding of their causes since it so neatly reflects many other stories I heard from young Brazilians. Most of them were relieved to be back to their parents' home because that meant they did not have to struggle with downward mobility, precarity, managing a budget, cooking, and cleaning anymore. However, it was a time of hardship at church. This contrasts with research with other Brazilian diasporic returnees. For instance, in her work on young Japanese Brazilians returning from Japan, Baeyer (2020: 155) noted that "although they missed Japan and struggled to adjust to life in Brazil, through religious spaces they were able to make new friends with similar values and beliefs, and thereby ease the process of return." Sheringham (2013: 142) also found that, for Brazilian migrants returning from London, "the support provided by religion was clearly very important, just as it had been in London in helping them to face the challenges of life there." However, for the Brazilians who went to Australia seeking a different style of church, that solace was not there as they returned home.

To be sure, the way they handled their "reverse culture shock" was not the same for all them because their contexts were different. They all tried to change their churches with different degrees of success. Some became so frustrated that they left their home churches and went shopping for a new church more in line with their new values. They found them among those churches that were part of the Hillsong Network or Family and/or copied its style. As we saw in the previous chapter, their senior pastors frequently go to Hillsong conferences and some churches fund the college studies of young pastors so that they can bring back what they learned there. For these pastors, change is desirable as a way to grow by attracting young people. However, Thiago's story demonstrates that even as one is called back to help reinvigorate one's father's church, the structures in place and the social and cultural contexts prevented change. Among those who were not able to find a suitable church, some made the decision to become churchless.

I contend that these returnees' stories of quitting their home churches are not only a consequence of disorientation caused by return migration and different church styles. It is also due to two other factors: lack of community and agency. As I showed in Chapter 3, for these young people who traveled to Australia without their families, church became even more of "total social institutions" or "total environments" (Wade 2015; Wellman et al. 2020) than is usually the case for megachurch congregations and for migrants. Many lived in shared accommodations with fellow church members and felt they were living like the biblical church community. However, as they returned home, church was just another activity in people's lives and that was felt as a loss for these returnees. In addition, through their work as volunteers assisting the day-to-day management of services, Hillsong gave them more agency than their home churches, as we saw in the previous chapter. By contrast, Brazilian Pentecostal churches—with their rigid hierarchy which offers privileges for those at the top, and clear roles based on gender, age, and marital status and which reflects Brazilian society—made it impossible for them to make changes in their home churches.

Significantly, I show that their return prompted a stronger attachment to Hillsong and Australia. I suggest that as they feel stuck in Brazil, they strengthen their desire to reach out to the Global North and reinforce their cosmopolitan identities. Rather like those in exile, they are nostalgic for what they regarded as their "dreamlike" previous lives. Speaking English and traveling internationally are, as I have shown throughout this book, ways of accumulating cultural capital that is used for social distinction. Hence, many keep in touch with other college alumni located in other parts of the country, and in these interactions reminisce of their lives in Australia and speak English (or at least pepper their sentences with Australian English vernacular, as Thiago did in the interview). They also chat online with and travel to visit their international friends from Hillsong College now back in their homelands. Like Thiago, many keep regular contact with their college teachers. After Hillsong opened in São Paulo in late 2016, like Thiago, some left their families behind once again, this time to join the church in Brazil. Significantly, their narratives of return demonstrate that, in the homeland, it is through Hillsong that their feeling of cosmopolitanism is generated, bolstered, and lived.

Attempting Changes

Time and again young Brazilians who studied or served at Hillsong told me of their frustration when they tried to change things at their own churches upon return. For those whose parents were pastors, there was a fine line between being good children and fighting to bring changes that they thought would improve their churches. They had little choice but to stay and try to change things from inside. The reader may remember Paula, whose story I described in Chapter 2. After serving at Hillsong for a year, she returned to Brazil to find that there was very little she could change in her own church. She had meetings with church leaders during which she told them of her experiences in Australia; she wrote a letter to the worship ministry offering ideas to improve things. Yet when I spoke with her five years after her return, they had not implemented much of what she had suggested. Her church still did not have a youth group or a dedicated youth pastor, as Hillsong does. Her sadness was compounded by the fact that the church leaders did not allow her to lead the worship ministry, as she desired, because she was not married at the time.

Patrícia, who studied at Hillsong College and whose parents pastored a church in a large city in the state of São Paulo, has had a little more luck in trying to implement things that she learned at college. She noted that it was not just her parents that she had to convince to make changes:

> The board of directors has also to approve changes. They usually ask: "Why do you want to change something that is working?" So, it's not easy. My church has changed dramatically from what it was before [I went] but one thing that I always wanted to change is the pulpit with the Ark of the Covenant right there at the center of the stage. I said: "Guys, there's no need for that. Put a portable pulpit there, so that you can remove it to leave the stage free." We would have the whole stage for us to use! What happens during worship? The pulpit is in the middle of the stage, and half the band is

on one side of it and half on the other. Nobody is at the center! It's weird. But it was something that I couldn't change.

Patrícia was able to change other things mainly because these changes were already taking place in other Pentecostal churches in Brazil:

> For example, there is more freedom now. People may dance and jump up and down during worship, thank God! Before, the worship ministry used to play wearing a shirt and tie, and today they can play wearing a polo shirt. It's not just the church leadership that finds new things strange. Sometimes you put something on and people ask, "Wow, what's that guy doing on the platform wearing a T-shirt?" At Hillsong they play wearing ripped jeans! We are changing people's minds bit by bit. We must show that it is just clothing; it is not something that influences [our faith].

For those whose parents were not pastors, it was easier to go church shopping after they returned. Carla is one of them. She missed Hillsong's "massive structure, the worship" in her home church, and also thought the pastors' theology was "weak." "They had no vision, so I couldn't submit to the church," she explained.[7] After a while, she left and tried several churches. One of them was Bola de Neve, a Brazilian megachurch famous for its youth focus, informality, and surfing culture: the altar is a surf board, and most followers sport tattoos and piercings (Maranhão 2013). However, the visit left her "horrified":

> It is not my style. They are into *reteté*, you know; they like to scream. It's like they are having a fit. People do all sorts of strange things. At Hillsong, you won't see anyone lose control. I don't like pastors who scream. This is something *crentes* [literally believers, i.e., Pentecostals] do. You don't have to scream; I can hear you.

She also took exception with the length of Bola de Neve's services:

> Bola de Neve has no timekeeping. Praise takes an hour, and after 30 minutes I'm like, "Please! When is preaching going to start?" And preaching finally starts, and that is not forty minutes [as in Hillsong], it goes on for one, two hours. I can't handle it. I like that [at Hillsong] there is a time to start and a

time to finish. "If you are here, we are going to respect your time." It is a very Australian thing: you set a time and they arrive on time.

In Chapter 1, I discussed the ways in which *crente* and *reteté* are used as derogatory terms for poor Pentecostals and their church practices. What I find noteworthy in this case is that Carla rejects a church that is fully dedicated to youth culture and more in line with Seeker churches because it still retains traits of Brazilian Pentecostal churches (screaming, losing control, lack of timekeeping). After many false stars, Carla finally settled in a church that is part of the Hillsong Network. She met its pastors when they participated in a Hillsong conference in Sydney while she was at Hillsong College. Once she was back in Brazil, they invited her to visit their church when Hillsong pastor Chris Mendez came to preach there. She feels that her new Brazilian church has "a vision" because they are open to learning from other more successful churches like Hillsong.

Some who left their home church were not so successful in finding a more suitable church and remained churchless until Hillsong established a campus in São Paulo. After studying three years at Hillsong College, Claudia whom we met in Chapter 4, said that she was frustrated that she was made to serve at the kids' ministry at her church in Brazil. She felt she had no talent for it. She was not able to lead the video-making ministry, the discipline she graduated from at Hillsong College, because as a single woman she was not allowed to lead men and women. She sought other churches, but the problems of sexism and disorganization persisted. Like many other Brazilian returnees whom I interviewed, her frustration was so great that she gave up going to church altogether. She had made many good Brazilian and foreign friends at the college and found comfort from keeping in touch with them through social media, online calls, and actual visits. Like Thiago, when Hillsong announced they were opening a branch in São Paulo, she decided to move to the city to volunteer at the church. She was finally using what she had learned in leadership to run a group of volunteers who work on the cameras during service. However, she also had to teach the same things she learned at Hillsong College—excellence, being on time, planning, and encouragement—to her team of young Brazilians who have not studied at the college. In her study of Hillsong in the Netherlands, Klaver (2021: 44) found a similar situation. Young people of migrant backgrounds frequently felt that in their parents' church they were barred from taking positions of power because they were not married or had a family. She noted: "By contrast, they feel highly valued and appreciated at Hillsong Church by being involved as a volunteer and having opportunities to obtain leadership positions."

A Brazilian pastor of a church that belongs to the Hillsong Family and who studied with her husband at the college for a year identified the power inequalities at Brazilian churches as a reason returnees get frustrated. She described how after six months at the college she and her husband became reception leaders for a service at the chapel at the Hillsong headquarters compound. She explained that because they were expecting a lot of people, they had to bring extra chairs from the main building:

> Many of the pastors in that service were sort of under our authority. One of those pastors was Ben Houston, who is in Los Angeles, who is Brian's son! Ben was there like everyone else, carrying chairs and pointing [at] them for people to sit. So, this for Brazilian culture . . . We have cases of people coming here to the church . . . [for example] a couple that we went out to dinner with, and he said: "I don't believe that I'm having dinner with my pastors! In my other church it was very difficult to have access to my pastor."

Her husband added: "Pastors are demigods [in Brazil]. When I'm not preaching, I am serving in the parking lot. And people go 'Huh?!' Because what is the [Brazilian] culture? 'My pastor is a demigod.'" It is understandable that Brazilians, who are raised in a highly inequal and authoritarian society, where power means being above the rules and the law (Chaui 2012; DaMatta 1979), find remarkable Australian Hillsong pastors' self-effacing attitude. This is something Thiago also noted in his dealings with Brazilian pastors in his father's church, as we saw earlier. Australian society's egalitarian trait can be explained by its historical anti-authoritarianism and anti-classism as a way to counter classist British mores (Elder 2007). Historian Russel Ward (1992: 179–180) has argued that anti-authoritarianism has historically been part of the "Australian national character":

> According and to the myth, the "typical Australian" is a practical man, rough and ready in his manners and quick to decry any appearance of affectation in others. He's a great improviser, ever willing "to have a go" at anything. . . . He believes that Jack is not only as good as his master but, at least in principle, probably a good deal better, and so he is a great "knocker" of eminent people. . . . He's a fiercely independent person who hates officiousness and

authority, especially when these qualities are embodied in military officers and policemen.

For Ward (1992: 180), this national character was constructed with characteristics derived from the bushmen ("outback employees, semi-nomadic drovers, shepherds, shearers, bullock-drivers, stockmen, boundary-riders, and station-hands") of the nineteenth century. Most of these were, in fact, Irish convicts or ex-convicts who had to deal with British officers in the colony. Although Ward paints a patriarchal and historical picture, and class differences have been growing in contemporary Australia, this national myth nonetheless continues to affect how the nation perceives itself. Kapferer (1988) argues that over time these qualities have translated in the contemporary concepts of "mateship," "fair go" (equality), and the "true blue" (real) Australian.

The owner of Christians Abroad—the student-exchange company that sends Brazilians to Australia and Hillsong College mentioned in the last chapter—was very aware of his clients' difficulties as they returned to Brazil. In an interview in the company's headquarters in Curitiba, he explained that returnees suffered from "reverse cultural shock." They did not feel that they belonged in the homeland anymore since their friends and the country had changed while they were away. In addition, those who studied ministry overseas often felt frustrated that they were not able to apply what they had learned in their home churches. He told me: "Sometimes the pastor is really closed-minded—the church doesn't have that *pegada* (vibe)—so you sort of have to bury what you learned. Not being able to make even a small change... That is really frustrating!" Echoing Carla, one of the examples he gave me of Brazilians' reverse culture shock was time management. Hillsong's precise service schedule, where services start and finish at the exact time, were important to them but not found in their home churches:

> In Australia [Brazilian] students at the College are impressed by [time-keeping]... When it's the time to start the service, they play the first musical note; the service closes exactly at the right time, when the last note is played. Think about the shock for a guy returning [to his church] when the service is beginning and the pastor is still at the door welcoming people arriving late as usual, and you never know when the service will end! So, they say to the pastor: "We have to have a time for each thing. We need to

organize the service." And the pastor replies: "This doesn't work like this here, you're very enthusiastic, but..."

The reader may remember that students learned and admired the modernist attitude to timekeeping and time discipline, which they associated with Australia's "First World" status, something also mentioned earlier by Carla. It is this association that is in play here. The way Christians Abroad supports their clients is through a Christian perspective:

> Reverse cultural shock is mitigated when you understand that you are not a citizen of this world. You were born in Brazil, but you're passing through both Brazil and any other places here on Earth. When you focus on eternity, people become more flexible.

Their approach is then to relativize the deeply cultural experiences his clients have in different countries and make them subservient to the larger, all-encompassing Kingdom's culture. The cosmopolitan experiences of being born in Brazil and living in other "places on Earth" is shifted on to the large culture where everyone belongs. This rationalization is similar to that of young Brazilians who felt lost and suffered downward mobility in Australia, as we saw in Chapter 3. They asserted that their citizenship was in the Kingdom of God. Nevertheless, local culture is still important. Their life in Australia transforms their subjectivity. There, they start to see their own society and its Pentecostal culture through different eyes, as we saw in Thiago's perceptive narrative earlier.

Becoming Churchless

As a result of failed attempts to find Brazilian churches that were like Hillsong, many returnees ended up becoming churchless altogether. Roberto, who studied for three years at Hillsong College, told me: "[When I returned] Young people were leaving the church. The church was a disaster; everybody was leaving because the church was boring. It was like a church for old people." He explained that out of thirty of his friends who returned after serving or studying at Hillsong, only three or four were still in church. His friends justified their decision by saying: "It's because I haven't found a church that was like me"; "I had problems with my pastor"; "I went back to my church, and it was nothing like I wanted and now I'm kind of lost"; or "I'm going to different churches here and there." Roberto added another important element for returnees' despair: "They want the *perfection* that exists there, but you won't find it anywhere else." Perfection, as we have seen, is part of the imaginary Brazilians have of the Global North, something which is made real by Hillsong's emphasis on time management, excellence, and the high production values of its services and products.

These findings were reflected in a Datafolha poll conducted with Brazilian youth between 16 and 24 years old in May 2022 (Carrança 2022). Nationally 25% of this cohort said they had no religion (as compared to 14% among the adult population). In the country's most populous and developed cities, that figure was higher. In São Paulo, 30% said they had no religion, a figure above the city's number of Protestants (27%), Catholics (24%), and other religions (19%). In Rio de Janeiro, 34% had no religion, again a figure above the city's Protestants (32%), Catholics (17%), and other religions (17%). As in other parts of the world, no religion does not mean that they were atheists but that they have a fluid religiosity and do not belong to a religious institution. Scholars attributed the growth of "nones" among the youth to two factors: the historical decline of Catholicism and young people leaving Pentecostal churches. In the same report, sociologist Regina Novaes noted:

> The young generation of evangelicals raised in the church are starting to have problems with their pastors for moral, behavioral, political criticism or in relation to the way they are conducting the church. Many of these young people go to other churches, such as those that are inclusive. But there is another group: the "unchurched," young people who continue to share in the evangelical world, but who are left without a church.

In another report on the poll results, theologian Rodolfo Capler (2022) explained the phenomenon with these words:

> The profile of Pentecostals has changed drastically. Today they want to participate in the institutional decisions of their faith communities. They aspire to more democratic and transparent environments, and they are much more flexible regarding behavior.

These factors—the conservativism and authoritarianism of Brazilian churches and young peoples' awareness of a larger world—are similar to those that make returnees from Hillsong headquarters in Australia move churches or become churchless. In addition, I suggest a difference in sensational forms is also a significant reason. The lack of excellence, low production values, and interminable services in brightly lit rooms do not offer the same bodily, emotional, and spiritual experience they had at Hillsong services.

Strengthening Cosmopolitan Identities

Glick Schiller et al. (2011: 402) coined the concept "cosmopolitan sociability" to explore the everyday interactions in which "people gather in the same place or in cyberspace around some point of shared interest that is not primarily utilitarian." According to them (2011: 402), cosmopolitan sociability, "consists of forms of competence and communication skills that are based on the human capacity to create social relations of inclusiveness and openness to the world." In Chapter 2, we saw how these young Brazilians, who shared the dream of joining Hillsong in Australia, actively connected with each other via affect and everyday practices oriented toward cosmopolitan identities. They joined fan clubs dedicated to Hillsong on social media, exchanged CDs, met at local concerts of its worship bands, followed celebrity pastors online, learned English, and so forth. Rather than "utilitarian," these gatherings and exchanges were about affect, dreams, and aspirations for a life and a church that could be otherwise.

As they returned, they again exercised everyday relational practices of cosmopolitan sociability. Returnees told me that their time in Australia was not only a time of learning about themselves and becoming adults. They also had learned English and made friends from all over the world. While the Internet offered them a possibility of talking on a daily or weekly basis with their new friends, their middle-class status made it possible for them to travel to see Brazilian friends who lived in other cities as well as their international friends who were celebrating milestones in their lives such as weddings. Claudia remarked that her college friendships continued after her return:

> For example, I went on vacations in Florianópolis because a friend of mine from Hillsong was arriving from Australia to spend nine days at her parents' house. I ended up spending a month at her parents'! I went to Curitiba to

see another friend who had lived with me. The day I arrived in Curitiba, another four people who were also from Hillsong arrived. So we end up seeing everyone all the time. As much as it seems like you've gone six months without seeing anyone, you're always seeing someone. [It's a] network. And [this network] is helpful to vent the frustrations that we all have.

In getting together with friends from all over Brazil, Claudia formed a network of nostalgia and care. This is also clear in how her friend's parents took her in for a whole month as a daughter when their own daughter returned to Australia. When I asked Claudia if she had missed Brazil while she lived in Australia for three years, she replied: "It's the other way around! When I arrived in Brazil, I missed Australia more than I missed Brazil when I was there." Such nostalgia shows the significance of her overseas experience in her life and the difficulties she found on her return.

This network of nostalgia and care was also the key factor for some returnees organizing more formal meetings among Brazilian College alumni and their Australian teachers. These transnational "reunions" happened in several Brazilian cities over the years. That they used the English word *reunion* rather than its corresponding Portuguese word (*reunião*) shows the importance of English in Brazil and the consequent key role of the language to these young people's experience at Hillsong. In order to connect with fellow returnees and Australian teachers, they used a hybrid mode. Brazilians flew in to meet in person and connected with the college staff online on Google Hangout. In these reunions, they first worshipped, read passages of the Bible and prayed among themselves, and then livestreamed with the staff. These meetings were set up for the students to discuss their frustrations with reverse culture shock and get encouragement and strategies to address these problems from the college staff. The affordances of online calls made them feel co-present at Hillsong with their old teachers and fellow students in Brazil. Years later, this group of college alumni formed the core of volunteers when Hillsong established a branch in Brazil, as we will see in the next chapter. Sheringham (2013: 137–138) found a similar role of the Internet in her research on Brazilians returning from London:

> The use of the Internet among return migrants to remain in contact with their religious lives in London reveals another way in which the boundaries between here and there, before and after, are blurred as migrants participate in a transnational religious space.

Returnees also kept their connections with the foreign friends they had made in college. For instance, Juliana traveled to Alabama to be a bridesmaid for her best friend's wedding. At the wedding, there was a large group of her college friends from all over the world. After the party, Juliana and a Bolivian College friend traveled to Miami on holidays. Juliana told me they were "friends for life." She also felt that she would have a place to stay anywhere in the world because the students she met at college. Clearly, the college offered Juliana an opportunity to hone her cosmopolitan sociability skills and be open to the world.

But for Thiago, whom we met earlier in this chapter, his post-college status offered him an opportunity to participate in Hillsong's celebrity culture. He was invited to volunteer as "guest relations" for the first Los Angeles Hillsong conference. He explained:

> Guest relations is a part of our church that needs people who already know the job and are trustworthy. I had done that at the College. I drove the main pastors around; [I drove] the guy who's Justin Bieber's stylist. You have to be professional. You can't say, "Get me a ticket for Justin's concert," you know?

He went on to describe his job: "I had to arrive early in L.A. to learn my way around the airport, the city, etc. The conference was at Nokia Theatre, where they have the Grammy! I paid for my flights, but they covered the accommodation and the car." His job also involved shielding Hillsong celebrities from their adoring fans, a similar situation that happens to secular celebrities:

> I had to pick up Carl [Lentz] and Judah Smith and walk ahead of them, greeting the people who wanted to greet them while they walked to the Guest Lounge. If I didn't do that, they wouldn't be able to walk! At the end of the conference, people were going crazy asking Taya [Gaukrodger] for photos.[8]

More recently, some Hillsong College students from the Global North and members of the New York City Hillsong congregation have complained about this extra volunteering work as exploitative, as we saw in the previous chapter. The Discovery + podcast *Hillsong: A Megachurch Shattered* also carried interviews with youth who served in New York and who expressed anger at the obligation of having to drive Lentz and other VIP pastors around in the city. However, for Thiago and other Brazilians, this volunteer work offered a gateway into a dream of celebrity culture and cosmopolitanism. That Thiago would pay for his own flights to do this work for free shows his social class and his emotional investment in the megachurch. He also felt valued as a trustworthy person, someone who had received the right training to do this job.

Conclusion

In this chapter, we saw how locality is still important in the global expansion of Pentecostalism. It is differences in style between Hillsong and Brazilian churches, derived not only a diverse focus on age and class but also from the societies where they originated, that makes young Brazilians' return to their home churches so difficult. Hillsong's sensational forms are similar to those of Seeker churches, as we have seen throughout this book. But its organizational style and more egalitarian everyday interactions that allow volunteers and college students to run many of the church's day-to-day activities irrespective of their gender, age, and marital status align with Australian society's egalitarianism. During their time in Australia, Brazilians learn a new way of being Pentecostal—striving for excellence, being punctual, becoming leaders as they volunteer, treating others who are superior as equals. As Meyer (2009: 10-11) reminds us, this shared aesthetic style "is central to processes of subjectivation [and] modulate ... persons into a socio-religious formation," particularly when they are so young and are alone in a new country.

They return from their immersive experience at Hillsong full of enthusiasm to change their churches into positive examples for Brazilian society. Yet their pastors resist change. Brazilian churches' organizational style has to do with the country's history and society, where power and associated privileges are usually concentrated in the hands of men—fathers, politicians, pastors. Those whose parents were pastors had the difficult task of trying to make changes but not upsetting their parents. Others left their home churches and went church shopping for a church that followed the Hillsong-like style. Many could not find one and became unchurched. I would argue that for Brazilians there is also an ethical dimension to it. Many of the people I interviewed saw the less rigid social distinctions in Australian society, the way pastors related to them informally and on a more equal basis, and how they were accountable as a desirable and moral way of "doing church."

Crucially, upon their return, they strove to keep their cosmopolitan outlook. They forged online and offline transnational networks of nostalgia and care. College alumni and teachers supported them through their painful return. In the next chapter, we will see how Hillsong dealt with Brazilian social mores and offered these young people a home when it established a branch in the country.

7

Taking Root and Spreading Shoots

> When Hillsong establishes a campus in São Paulo, it will not be easy to transform a crowd into a family. Everyone will arrive from a different church culture and Hillsong will have to deconstruct their culture and rebuild it. In Sydney, it is easier because Hillsong is the local church, but in Brazil the local church cultures are stronger than the Hillsong culture.
>
> —Brazilian Hillsong College student in Sydney

In this final chapter, I explore the establishment of Hillsong São Paulo and how the Hillsong style spreads in the country, both online and offline. I am interested in how the challenges the megachurch faced in Brazil bring to the fore not only Hillsong's own problems caused by its global expansion through branding and fandom. They also show the inherent tensions that exist when a global network takes root locally. I content that as a megachurch with branches in many countries which have different Pentecostal cultures, the Hillsong style needs to be fine-tuned—inclusive enough to be relevant to youth but also conservative enough to allow its global expansion. In Brazil, Hillsong's inclusivity and in many ways flatter organizational structure at the bottom needed to be accommodated within the more conservative and authoritarian style of Brazilian Pentecostal churches. While in the previous chapter we explored the conflicts created when young Brazilians returned from Australia, here I analyze these differences in style focusing on churches as institutions. Before opening in São Paulo, Hillsong had to train an army of volunteers that would be able to reproduce the Hillsong service experience. That posed its own challenges, given that volunteers were steeped in a more conservative culture. Moreover, fearful that they would lose their youth to Hillsong, Brazilian churches reacted by either criticizing the megachurch or adopting and adapting its style. Thus, the Hillsong style spreads in the country by not only taking root (through church planting by Hillsong) but also by spreading rhizomatic shoots (through other churches' adoption and adaptation of its style).

Planting the São Paulo Extension

After successfully establishing branches in London (1992), Paris (2005), Stockholm (2009), New York City (2010), Amsterdam (2012), and other global cities, Hillsong moved on to conquer South America. In July 2015, Australian Pastor Chris Mendez, whose Argentinian parents had migrated to Australia in the 1970s, moved with his family to Buenos Aires to plant a new Hillsong campus. This would become the headquarters for Latin America. At the same time, Mendez started traveling to Brazil to sow the seeds of another campus in São Paulo city. There, many young Brazilians, who had served in Sydney, London, New York, and other branches or studied at Hillsong College and had returned, were eagerly waiting for a call to volunteer at the church. Others, who were fans of Hillsong worship bands, were also enthusiastic to join the church. After all, they had been begging the church to come to Brazil in person, during concerts in Brazil, and on social media for years.

As expected then, from February 2015, when the news broke of a future opening of a campus in São Paulo, there was a frenzy of messages and gossip on Brazilian social media, Pentecostal news sites, and even on mainstream media. In May, when the official Facebook account for Hillsong São Paulo announced an information night in a mansion-turned-party venue in Jardim Europa, an upmarket suburb, the site was inundated with comments and queries. Many asked whether they had to buy tickets to the event, demonstrating the strong overlap between the church and its worship band concerts in young Brazilians' imagination. The event was booked out in hours. A later time in that same evening was set for a second information session. A few months later, when the then Senior Global Pastor Brian Houston came in person to lead another information night, the crowd was so large that while 2,000 people got in, another 2,500 people were turned back after waiting for hours in the queue under the rain on a weeknight. People had traveled from all over Brazil for the event; even Hillsong leaders were not expecting such astounding success. Through the next two years, successive information and DNA Nights[1] also attracted so many people and they had to be repeated a second time in the same evening. In addition, Hillsong pastors based in Australia and elsewhere started participating in these events, usually after their visit to the Buenos Aires headquarters. The church finally officially opened in late October 2016. When I asked the Brazilian Hillsong pastors why there was an almost two-year gap between the announcement and the opening of the church, they gave me several reasons. The church was focusing first on establishing the Buenos Aires campus. They were solving teething issues (looking for a site, training volunteers, translating and publishing Brian Houston's books, working on legal documents). They were also making sure there was a large number of trained volunteers and people in attendance during services. As Porter (2017: 172) observed for the planting of Hillsong Oxford, "Scale is important in order to produce the proper Hillsong experience." I would suggest that this attention to detail has to do with the need to preserve one of its most important hallmarks, and one which is particularly important to Brazilians: excellence.

Meanwhile, the announcement that Hillsong was coming to the country caused a stir in Brazilian evangelical circles. Hillsong was just emerging from a scandal regarding a gay couple who had led the New York branch church choir, as we saw in Chapter 1. Many Brazilian pastors condemned Hillsong's acceptance of gays. In addition, they were fearful of the competition and losing their young members. To counter the bad reviews, pastor Mendez engaged in a strategy of good neighborly relations. He began traveling around Brazil to meet with local pastors to assure them that Hillsong did not intend to woo young people from their churches. He asserted the same intent every time he spoke to anyone in the country and on those Information Nights I participated in Brazil. For instance, an Evangelical news site reproduced Mendez's talk during the first Information Night in May 2015:

> We are not coming to São Paulo thinking that the church is an answer to anything. The answer is Jesus. A church such as Hillsong, which is very well known—many of you are here because you met our worship team—brings a lot of excitement to people. But if you are planted in another church, please, don't leave your church because Hillsong is coming to São Paulo. The best thing you can do for the Kingdom of God is to continue planted. The Word says: "Those who are planted in the House of God will flourish." We're not coming to build a church that will take Christians from other churches; we're coming to build a church where the lost can be saved in a town with millions of inhabitants. (Novaes 2015)

As we can see, Mendez was at pains to deflect attention from Hillsong to Jesus and by doing so reaffirm the worth of every other (not so hip) church as a path to him. That he had to do it so frequently shows the immense appeal and celebrity power of Hillsong in Brazil. Similarly, Porter (2017: 166–167) found that when Hillsong planted a campus in Oxford, England, the pastors also tried to reassure other churches that they were not there to "steal sheep." Rather, they "emphasized that the purpose of the church was reaching new converts, of bringing people into the Christian faith that other churches had yet to reach, [and that] they would discourage people from other churches from joining." However, Porter noted that given the decline in church membership in the United Kingdom, Hillsong's large number of attendees came from other churches, in addition to those Christians moving to Oxford, tourists to Oxford who took the opportunity to visit Hillsong, and new converts. Pentecostalism is not in decline in Brazil, but the composition of the congregation in São Paulo is similar. It includes those who had joined Hillsong overseas (particularly Australia, London, and New York) and had returned, visitors from other parts of Brazil, those leaving their own churches, and new converts.

By contrast, in her research on Hillsong extensions in Amsterdam and New York City, Klaver (2021: 78–79) found that Hillsong did not engage with local churches while planting its own branch. In fact, the pastor establishing the Amsterdam branch told her that 'the first priority was to build the Hillsong church so that other churches would eventually learn from them how to do church in the twenty-first century." Klaver attributes this attitude to two aspects that give the megachurch its identity: revival and pioneering. While revival defines Hillsong's identity vis-à-vis a declining mainline Christianity, pioneering is about growth and conquering new territories. Both mean that Hillsong ignored the "the possible other places that God might be at work" (2021: 79). I suggest that Hillsong had a much less arrogant stance when planting a branch in Brazil because of the large number of churches and the political, cultural, and spiritual power of Pentecostal pastors in the country. There, negotiation and appeasement were paramount for the success of the megachurch.

When Hillsong São Paulo finally announced the opening date on its Facebook account, the church posted an excerpt of Brian Houston's 2014 vision statement in Portuguese (Houston 2016):

> Positioned in the heart of culture, in great diverse urban centers, I see buildings that struggle to contain the increase of all that God is doing; occupying land and places that are miraculous in provision and impossible to ignore.

The statement was followed by the English translation, as it has become usual for every social media posting. The Portuguese statement was also made into a poster: it was superimposed over a sepia picture of skyscrapers in downtown São Paulo. The choice of statement, the use of the local and English languages, and the picture imparted a sense of excitement to future congregants. From them, they gathered that not only is the Kingdom of God taking over territory and cannot be stopped but also São Paulo was part of this powerful global church expansion, and as Klaver (2021: 77–78) argued in her work, a global revival.

Many of those who went to the opening night posted their experiences on the Hillsong Facebook account, demonstrating how their offline and online experiences are entangled.[2] In addition, it shows the significance of social media and its capillarity in spreading the news of the church's arrival and people's impressions to newer audiences (friends and other readers), and also back to the church. One person noted: "Brilliant! They should have sung in English to make it even better." A few comments later, another visitor wrote: "Loved it! Just wished they had sung worship songs in the original English. . . . But the best thing was the service in three languages. For those who know English and Spanish, or want to learn, you can worship and practice at the same time! 😄 😄 😄 🙏 🙏." One young man planned to skip his own church's services to go to Hillsong's and wrote: "Do you think our pastors will kills us if we don't go to their service?" Some, more conservative, wondered why a church service was taking place at a nightclub, noting: "Ok, I don't disagree that wherever God's spirit goes, it purifies [the site], and that the church are its people not the place. Still, this place attracts bad stuff, evil spirits." To which others replied: "Where do you think Jesus would be? At nightclubs going after lost sheep or at the church? God is omnipresent 🖤." These posts reflected three key issues pertaining Hillsong in Brazil that I have been discussing in this book. First is the prestige ascribed to the megachurch's foreign origin and use of English language (and also Spanish due to Mendez's role as Lead Pastor), and how they work to create a sense of cosmopolitanism and a marker of class for Brazilians. Second is the question whether young people would leave their churches to join Hillsong. Finally, there is the collision between Hillsong's more tolerant and permissive culture and the Brazilian conservative Pentecostal culture.

In their reports of the opening, Brazilian mainstream media dubbed it "Justin Bieber's Church," lending additional kudos to the church. Soon some Brazilian companies also saw an opportunity to profit from Hillsong's fame, in a similar strategy adopted by Brazilian Pentecostal musicians and bands who recorded Hillsong United songs before the church arrived in Brazil (see Chapter 2). From the early twenty-first century, Brazilian Grupo Globo, the largest media conglomerate In Latin America, had engaged with the growing gospel industry by organizing Christian music festivals and awards, and recording albums by many worship bands (Rosas 2015: 127).[3] In early 2017, a few months after Hillsong São Paulo was inaugurated, Globo TV exhibited the documentary *Let Hope Rise* (Port.: *Hillsong: Uma Canção de Fé*), a feature film that tells the story of Hillsong United. Social media in Brazil went into overdrive, and for a while, it was the most commented-upon topic on Brazilian Twitter. Although it was exhibited in the early hours of the morning of a weekday, it was watched in around 410,000 households in the city of São Paulo alone (Feltrin 2017). Here we see how the online, offline, and culture industry products such as a feature film work in tandem not only to spread the news but also create an imaginary of the megachurch as it finally arrived in Brazil.

Teaching the Hillsong Style

While Chris and Lucy Mendez are the Lead Pastors for Latin America, overseeing churches in Argentina, Uruguay, Brazil, and Mexico, the São Paulo branch's day-to-day activities and some of the Sunday preaching are taken up by three Brazilian couples who studied at the college and returned home. I had known one of these couples for many years in Australia. At the time they were studying at Hillsong College and later pursued a bachelor of theology degree at Alphacrucis College. After they finished their studies, they felt that God was calling them to return to Brazil. On hearing of their decision, Brian Houston and Chris Mendez approached them to help establish the Brazilian extension. Over the years, whenever I returned to Brazil for fieldwork, I met with them for a meal and a chat. In these meetings, we discussed, among other things, the challenges they encountered to plant Hillsong in the country. Most issues arose from the differences between the Hillsong style and the more conservative Brazilian Pentecostal culture. However, the very first problem they mentioned was finding and training the right people to volunteer at the church. Many of those who signing up were enthusiastic fans of the church. The Brazilian pastors found this problematic, although, as we have seen, affect and fandom are significant drivers of church growth. The male pastor clarified:

> I think [the main problem is] trying to make sure that people don't make decisions out of sheer emotion. Because Chris [Mendez] always says that . . . *the church is not going to be built by fans*. It's going to be built by people who really have conviction, who have direction from God that's for them to be here right now. There's really no way to build a church with fans.

He shook his head when he told me that people were even becoming fans of him and his wife. Here the perennial issue that Hillsong faces presents an obstacle to church planting. The church grows through celebrification, but then its celebrity pastors and worship leaders need constantly to redirect the focus to Jesus, "the real famous one," as Wagner (2020: 13) noted in his study of Hillsong London. Significantly, while Pentecostalism is a type of Christianity that praises an emotional experience of God, fandom is deemed as the wrong kind of emotion. Fandom is a fleeting emotion, not born of religious conviction—the awareness of sin given by the Holy Spirit that will draw one to become born again.[4] Conviction, Chris Mendez contends, will help the church grow strong roots.

In addition to the problem of fandom, the Brazilian pastors noted that many of these potential volunteers arrived wishing to take center stage during services, a similar attitude to their arrival at Hillsong Sydney, as we saw in Chapter 3. In a way, they wanted to become celebrities themselves, by preaching, singing, or playing in the worship band. The pastor told me:

> We see a lot of people who tell us, "My call is prophetic; my call is praise." Many people have this perception [in Brazil]. So, in our meetings—we hold two induction meetings for every volunteer—we deal with these questions. We say, "People, your call is much bigger than that. If you are asked to clean the bathroom or something else, do not think, 'Oh, I was not made for this!'"

It is remarkable that he chose cleaning bathrooms as an example of a sticking point for new volunteers. An aversion to cleaning bathrooms came up again and again during fieldwork. As we saw in Chapter 3, Brazilians, particularly from the (upper) middle classes, look down on unskilled jobs since these are taken up by the poor. Most grew up with cleaners at home and feel humiliated when performing these jobs. Their reaction against cleaning bathrooms is even more understandable when class and religion intersect. They feel they have a supernatural call from God to perform a skilled and prestigious job. After a while, some of these fans who are denied their wishes become disappointed and leave. Sometimes, they post their grievances on social media. The wife of the pastor noted: "The Brazilian culture of criticism is very heavy. Everyone has an opinion. If somebody doesn't like something or we don't give them what they want, some people go on social media and destroy the church or bring their frustrations to the WhatsApp group." Her husband went on to say:

> The people we usually ask [to be on the platform] are the ones who we see that their heart is not set on being a star. They are people whose heart is to serve God. We can feel that. If I put you to serve somewhere, and you say: "Oh, this is not for me, my thing is singing," you are certainly not going to [be placed] on the stage, you know?

The pastor explained that people arrived thinking that there was a hierarchy of jobs—some more prestigious than others—which was typical of other Brazilian churches. According to him, at Hillsong there is a "church structure," but all jobs are equally important. Actually, as Klaver (2021: 12) has shown, Hillsong's "centralized hierarchical leadership structures offer little to no space for believers to influence church policy and processes of decision-making." While that is true in everyday interactions, people overseeing different lower ministries are expected to make decisions, and those who are single can also occupy positions of leadership as opposed to what happens in Brazilian churches. This was something Brazilian Hillsong College students, who had to volunteer at church and conferences, told me again and again. As we saw in Chapter 4, affective labor through volunteering is very important for both the church and young Brazilians transitioning to adulthood. They also felt that they were learning to be more like Australians, who did not focus on class distinctions.

Another difficult aspect of the Hillsong style for people to learn is inclusivity. Brazilian Pentecostal churches frequently place obstacles for people to join them, mostly in terms of acceptable behavior. As volunteers come from other churches, they have to learn a new style of "doing church," including how to be inclusive, the appropriate use of language, the close engagement with the secular world, and that pastors are not the all-knowing authorities. The Brazilian male pastor emphasized that they wanted people to feel comfortable at Hillsong even if they were not Christian or Protestant, and language was a significant aspect of this. As we discussed in Chapter 2, producing comfortable subjects is key to Hillsong's success (Wade and Hynes 2013). He further explained:

> Jesus was a person who communicated with all kinds of people, from the religious to the excluded. We want our church to be for all kinds of people. [We want] Spiritists[5] to come to our church and feel good; if they come from a Catholic family, [we want] them to feel good. Hence, we really have to train our teams. [We tell them:] "People, let's not talk *crentense* [a neologism that literally means, 'believer language']!"[6] You know, "May the peace of the lord . . ." Not that this is wrong but we have to assume that all this is new to them. People are welcome with their convictions. *They don't need to change to belong.*

Welcoming all before they convert is typical of Seeker Churches (Sargeant 2000) since they desire to reach the unchurched. Rather than proselytizing to the "unsaved," the aim is to first gain the attention, and then the respect of the "seeker" (Twitchell 2004), while also avoiding any kind of "cultural shock" that may deter further inquiry (Ellingson 2013). However, this is a radical attitude within Brazilian Pentecostalism, and it takes time for volunteers to unlearn the culture that they have been taught in other churches. Indeed, the pastor conceded that "this is very, very different from what takes place in Brazilian churches. We can't generalize, but in many churches, you have to behave a certain way to belong." He then gave me a list of *crentense* terms to avoid and the neutral ones volunteers should use. Services (*cultos*) should be called "meetings" (*reuniões*). Rather than saying at the church door, "May the peace of the Lord be with you," they should say, "Welcome to church." They also should not use the term "to convert" because it may cause "discomfort" in people since it excludes those who have not done so.

He gave an example of a Brazilian volunteer who was giving away Bibles after the service, as it is usual at Hillsong for those who raise their hands at the altar call. When a woman came to pick up a Bible, the volunteer asked whether she had converted. Since the woman said she was actually Catholic, the volunteer said she could not have the Bible. At this point, he raised his hands in midair and said: "When we heard of this, we called the whole team for a talk. [We said to them] 'People, we are never going to create an obstacle for a person to pick up a Bible and we will not use the word convert anymore.'" Likewise, they should not ask whether people were *evangélicos* (Pentecostal) at the start of conversations, as they noticed volunteers doing. "If the person is not *evangélica*, s/he will feel excluded." The same rationale of inclusivity is used to ask people not to make jokes about gays, blonds, the Portuguese,[7] and so forth, or talk about their politics and take sides in the highly polarized Brazilian political scene inside the church. This again is a departure from the Pentecostal scene in Brazil, where a majority of churches openly supported the former far-right President Jair Bolsonaro.[8]

When I asked a little more about this use of secular, everyday language at church, he explained that at Hillsong they did not differentiate between the secular and the religious:

> Chris [Mendez] says that for us there isn't such a thing as the mundane. "Oh, this is of the world; this music is of the world; these clothes are of the world." We are in the world! We don't try to divide things. A song may not speak of God, but it expresses God with its art. It is not because it doesn't speak of God that I will not listen to it. Here in Brazil many churches have a problem with secular music, [they say,] "What are you doing bringing the world [into the church]?"

He told me that Hillsong does not engage with these criticisms or criticizes other churches. They do have a section of the Hillsong website where they defend the church against negative media reports, but they never do it on the platform. In this way they make people feel comfortable and avoid division and discord. As we discussed in Chapter 1, this engagement with the secular world—be it through music, fashion, social media, celebrity culture, marketing, branding, and so on—is typical of megachurches, and in particular Seeker churches, in their desire to stay relevant in a secularized world (Coleman and Chattoo 2020; Hunt 2020; Sargeant 2000; Twitchell 2007; Wagner 2020). By contrast, although Brazilian Pentecostal churches and worship bands do make use of business strategies to grow, the line between the world and the church is constantly emphasized. For instance, in his study of electronic media and Pentecostal music in Brazil, Oosterbaan (2015: 162) posits that when Brazilian Pentecostal musicians become celebrities, there is a potential gain and loss of charisma. Musicians employ electronic media to expand their audiences, but that means that "new circuits of transmission regularly invoke theological and normative conflicts about the borders between the sacred and the profane." The solution these singers found is to include testimonials in their singing in which they emphasize that their musical talent is God's gift. Thus, rather than just ordinary singers, they are in fact "anointed" by God to convey His message and mediate His presence (2015: 166).

Furthermore, the way Hillsong approached holy communion and baptism caused confusion among volunteers. The Brazilian pastor observed:

> A lot of people come from churches that in order to join in the holy communion, they must be baptized, be over twelve years old, etc. In our church, whoever wants to participate can do it. So, we have many people saying, "I came from a church that it was not like this. My whole life I thought it was different."

Hillsong allows anyone to join in the holy communion under the same principle that "people don't need to change to belong." A visiting pastor from Melbourne to Hillsong São Paulo affirmed a similar thing in one of the DNA nights I attended: "Stay inclusive. Your job is to love and include, help people in the journey. You don't have to be the police. Let the Holy Spirit do its job and transform people." But inclusivity does not mean that people can be baptized again and again as they change churches. The Brazilian pastors told me that many people ask to be baptized at Hillsong, although they have already done so in other churches. Then they have to explain that "the Bible is clear in relation to baptism. Baptism is a one-off, it is a decision.... Baptism is not something you do because of the name of the church; baptism is what you do on your path with God." In Chapter 3, I mentioned the story of a man who had been baptized in Brazil but was excited to be baptized again at Hillsong Sydney. I suggest that for these young people, baptism is not perceived only in terms of conversion but also to be closely associated to Hillsong (or "because of the name of the church," as the pastor stated). No matter how hard pastors emphasized that the focus should be on Jesus and Kingdom culture rather than Hillsong, for most Brazilians I interviewed and spoke to informally the appeal of the church was as important in their Christian lives as their conversion.

A last challenge in establishing the church in Brazil was the focus on the pastor as the sole authority of the church on spiritual and everyday matters. According to the pastor couple, Brazilians wanted to greet the pastors personally at the beginning and end of services, expected pastors to pray at their homes, and wanted the pastors' opinion on everything, even on intimate decisions such as who they should date. At Hillsong, they told me, they were "trying to break with this attitude of putting the pastor on a pedestal." He went on to explain:

> There are many church people who have this "culture of pastor." They say, "I have to receive a prayer from my pastor," "I have to talk to my pastor." [At Hillsong] we don't have that. Chris [Mendez] once said, "If you're looking for a church where you're going to have direct access to the pastor all the time, [focusing on] just the pastor, maybe this isn't your church." We understand that the Word says, "The prayer of the righteous is effective."[9] Who is righteous? Everyone who receives Jesus.

Such an attitude of subordination to the pastor has its origins not only in church history but also in religious leaders' charisma and standing in spiritual matters. However, as we previously saw, in Brazil, it is inflected by premodern, authoritarian relations which are widespread in society as well as a system of privileges supported by the law (Chaui 2012). In Thiago's narrative in the last chapter, we saw that those who aspired to positions of power in his father's church actually desired the privileges associated to them rather than serving the community. His own father, a pastor, was able to flout ordinary church rules because of his position. By contrast, Miller (2015: 287) has shown, Hillsong encourages late-modernity neoliberalism based on individual responsibility and autonomy (although the more involved one is in the church, the more it tends to control followers' behavior to fit a Pentecostal outlook). Indeed, rather than following the pastor blindly, Brazilians told me that pastors gave them the tools to interpret the Bible and think for themselves, as we saw in Chapter 4.

In the next section, we will see how the Hillsong style spreads in Brazil via churches affiliated to the megachurch's Family and Network as well as Brazilian churches adopting its features. We will see how their adoption of the megachurch's clubbing-like services and use of English language offers Brazilians a sense of excitement, pleasure, and cosmopolitanism.

Spreading Shoots

In August 2016, I traveled to the northeast of Brazil to visit a branch of the only Brazilian church that is part of the Hillsong Family. These churches have a close connection with Hillsong but are independent. When I arrived, I had the strange sensation of being at a mini Hillsong, albeit not so sophisticated. The use of English language and Hillsong features were everywhere, conveying a feeling of co-presence of Brazil and the English-speaking world. The church operates from a modern two-story box-like building featuring no crosses or outward signs of being a church, just a big logo with its name in cursive letters (similar to Hillsong's) over the large glass doors. When I went through the doors, I was greeted by young people wearing black T-shirts emblazoned with the word *voluntário* (volunteer). They offered me candy, and just like at Hillsong Sydney, intoned, *Bem vinda à Igreja!* (Welcome to church!). In the foyer, some of the volunteers had earpieces and walkie-talkies to coordinate the flow of people coming in and out. At the right of the reception area, there was a small blackboard with the word "shop" written in chalk in English, indicating the area where they sold their merchandise. This included T-shirts with the English phrases "True Love" and "One is Three, Three is One"; books by Brian Houston, Joseph Prince and Rick Warren, among others, translated into Portuguese; CDs by their own worship band, Hillsong, and other bands; as well as diaries, mugs, Bibles for children and adults, and other merchandise. Inside the church, the walls were painted black, and there were large screens on the stage featuring the well-known Hillsong motto, "Come as You Are." As the service started, it was clear that it followed the Hillsong script: the countdown, then worship, offering, videoclips containing church news and testimonials, preaching, and some more worship songs. The congregation was also similar to Hillsong's: a large majority of young people and couples with young children. They were all well-dressed and middle class—women in fashionable dresses or mini-skirts, wearing jewelry and carrying leather bags, and men in T-shirts, skinny jeans, and sneakers. The male pastor followed the Hillsong style: a long-sleeved black T-shirt, black skinny jeans, and boots. His wife wore a shoulder-less top, fashionable at the time in Brazil, skinny jeans, and high heels.

After the service finished, like everyone else, I lingered around the reception area and chatted with people. A worship singer told me that she had been to the Hillsong conference the previous year and was about to fly that week to start her studies at Hillsong College. Needless to say, she was very excited about her trip, although a little worried because her language skills were not so good. A young man said he had graduated in business administration and fashion design and was part of the church staff. He explained that, like at Hillsong, young churchgoers were divided into "tribes," and he was the head of the "Legacy" tribe. When I enquired why the use of an English word for his tribe, he replied, "It is more global. Imagine if it were called *Legado*! That wouldn't do [*Não dá*]. English is a global language." Once more, we can see the importance of English in providing churchgoers with a sense of cosmopolitanism. He really wanted to study at the college but had to wait his turn because staff numbers were small and two of them were in Sydney at the time. He watched the Hillsong Sunday service in Sydney every week on YouTube as a way of learning and keeping up with what happened there. As we talked, I could see a tattoo on his arm with the words, *Amor Verdadeiro* (Real Love), the title in Portuguese of a Hillsong Y&F worship song frequently played at services in Sydney. In every detail, the church and its congregation were oriented toward Hillsong Sydney. The megachurch worked as a mattering map. A few days later, when I returned to the church to interview the pastor couple, I learned that, in fact, they were adopting the Hillsong style not only to make their church relevant to new generations but also in a bid to change the church culture in Brazil, a similar desire to other Brazilians with whom I spoke.

We met at their office above the church. In true Seeker Church style, it looked like a corporate office: there were comfortable leather chairs, a wooden desk, and a matching wooden bookshelf on the back wall with books, ornaments, and potted plants. On the corner, by the window, there was a large potted cactus. They were welcoming and gracious throughout the interview. They started by clarifying why they used the Hillsong style:

> We are Family. We don't have to be the same but we should have the same blood, if we can put it this way, the same last name, to become a family. So, in our church, our culture looks a lot like the culture that they have there [in Australia]. Our methods are very similar. The songs that we play are their songs.

The reference to bloodline to explain this fictive, transnational family is telling. As Ikeuchi (2019: 183) reminds us, "The blood of Jesus, as the medium of charismatic kinship, unites 'brothers and sisters in faith.'" Thus, it seems that there are two sets of belonging operating concomitantly—on the one hand, belonging through the materiality of blood to a larger global Hillsong family, and on the other, belonging to God's spiritual family in the kingdom of God. It is through these two kinds of belonging that they are able to create an "alternative geography of belonging" (van de Kamp 2017: 2), as we have been discussing throughout this book. Indeed, they then went on to say that because their church is inspired by Hillsong, anyone who comes from Hillsong "won't feel lost. They'll feel at home." Here, they are referring to the common Hillsong slogan for its global structure, "One house, many rooms," and also, and more importantly, the idea that people should feel comfortable at church, something I have analyzed in previous chapters.

Prior to Hillsong, the church was drawing lessons from US megachurches, such as Willow Creek and Saddleback, where they traveled to participate in their conferences. The Senior Pastors' own daughter is a pastor of the equally famous Californian church Churchome (previously called City Church) led by Judah and Chelsea Smith, who have preached at Hillsong conferences many times. This strong connection with the US church culture was something present in every Brazilian church which had links with Hillsong. Brazilian pastors frequently perceived Hillsong and these American megachurches as one single ecosystem that they could draw on to keep their churches updated. The reader may remember that in Chapter 2, I noted the strong influence the United States has exerted over Brazilian Pentecostalism and how Hillsong music also arrived in Brazil via the United States. This is easily explainable by the strong power the United States and its culture exert on Brazilian society, economy, and culture. Nevertheless, the senior pastors preferred to invest in their relationship with Hillsong because,

> Willow Creek ['s services are] much more sedate. [In addition,] Hillsong gives you the opportunity of living and studying there up to three years. . . . It gives you tools to return and make a difference in your local church. Hillsong's way of doing church is more vibrant, so it is more like us, has more to do with our [Brazilian] outlook [*nosso jeito e nossa pegada*]. . . . And let's face it, Hillsong is taking over the world.

In their choice of Hillsong, two things stand out. First, the idea that there are similarities between Hillsong, their church, and Brazilian culture. They all have "vibrant" cultures. Accordingly, there is a "natural" kinship between them, as we saw in the pastors' reference to blood ties earlier. I suggest that this view originates in the imaginary of Australia that circulates in Brazil of both countries being similar (both are located in the Southern Hemisphere, with a large migrant population, beach culture, and laidback lifestyle) but different (Australia became a developed country). This is neatly encapsulated in the phrase Brazilians in Australia often utter, *A Austrália é o Brasil que deu certo* (literally, Australia is what Brazil would have been like if it were successful/developed) (Rocha 2014). Second, it is the idea of (global) success, so dear to Pentecostal churches since it is synonymous with being favored by God. These pastors attribute the success of their own church to Hillsong. They explained that before the senior pastors' son returned from studying at Hillsong College, their church was "just like any ordinary church" and was not growing. After he arrived, he established the "Hillsong culture" and the church has grown exponentially ever since.

A few years after the senior pastors' son returned, the couple also left to study at Hillsong College. When they arrived back in Brazil, the challenge for them was not so much implementing change at their church since the senior pastor was already adopting the Hillsong style. They had to face other churches' criticisms. They felt other churches criticized them because they gave people freedom to behave as they wanted (drink alcohol in moderation, listen to secular music, wear what they wanted, have tattoos, etc.), and pastors did not wear suits on the platform but ripped jeans. Such criticism can also be explained by the location of this church in the northeast of Brazil, a much more conservative region than the southeast, where São Paulo and Rio de Janeiro are located. They went on to say:

> Instead of saying, "What is this church doing differently that I can also do?" The Brazilian culture is to say, "This church sucks! Do not go to this church because what they are doing is not of God." [This happens] because Brazilians sometimes get too focused on traditionalism. What we have to understand is that over time, the methods change, the essence the word of God does not change.

In defending their church, they used Hillsong's usual explanation for engagement with youth culture as just a method, or a strategy, to reach this cohort. According to them, this method appealed to people—around ten of their pastors had left their own churches because they were attracted to this new way of "doing church." Their strategy to spread the Hillsong style is to go slowly in their training courses and, whenever possible, to bring Hillsong pastors to preach. A few weeks before we met, Chris Mendez had spent three days teaching the Hillsong style at the church. Another strategy is using translated books by international pastors. In addition to Brian Houston's books, they direct the church leadership to read books by senior pastors of US megachurches, such as Bill Hybels (Willow Creek) and Andy Stanley (North Point Ministries). They also ask the creative and worship leaders to watch the Australian Hillsong services to be up to date with what is going on at the headquarters. In a nutshell, "The way we found to bring Hillsong culture here is through our language, in the way we communicate, in our training and through books."

We can see from this example that the Hillsong style arrives in Brazil not only through Hillsong itself but also from US megachurches, as the US-Brazil route of cultural flows is historically more established than the Australia-Brazil one. Nevertheless, once Hillsong became recognized as a church with its own culture, and not only a worship band, then flows moved directly from and to Australia. In the next section, we will see how other churches that have not developed any official link with Hillsong may copy or adapt its style as a way of appealing to young people.

Copying

Elsewhere I have discussed how Brazil's colonial past and historical position in the Global South has made it doubt its modernity and copy the cultural products of the North as a way to enter modernity (Rocha 2006a). Brazilian churches are no exception. As Hillsong became famous among Pentecostal circles in Brazil, some churches started adopting its aesthetic style. They learned it by sending their own pastors to conferences and study at the college or just by copying what they saw online. In this they are following other churches in the world in a process that ensued the "Hillsongization of Christianity," as Martí (2017: 382) noted. For Marti, "Doing church in a Hillsong way becomes learning how to mobilize and produce affect in a particular manner, one that is viewed as distinctly cosmopolitan."

The Brazilian Renewed Baptist megachurch Lagoinha is a good example of the Hillsong style spreading via digital media. The reader may remember that Lagoinha's well-known worship band *Diante do Trono* was the first to officially record Hillsong music in Portuguese (Chapter 2). With allegedly 90,000 members, Lagoinha has several branches in Brazil and globally (these mainly cater to Brazilians abroad). I visited its headquarters in Belo Horizonte in one of my periods of fieldwork. After I climbed up the stairs of the concrete circular building, youth wearing black T-shirts emblazoned with the word *voluntário* (volunteer) were welcoming congregants. A young female volunteer directed me to a seat among 2,000 others in the large auditorium. As the service started, I was faced with a slightly hybrid set-up: it mostly followed a Brazilian church style, but there were international megachurch tinges here and there. There was the usual large screen on the background, but it was actually composed of many smaller screens so that black lines cut the image in many square pieces. The senior pastor was wearing a suit, but his pastor son, in his thirties, was dressed in a polo shirt and jeans. Polo shirts are acceptable men's business casual attire for the middle classes in Brazil, particularly if they are branded. The service was televised through their own Rede Super, so that there were cameras on long poles hovering over the congregation as well as cameramen walking around filming people whenever they displayed emotional outbursts. The bright fluorescent lights meant that as people worshipped, cried, and raised their arms, they could be filmed and watched by everyone else. There was a complete lack of privacy, in contrast to Hillsong, where the cameras only point at the pastors on the platform. The congregants are only filmed as a crowd in the dark theater. The whole experience was very different from the immersive services that Hillsong offers.

Speaking to a Lagoinha youth pastor the next day, he explained how the Lagoinha headquarters ended up adopting some aspects of the Hillsong style influenced by a younger generation of pastors. When the senior pastor's daughter and her husband decided to establish a new branch in Niterói, in the state of Rio de Janeiro, they fashioned it as a carbon copy of Hillsong (infrastructure, services, graphic design, etc.). They had never been to a Hillsong church but learned its style online. They also redesigned the church logo to look like Hillsong's (a black circle enclosing the church's cursive name written in white). In time, the new branch's success influenced the headquarters, and it started adopting some of these features. However, the changes became a source of heated debate. He clarified: "Our church [walls] was not black; a year ago we painted it black ... we put new lights; the pulpit changed ... everything changed. The old people kept saying, 'Lagoinha is going to become a Satanist church.'" A condition for the approval of the black walls was that the fluorescent lights were to be kept on at all times as a sign of God's presence. Here we see how aesthetics and belief are intertwined, and the ways new aesthetics arriving from overseas are localized in the church. He then offered more examples of how Lagoinha had adopted Hillsong features:

We have the black *voluntário* T-shirt, written "Lagoinha." The musical style is very Hillsong; it's pop rock. I think our model of church today, overall, has very, very much to do with Hillsong: the music, the structure of worship, how the service works. Hillsong ended up kind of monopolizing, kind of setting a parameter [for other churches].

When I asked why this impulse to copy, he mentioned the power of English-speaking culture from the Global North on Brazilian Pentecostalism. He told me:

You know that for Brazilians everything that comes from outside is better. Especially in regard to the language—everything that arrives in English, whether from England, the United States, Australia. Pentecostalism in Brazil is also very much influenced by foreign movements.

I asked for an example of foreign movements, and he replied:

Hillsong is super influential. It eventually became a model for everything, from music to ecclesiology to doctrine. I think it's hard to find a church in Brazil today that doesn't have "a reception structure" with people dressed in black T-shirts giving away sweets, etc. That's totally Hillsong.

Indeed, in all the churches I visited during fieldwork in Brazil, I was welcome in that way. At Hillsong, visitors are not given sweets, but first timers are offered free coffee after the service, something that I also saw in more affluent churches in Brazil. He offered other examples of foreign churches that influenced Pentecostalism in Brazil such as the Australian Planetshakers, and the Americans Bethel, Willow Creek, Gateway, and before it was closed down, Mars Hills. That he could easily name these churches and explain their ministries although he does not speak English shows how influential they are in Brazil. He understood this influence as part of the entertainment industry, where the latest fashion coming from overseas becomes trendy:

It's because this church is a new fad. It's fashionable. The culture of entertainment is all over the world, isn't it? So, everyone is after the latest novelty; everyone wants a new phone, new watch, a new outfit to follow the fashion trend. It turns out that this influence of entertainment culture also sometimes influences many people in their choice of church, you know. Hillsong is a big name, and it appeals to the crowd.

Here we see how Brazil's position in the Global South and a desire for modernity that seems to be located in the Global North influences what kind of Pentecostalism is imported. Even a powerful and successful Brazilian megachurch such as Lagoinha adopts trends coming from overseas as a way to grow.

Other Brazilian churches have followed closely the Hillsong style. For instance, Aguiar (2020) has studied "Brasa Church," a growing youth ministry established in 2013 and affiliated with Igreja Brasa, a renewed Baptist church, located in Porto Alegre, the capital of Rio Grande do Sul state. Aguiar has shown that Brasa Church has a middle-class congregation comprised of university students and professionals, and it aspires to reproduce the worship style so characteristic of Hillsong and Bethel churches. Brasa Church's youth pastor was inspired by a visit to both churches in the United States in 2013. This again attests to the significance of Pentecostal flows arriving from the United States, and how key the Hillsong New York extension was for its expansion in Brazil. Its Saturday nights services and infrastructures follow closely Hillsong aesthetics and infrastructures. There are the usual young volunteers wearing black T-shirts welcoming and directing people; the church is dark with large screens and professional lighting; services are informal and worship songs take center stage. There is a strong focus on welcoming people so that they feel comfortable and loved, a similar attitude to the "Welcome Home" message at Hillsong. Worship songs are translations of Hillsong United, Jesus Culture, and Bethel Music. The frequent use of English words, "next steps," "Start" courses for new Christians, "Hub" for cell groups, and even the adoption of the word "Church" in its name (Brasa Church) instead of *Igreja* reinforces an aspiration for the life of those in the English-speaking world.

Da Silva Moreira (2018) also noted a pattern of some Brazilian middle-class churches imitating North American churches' aesthetic style such as concert-like services, big screens, youth-oriented language, communicating through social media, and so forth. He (2018: 131) observed that "compared with its North American counterpart, the Brazilian churches . . . seem to be very modest and somehow amateur." This is something I noticed at the Lagoinha headquarters as well. The long poles of the TV cameras swerving very close to people's heads, the poorly built concrete building, the small platform, the lack of a reception area with a café all made the "experience" different from services at Hillsong São Paulo, located at an upmarket nightclub described in Chapter 5. To be sure, the newly built Niterói branch offers a much closer aesthetic experience to Hillsong's. Da Silva Moreira (2018: 128, 131) also mentioned two other features of these churches that are similar to my findings: their pastors had never visited the US churches and had seen it only on the Internet, and they adopted an English name or English words in their structure.

The importance of English language was remarked on by a pastor of another church that adopted the Hillsong style. *Igreja no Cinema* (Church in the Cinema [INC]) was founded in 2013 by two young pastors who have been going to Hillsong conferences in Australia and Hillsong United concerts in Brazil for many years. As its name indicates, their services take place in shopping mall cinemas on Sunday morning, before the malls open at 2 p.m. When I asked the two founding pastors why the church used English terms such as "hangout," "lead pastor," "senior pastor," and so on, they told me:

> This either appeals to people or generates anger because it shows people's weakness. In Brazil, just one percent of the population is fluent in English. This shows how behind we are! Many people come (to INC) because they think, "I need to learn English. I'm going there; they will help me, encourage me."

For them, speaking English was synonymous with modernity and hence the idea of Brazil being "behind" the Global North because its population is not fluent in the language. But also, they feel the use of English terms is appealing to Brazilians who want to learn the language, in a similar process to how Hillsong appeals to them. It is clear that the pastors feel that their church becomes relevant to this cohort not only for religious reasons but also for the cosmopolitan opportunities it offers its congregants. As for why they use the Hillsong style, one of the pastors noted:

> Hillsong was the only church that has influenced me in the whole world. Hillsong is an answer to a church that was dying. There is a special grace there. Hillsong makes the same song be sung in every country on earth.

For him, Hillsong was countering the decline of Christianity in the world. He saw this as a special anointing by God. Nevertheless, not everyone is happy with Brazilian churches copying the Hillsong style. A young Brazilian who lived in Sydney for over a decade and was very involved with the Christians Abroad student agency thought copying was problematic. For him, churches should be an organic part of the community and as such not a copy of other places. Brazilian Hillsong pastors are very aware of this trend. I asked what they thought of other churches copying the Hillsong service aesthetics. In their reply they also argued for adaptation rather than copy:

> The problem of copying sometimes ... Chris always says that to us: people, we are in Brazil; the way we communicate will be different. The method we use will perhaps change. For example, if you look at the creative part of London, they have a very London quality. You can see the difference from London to Australia. The photos they take, the way they do the decoration, it's different. It's the same vision, same house, a lot of similar things, but they have their own touch. I think it's important that you adapt. The problem is, when people stop thinking, they just copy. "Copy and paste" is perhaps good for the church that is copied, cool, but then what?

Conclusion

New sensational forms have to be negotiated and learned to become authorized. The arrival of Hillsong Church in Brazil was a highly anticipated event. Brazilians had spent the previous decade asking the church to come to Brazil, as we saw in Chapter 2. However, after the announcement was made by the headquarters, it took almost two years for the church to start holding services. Hillsong's brand is associated with excellence, and its services are synonymous with high-quality immersive experiences. In addition to finding a suitable building and sourcing the technology for its services, it needed an army of well-trained volunteers to reproduce the sensational forms that made it famous in Brazil. The challenges it faced were similar to those that returned Brazilians faced when they endeavored to change their home churches. Hillsong São Paulo pastors had to allay fears they were "stealing sheep," teach inclusivity and tolerance to other religions, persuade volunteers that their church jobs (even the lowly ones) were equally important, coach them to avoid *crentense* expressions in favor of secular ones, and convince them to stop putting pastors on a pedestal and treat them as celebrities. In short, Hillsong had to negotiate its aesthetic style with the conservative, unequal, and more authoritarian Brazilian Pentecostal style that is stigmatized in the country.

As Hillsong became famous in the last two decades, Brazilian churches started adopting some of its features. A few joined the Hillsong Network and Family and thus received resources and sent pastors to train at Hillsong College in Sydney. Others copied from what they saw on the Internet—from its logo to outward Seeker church features (performative, clubbing-like services and youth-oriented activities). In all of them, the use of the English language was key in their makeover. Both the desire to mimic fashion trends from the Global North and the use of English expressions show how these traits are associated with modernity and the power they hold in countries in the Global South.

Conclusion

In December 2021, I watched the Christmas Spectacle held at Hillsong São Paulo, an annual event that is re-created in each of the megachurch's global campuses.[1] Certainly, it was not a superproduction like the one held in Sydney (involving dance, music, theater, and film). It nonetheless included many of the elements that made the event well known to its congregants globally. The stage was decorated with two white Christmas trees, adorned with golden and silver baubles, on each side of the platform. There were two white neon stars hanging above the trees. The two female singers wore white evening gowns, while the two male singers wore black-tie. The musicians wore black shirts and trousers and red bowties. In the audience, chairs were placed one meter apart and people in the congregation and musicians were wearing masks. The omicron variant was still a few weeks away from exploding in the country, so the service was held face to face.

After a few worship songs, Chris Mendez (the now Lead Pastor for Hillsong Brazil, Argentina, Uruguay, and Mexico) walked onto the stage with Raphael Galante, a Brazilian pastor who returned to Brazil after having studied at Hillsong College and later teaching pastoral leadership for some years at the college. Galante was there to translate from the Spanish for Mendez. Mendez was the event's MC, preacher, and entertainer. One of the first things Mendez noted in an ironic tone was that the dressed-up singers looked like "perfect Christians." He then made his first joke by asking the congregation: "Who thinks they should be dressed like that every Sunday?" He immediately segued with: "No, not at Hillsong!" Everyone laughed. With that he affirmed the Hillsong style, while distinguishing it from churches in Brazil where pastors and congregation wear formal clothes. Mendez was doing boundary work and creating community. He himself had made no concession to Christmas. He followed the Hillsong style as usual: he wore a wrinkled white shirt, jeans jacket, and black skinny jeans. Galante sported a short-sleeved shirt and black, ripped, skinny jeans and boots.

Like in Sydney, all activities were chosen and done in a way that conveyed growth, success, and excitement, a sure sign of God's strength and favor. As

Cool Christianity. Cristina Rocha, Oxford University Press. © Oxford University Press 2024.
DOI: 10.1093/oso/9780197673195.003.0009

Goh (2008: 296) put it so well, the activities were about a "performance of the mega." Mendez started by showing a video of 200 baptisms performed the day before because they had been cancelled for a while due to the pandemic. The video showed the usual emotional scenes of people hugging and crying as they came out of the pool. In the last scene, the camera (probably attached to a drone) rose from the pool, through the open retractable roof of the rented nightclub where Hillsong congregates, and panned down on the baptism scene. The words "Hillsong São Paulo" and the Hillsong logo were placed over it. When the lights returned, Mendez excitedly announced the opening of Hillsong Montevideo. He told the congregation that it was the first campus fully funded by Hillsong Latin America. Everyone clapped to the news. He then moved to the highlight of the evening.

Endeavoring to stir people's imaginations, Mendez asked them not to post what he was going to say on social media. It was to be a "surprise" for those in the next *reunião* (service). He noted that the annual Hillsong "Heart for the House" campaign had started in 2018 in Brazil.[2] The surprise was the large amount the church had raised in donations during these campaigns since then. As he spoke, the sums were projected in large numbers on the big screens on the stage. He started by giving the 2018 figure (R$459,000, roughly US$86,000). As he mentioned the 2019 figure (R$879,000), he told the congregation that they had obviously "captured the vision, the heart of our house" because the donations had doubled. Before the figures for 2020 were projected, he noted that, as the pandemic and the economic crisis hit, he and this wife, Lucy, had wondered whether to proceed with the annual campaign. They went ahead because getting "something was better than nothing." At this point, he switched his speech from the congregation donating on their own volition, to God favoring the church. According to Mendez, God surprised them as they were able to raise a similar figure to 2019 (R$868,000).

He continued to create suspense and excitement by exclaiming: "Let's see what God did in 2021." He then asked everyone to stand up. The amounts projected on the large screen started increasing faster as music was played in a crescendo. The numbers first stopped at R$89,000, and Mendez remarked, "No, that's not it. Let's continue." The numbers kept stopping at random higher amounts, while Mendez kept saying in an ever more excited voice: "It's getting better, but it is still short," or "That's good, but we should keep going." People started clapping as the music got louder. When the final amount was on the screen, both Mendez and Galante shouted in unison as if they were TV presenters giving off a prize: "Heart for the House 2021! ONE MILLION AND ONE HUNDRED AND FOURTEEN THOUSAND REALS! GLORY

TO GOD! LET'S CELEBRATE CHURCH! LET'S WORSHIP OUR GOD!" That was the clue for the band to started playing "He Shall Reign"[3] by Hillsong Worship translated into Portuguese. This was a befitting choice of song to convey the power of God demonstrated by the amount on the screen. Everyone was singing with their arms stretched forward.

Once the song was over, Mendez seemed to assume the role of a CFO explaining the annual financial report to the board or employees of a company. However, his report mixed finances and religion. For him, God was moving in this world and supporting the church's growth:

> Lucy and I are so impressed! With the pandemic, there are fewer people coming to church despite the precautions we are taking. Not only in our church but all churches. But with fewer people, we had a record revenue for the Heart for the House. In the middle of crisis, God continues to be God. When compared to last year, there was an increase of 30 percent in revenue and 130 more people donated. With less we made more. The largest offering was R$111 thousand and we had around four donors who gave between R$20 and 100 thousand. This means that the rest of the church shared the load. This is because we understand that together we are better. From Lucy and I and the founding pastors, Brian and Bobbie Houston, we thank the church for your generosity, for your heart, for sharing the load. We will start Montevideo from a position of strength. We'll continue to support Monterrey and raise the level of what we do with CityCare [the social justice arm of Hillsong].

At this point, Mendez became more personal. He asked the cameraperson to do a close-up of his face, and he spoke in a low tone to the audience and those following online:

> Listen, 2022 will be full of surprises. Listen, listen. February is arriving. Those who belong to our church understand what happens in February. Glory to God for the Heart for the House. Amen? You can sit now. But as I said, please don't share this information. It is something just among us [*interno*]. On a continental level, it was a record year. In Monterrey, there was also a growth [in donations] of 25 percent in relation to the last year. In Buenos Aires, there was an increase of 110 percent. On a continental level, we are well positioned. Glory to God. This is a special Sunday. We are focusing on the life of Jesus. Let's now enjoy what the team has prepared for us.

The lights went off. When they returned, one of the female singers intoned *Silent Night* accompanied by a woman playing the harp. The next thirty minutes were dedicated to worship songs, then a performance related to the story of Christmas, and preaching by another Brazilian pastor.

The service brought together all elements that make Hillsong services appealing to followers. Key to them was affect. The service created a sense of family, community, love, and intimacy ("It is just among us [*interno*]"). There was much excitement and surprise for what God was doing at present. There was growth and success in the future (increasing donations and new branches being established). The latter is common in Pentecostalism through the idea of prosperity. At Hillsong, this is translated in pastors usually saying: "The best is yet to come!" All this was packaged as entertainment. Through spectacle, music, excitement, money, and success, God was made present. The standardized Christmas Spectacle, like other annual events in the megachurch calendar, also demonstrated how the Hillsong style is practiced globally. It is this standardization that holds the network firmly together. However, such uniformity and tight connection can bring trouble. When one of the nodes is engulfed in scandal, it can spread rapidly through the network and thus communication needs to be carefully controlled. Nevertheless, the local sociocultural context may also stop scandals in their tracks, as has been the case in Brazil.

Controlling the Fall

In late January 2022, a month after the Christmas Spectacle, Houston stepped down from his position as Hillsong Senior Global Pastor to deal with criminal charges for covering up his father's child sexual abuse. At the time, the church produced a film to be shown during services. As I watched the Sydney service online, I saw Brian and Bobbie Houston standing side by side to explain the situation. They started by talking about their early days establishing Hillsong, then denied the veracity of the charges, and asked everyone to pray for the church (but not for the victims). They finished their presentation by introducing Phil and Lucinda Dooley, the Australian Hillsong pastors for South Africa, who would be acting in their place till Houston's return at the end of the year. When Phil and Lucinda Dooley came onto the screen, they talked about their lives at the church: how they met at a church camp; how Brian Houston married them; how they worked on youth ministry; and how they moved to South Africa to establish Hillsong there.

All the while, old photos illustrated their narrative. In this way they established a lineage between the Houstons and themselves. The video offered a linear history of church from the Houston's beginnings in New Zealand to the global megachurch it is today, and how the Interim Senior Pastors fit in it.

Later on that very Sunday in Australia, I watched this same film in the Brazilian service which took place online on Sunday morning in Brazilian time. As it is usual on these occasions, the video was subtitled in Portuguese so that Brazilians could hear and understand what was said in English. The sound and images provided a strong feeling of belonging to the Hillsong global family. The video also ensured the message was controlled and uniform through the global Hillsong network. As I watched Brazilians post on the chat function of the Hillsong YouTube channel, it seemed that nothing had changed. They posted the usual emojis (praying hands, hearts, etc.), "amens," "I love Hillsong," and after the Dooleys were introduced, one person wrote "Phil Dooley has been to Hillsong SP. It was 🔥." Once the video was over, the Brazilian pastor moved on quickly to other matters with no further explanation on what the criminal charges were.

However, merely two months later, in March 2022, Phil Dooley called an urgent online staff meeting. According to what was leaked to the global press—from the Australians *ABC* and *Crikey* to *The Guardian* and the *New York Times*—Dooley announced to the 800 global staff that Houston had incurred in two breaches of the Hillsong pastors' code of conduct and had resigned from his church position. According to transcripts of the meeting on the Australian news website *Crikey* (Hardaker 2022) and in a press release on the megachurch website, Houston had been the subject of an investigation for flirting on a text message to a woman in 2013, and spending time with another in a hotel room under the influence of alcohol and sleeping pills during the annual conference in 2019. The Global Board, which is in charge of the church governance, had asked Houston to refrain from drinking and preaching for three months prior to this meeting, but he had not followed the board's directives. Dooley said that a few of the Church Elders in Australia were not happy with the situation and were leaking details of the breaches to staff. The story was about to come out on the media, so the Global Board had no other alternative but to ask Houston to resign from the church he founded.

The following Sunday, I watched the Hillsong São Paulo service online to see how this momentous event would be communicated in Brazil. Chris

Mendez was purposely vague. He mentioned that there was news on the media about the Founding Pastor Brian Houston resigning, and that the Global Board would issue a press release. He had also discussed the matter of Houston's resignation with Interim Senior Pastor Dooley. That was it. He then quickly switched to a theological stance: at the end of the day, God was in control. By doing this, he skipped the very secular details of the Senior Pastor's dismissal and moved on to a focus on God and the little agency anyone had comparing to Him. He was equally vague when he announced the day's preaching, obliquely mentioning it had to do with the church's situation. He told congregants he chose Psalms 23:1–6[4] because it was "an apt passage of the Bible for this moment" but did not explain exactly what "this moment" was.

As I watched the comments being posted on the chat function, again there were lots of emojis, amens, messages asking for prayers and praising the church, and good mornings from such and such Brazilian city. The church posted its usual messages offering prayers, asking for people's reasons for gratitude, announcing events, and asking for donations. Just two people seemed to pay much attention to the significance of this event in their church's history. A woman blamed Houston's troubles on "the enemy": "The enemy is not happy with the growth of the church on Earth and so it raises accusations from all sides. Everyone should intercede[5] for the pastor and the church," she wrote. Others responded with "Amen." Another woman wrote: "Thank you for being transparent! I'm grateful for this family who seeks God and its reign in such a genuine manner." A third woman replied: "Our focus is Christ." After preaching, Mendez announced the opening date (May 2022) of a second branch in São Paulo in a theater in the city's east. As he did this, he was again projecting an image of growth and success indicating God's favor. This generated much excitement among those watching online, and they wrote messages to this effect.

It was as if nothing much had happened. The contrast between the English-language media and discussions on social media, which were saturated with images and descriptions of Houston's fall, and the Brazilian service's calm sameness was jarring. It made me think hard of why the church structures were shown to be so resilient in Brazil. Klaver (2021: 194) has argued that because the churches like Hillsong are not part of a denomination, they rely on the "personalized religious authority and charisma of its leaders" to keep their global structure together and its congregants loyal. According to Weber ([1922] 1968), charismatic authority is unstable. It needs to be validated and recognized by followers. In this sense, charismatic authority is relational. Hence, Klaver noted:

> Because religious authority is based on personalized charisma, the leading pastors and their family act as role models and are authoritative examples of how one is to live out faith in everyday life. Leading by example necessitates hyper-visibility and presence, which can be observed in mediated performances emphasizing transparency and authenticity.

Therefore, shouldn't the fact that the Global Senior Pastor was forced to resign for incurring in less than godly behavior be problematic for Brazilian followers? I suggest that the two chat-function posts I mentioned earlier explain how charisma and authority can be kept if there is a supernatural explanation for the fall ("the enemy") and the response to the fall is deemed "authentic."

With the scandals mounting, the media circling, and American celebrities such as Justin Bieber and Selena Gomez disavowing the church, Hillsong went into damage control. They were vague on the press release but still named the supposed issues that led to Houston's resignation. At the same time, they kept his charisma by asking for prayers for him as if he were a vulnerable victim of alcohol and sleeping tablets. The women's side of the story was never mentioned or heard. In that way, the church censured him but also kept its loving, caring image. The press release on the church website read:

> We are a church that believes in grace, love, restoration and integrity; these are our guiding values. You can be assured that investigations into these complaints were treated extremely seriously.... We are here for you, and as we work through this together, we are available to help and offer you support.... We also believe this is a time to focus our attention on the God who restores and rebuilds and encourage you to continue to meet together regularly not just on Sundays but in connect groups.

Hillsong thus reinforced one of its key characteristics—a focus on grace and love rather than judgment, something Brazilians admired and which they saw as opposed to the Brazilian Pentecostal style. For the megachurch, members' focus should be on God and strengthening the church community through group activities. In their study of charismatic leadership in megachurches in the United States, Corcoran and Wellman (2016: 310) found that "Charismatic leaders in institutionalized religions do not have to worry about backstage encounters with followers or discussing their ordinary life, because being ordinary can be a part of their charisma." It is both their everydayness and extraordinary qualities that appealed to followers. If the pastor is a man just like anyone in the congregation, he can be tempted and fall like them. His authority may be reinstated through the story of Christianity—humans are not perfect, but they can be redeemed. In this light, it makes sense for Hillsong to ask the church community to pray for Brian Houston and offer grace and love so that he can be restored.

Yet, as Johnson (2020) demonstrated in her study of the demise of Mars Hill megachurch, a coordinated online campaign disrupted senior pastor Mark Driscoll's charismatic authority. Through websites, blogs, and social media posts, aggrieved church members were able to offer powerful counternarratives that led to Driscoll's fall and the closing down of the church. Johnson (2020: 121) noted: "The very online technologies used to spread Mars Hill's influence and accrue Driscoll international celebrity became instruments of empowerment [for the congregation] . . . by turning Driscoll's own words, teachings, and voice publicly against him." At the onset of the Hillsong scandals in late 2020, social media accounts were created to offer counternarratives to Hillsong's tight control on information. For instance, *Hillsong ACCountability*[6] (on Facebook and YouTube), *The Hillsong Kerfuffle* and *Religion.Shouldnt.Hurt* (on Instagram), and the blog *Hillsong Church Watch* frequently post news media reports on the abuse, and their critical views on church videos and the Houstons' own social media postings. In October 2022, the same creators of the Discovery + documentary series *Hillsong: A Megachurch Exposed* started streaming a podcast series, *Hillsong: A Megachurch Shattered*, mirroring Christianity Today's podcast *The Rise & Fall of Mars Hill*.

However, two things distinguish Mars Hills and Driscoll from Hillsong and Houston. First, while Driscoll was the sole charismatic authority of his church, Houston shares his with Hillsong's worship leaders (e.g., Darlene Zschech until 2007, and Taya Gaukrodger, Joel Houston, and JD/Jonathon Douglass since then) and other celebrity pastors. In fact, Houston's importance in the church is a later addition. As Hutchinson (2017: 46) argued:

> After the establishment of Hillsong Conference in March 1987, it would not be too much to say that the Church's worship team leaders, Geoff Bullock and Darlene Zschech, became better known abroad than its Senior Pastor.

The comparison from a standpoint of 15 years later, at a time when Brian Houston is seen as a dominant, "apostolic" figure, suggests that his rise and rise should not be discussed so much in terms of *personal* charisma, but in Weberian terms... *organizational/institutional charisma*.... The bigger the church, the more it needs to be able to call upon a charismatic leader, the charisma of which is constructed precisely to meet that need.

Thus, it was the megachurch growth that propelled Houston to become well known and not the other way around. A second difference is that Mars Hill had not expanded globally like Hillsong. The latter's global structure and local pastors offer more stability to the network since charisma and affect, which spread along the network, and is situated—it depends on the socioeconomic context of the branch's location. In this context, Hillsong may be able to sustain and continue to reproduce itself even if it loses its luster (particularly in the United States) due to scandals. To be sure, these scandals have led to a 12% drop in donations in Australia compared to the previous year and a considerable drop in attendance, according to Hillsong's 2021 annual report.[7] Most probably, this situation is echoed in the United States, although there are no reports for global locations.

However, if we believe Chris Mendez's figures during the Christmas service in São Paulo mentioned at the start of the conclusion, and the successful establishment of a second branch in the city in October 2022, this is not the case in Brazil. I suggest that the factors mentioned earlier have so far protected Hillsong in Brazil from the shockwaves that took place in Australia and the United States. In addition, things have not changed much for Brazilians after the Houstons' dismissal. Chris and Lucy Mendez and the Brazilian pastors are still in charge and present in their everyday lives. Moreover, like the Houstons, Phil and Lucinda Dooley are Australian and speak English, two traits that bring kudos to the church, as we have seen throughout this book. Hillsong pastors are still highly mobile and have continued to visit and preach in the São Paulo branches. On a mission to charm South Americans after the scandals, Phil Dooley himself preached in both São Paulo branches after his visit to Buenos Aires in November 2022.

Moreover, Hillsong continues to offer them experiences of excitement, pleasure, (vicarious) success, growth, Spanish and English speaking, and a sense of God's favor. It gives them some authority in their roles as ministry leaders (as they organize parking before services, clean toilets, or join the worship band). It does not discriminate in regard to gender, age, and marital status, as opposed to Brazilian churches. Finally, paradoxically, the firing of the Houstons reaffirmed Brazilians' perception that Hillsong was an ethical church, where the rule of law prevailed, and that in the megachurch pastors were not "demigods" as one interviewee noted. Both its ethical and egalitarian stance are deeply admired among the Brazilian congregation, as we saw throughout this book. In a nutshell, Hillsong afforded them a life that can be otherwise—global, cosmopolitan, rational, sophisticated, and modern.

And here lies the importance of this book. It shows that the local (as in both the origin and destination of religious flows) is key to how religion globalizes. Here I am referring not only to the fact that religions have to adapt to the new site where they settle. More importantly, this book demonstrated the ways in which the social conditions of the local generate affective imaginaries of other places and propel people to action. This could be in the form of fandom, (imaginary or actual) travel, and adoption of new sensational forms from elsewhere. By focusing on how Hillsong's Cool Christianity style spreads in Brazil (through middle-class aspiration for cosmopolitanism and social distinction, fandom, digital media, travel, and local churches adopting it), this volume showed how the work of imagination is mediated by power asymmetries between the Global North and South.

For instance, while American and Brazilian followers were attracted by Hillsong's celebrity culture, excellence, and excitement, they gained very different things from studying at Hillsong College or going to its services. For Americans living in Australia, the church's use of the English language and its teaching of work skills (such as punctuality and autonomy) were not key to its attraction for them. Australia may be an exciting place to live, but it is in the Global North like the United States. In addition, most Americans have work experience as teenagers in hospitality and other service jobs. As such, the long hours of volunteering at the college and church felt like exploitation. They can also switch to other megachurches with similar characteristics. By contrast, Brazilians were willing to put in the hours and submit to pastors' authority because they felt they were learning English and work skills, living in the Global North, and the pastors were far less authoritarian than those in Brazil. In addition, the church seemed transparent and ethical when it was able to fire its founder, something that never happened in Brazil. Perhaps, Hillsong has a brighter future in the Global South than North. Phil Dooley's recent speaking tour in South America in 2022 may suggest that the church thinks that as well.

Notes

Preface

1. See, for instance, the excellent website *The Shiloh Project: Rape Culture, Religion and the Bible* https://www.shilohproject.blog/. Established in 2017 by scholars of religion based in New Zealand and the United Kingdom, it brings essays, discussions, and resources by contributors from all over the world on gender-based violence in religious settings.

Introduction

1. Multiple religious affiliation and religious transit are common in Brazil. For more on this, see Prandi (1996). For more on Spiritism in Brazil, see Hess (1994); for Spiritism in Australia, see Rocha (2006b).
2. For instance, while in 2003 there were 51 Evangelical members of congress out of 594 total seats, in 2022 that number had grown to 115 elected members (Barreto and Chaves 2023).
3. Following Gordon (2020), in this book I capitalise Black to distinguish between "the black" who was produced by antiblackness racism, and "Black people" who claimed an identity in opposition to their dehumanisation. White does not carry the same capitalisation because white people are not discriminated against because of skin color.
4. I am grateful to an anonymous reviewer for pointing me to this reference.
5. For more on the UCKG in Brazil, see Almeida (2009). For the UCKG in Australia, see Openshaw (2018); in Mozambique, see van de Kamp (2016); and in South Africa, see van Wyk (2014).

Chapter 1

1. According to the Pew Research Centre (2021), around three in ten US adults were religiously unaffiliated in 2021. In addition, the percentage of Christians has decreased in the previous decade. While in 2011 they made up 75% of the US population, in 2021 they were 63%. The majority of these were Protestants (40%). A report titled "Europe's Young Adults and Religion" (Bullivant 2018) surveyed 16- to 29-year-olds who identified with "no religion" in 22 European countries. It found that Czech

Republic youth were the least religious (91%) while the most religious were located in Poland (17%). The figure for the United Kingdom was 70%, France 64%, Germany 45%, and Portugal 42%. For the UK population at large, the 2017 British Social Attitudes survey found that 52% of people had no religion (BBC 2017). Similarly, in the 2021 Australian census, 39% of the population ticked "no religion," while 30% did so in the 2016 census. Like elsewhere, Christianity is in decline in Australia. While the 2011 census found 61% were Christian, the figure for the 2016 census was 52%, and for the 2021 census was 44% (ABS 2022b). In Brazil, a Datafolha poll conducted with youth between 16 and 24 years old in May 2022 found that 25% of this cohort had no religion compared to 14% among the adult population (Carrança 2022).

2. Fear of God is allegedly one of the most influential streetwear labels in the United States. Lorenzo previously collaborated with fashion house Zegna and has recently partnered with Adidas to head its basketball and athletics divisions. Justifying this partnership, an Adidas executive board member affirmed: "The global impact that Jerry Lorenzo and Fear of God has had on culture and the industry is undeniable" (Wolf 2020). This high-end fashion label is endorsed and worn by Hillsong senior pastors. Fear of God has 2 million followers on Instagram, including Hillsong (Brazilian) pastors.

3. Here I follow Hjarvard's (2008: 113) definition of mediatization of society as "the process whereby society to an increasing degree is submitted to, or becomes dependent on, the media and their logic. This process is characterized by a duality in that the media have become integrated into the operations of other social institutions, while they also have acquired the status of social institutions in their own right. As a consequence, social interaction—within the respective institutions, between institutions, and in society at large—take place via the media."

4. The success of *Peaky Blinders*' 1920s style in 2019 is a case in point. See https://www.hellomagazine.com/fashion/news/2019091077523/primark-peaky-blinders-fashion-collection/.

5. For a good analysis of how these two moments within Prosperity Gospel influence worship music, see Bowler and Reagan (2014).

6. For instance, Rakow (2015: 16) notes that the megachurch Lakewood, located in Texas, has been accused of "'Christianity Lite' because of its emphasis on hope, empowerment, prosperity and inspiration without mentioning sin, suffering and redemption."

7. https://www.bbc.co.uk/programmes/m000y2g7

8. For instance, research by the Fórum Brasileiro de Segurança Pública (2022) found that cases of racism increased 31% between 2018 and 2021. It hypothesized that there has been more public debate on racism in the country, and thus those who suffer it are more aware of their rights. In addition, a study (Cerqueira et al. 2021: 49) by the Institute for the Research of Applied Economics (IPEA) of the Brazilian government observed the following: In 2019, Blacks (sum of Black and Brown people in the IBGE classification) represented 77% of homicide victims, with a homicide rate per 100,000 inhabitants of 29.2. In comparison, among non-Blacks (Asian, -white, and

Indigenous people) the rate was 11.2 per 100,000, which means that the chance of a Black person being murdered is 2.6 times greater than that of a non-Black person. In other words, in the last year, the rate of lethal violence against Black people was 162% higher than among non-Blacks.

9. I am grateful to an anonymous reviewer who pointed out Jairo Alves's powerful book to me.
10. Ethnographic work has shown that UCKG followers have agency. For instance, in his work on the UCKG among Cabo Verdean migrants in Boston, Premawardhana (2012: 85) found that rather than "victims of alienation or brainwashing," those who submitted to the pressure to tithe (many times beyond their means) found a "sense of empowerment" in the ritual. For him, "Their expressions of devotion are active and creative strategies of self-transformation in response to the precariousness of the migrant's life-world."

Chapter 2

1. The so-called *música gospel* in Brazil bears no relation to gospel music of African American churches.
2. Bowler and Reagan (2014) provide an excellent potted history of the development of new contemporary Christian music in megachurches in the United States—with its arena rock concerts, celebrity worship leaders, bands that tour the world, live recordings, charting, prizes, and copyright system. They (2014: 200–204) show the influence of Hillsong and worship leader Darlene Zschech in this process as well as the role of Integrity Music and other Christian record labels in distributing CCM.
3. For a good analysis of the historical influence of the Southern Baptist Convention on the Brazilian Baptist Convention resulting in the establishment of close transnational connections between them, and also with Brazilian Baptist churches in the United States that cater to the diaspora, see Chaves (2021).
4. March for Jesus (pt. *Marcha para Jesus*) is an annual global evangelical event which started as City March in London in 1987. The largest march in Brazil takes place in São Paulo with over 3 million participants. It ends with an all-night worship music concert featuring many Brazilian and international acts.
5. In September 2023, Taya Smith (now Gaukrodger) had 863,000 followers on Instagram.

Chapter 3

1. https://data.worldbank.org/indicator/SI.POV.GINI?locations=BR&most_recent_value_desc=true

Chapter 4

1. Hillsong has a scheme called College Housing that sublets accommodation to Hillsong College students. According to the college website, houses near the headquarters in the outskirts of Sydney are large (four bedrooms) and accommodate on average six to eight students, while apartments near the Hillsong city center are smaller (two bedrooms) for an average of four to six students to share. Students from all over the world live in close quarters with each other for long periods of time, creating close-knit cosmopolitan communities. For more on this, see https://hillsong.com/college/accommodation/.
2. This is in reference to the story in which Jesus invites Peter to walk on water and because of his little faith he starts sinking. In other words, it is a session on having complete faith in Jesus. For more, see "Jesus Walks on the Water," from Matthew 14:22–33 (NIV).
3. https://hillsong.com/college/.
4. For more on this, see https://trainers.hillsongcollege.edu.au/category/trainer/academic/.
5. In 2021, among the many scandals that came to light at Hillsong was the sexual assault of an American Hillsong College student by a drunk Hillsong worship leader and son of the church's Head of Human Resources. Although she reported the incident, the case was only investigated after her father, a pastor, pressed the church and went to the media. The perpetrator pleaded guilty at a magistrate's court but was able to return to work at the church later on. For more on this, see Blair (2021).
6. John Calvin Maxwell (born 1947) is an American author, speaker, and pastor who has written many books, primarily focusing on leadership. Titles include *The 21 Irrefutable Laws of Leadership* and *The 21 Indispensable Qualities of a Leader*. His books have sold millions of copies, with some on the *New York Times* Best Seller List. (https://en.wikipedia.org/wiki/John_C._Maxwell).
7. For more on the Australian national identity, see Elder (2007).
8. Hillsong College has two locations: at the headquarters in the outskirts of Sydney (Baulkham Hills campus) and at the city campus, near central station in the heart of Sydney.

Chapter 5

1. For Hillsong history, see Hutchinson (2017) and Riches (2010).
2. See https://hillsong.com/online/
3. As I mentioned in the Introduction, Marquezine is a soap opera star who posted her visits to Hillsong Los Angeles on her Instagram account to her 45 million fans.
4. Meaning they watched the English version streamed before the Brazilian one, probably on the headquarters' site.
5. Christians Abroad is a pseudonym.

Chapter 6

1. Valdemiro Santiago established the *Igreja Mundial do Poder the Deus* (World Church of God's Power, WCGP) in 1998 after he left the UCKG due to a disagreement with its founder, Edir Macedo. Today, the WCGP is one of the largest megachurches in Brazil, with branches in 27 countries, according to the church website (https://impd.org.br/igrejas).
2. The founding pastors of *Renascer em Cristo* (Reborn in Christ) church were charged and jailed for money laundering after the FBI found they were smuggling large sums into the United States (FBI Arrests Two Brazilian Bishops in Miami 2007).
3. Gaw (2000: 83–84) defines reverse culture shock as "the process of readjusting, reacculturating, and reassimilating into one's own home culture after living in a different culture for a significant period of time." While people usually expect culture shock as they move to other countries, most do not expect issues when they return, imagining that their own cultures and families have remained unchanged. Gaw observes that it can lead to "psychological problems such as academic problems, cultural identity conflict, social withdrawal, depression, anxiety, and interpersonal difficulties."
4. According to the Hillsong website, "In the early church, elders were appointed in order to provide example, guidance and spiritual oversight to the churches (Acts 14:23). Their primary focus was the spiritual health of the church (1 Tim 4:14) (1 Tim 5:17–22) (James 5:14). They were chosen for their pastoral leadership, exemplary lifestyle and willingness to serve (Titus 1:5–9) (1 Peter 5:1–5). In Hillsong Church, the global senior pastors and the leadership team have appointed 11 elders" (https://hillsong.com/australia/eldership). After Houston was ousted in March 2022, one of the elders resigned when the group of elders were pitched against the global board over the future of the church (Hardy 2022).
5. For a good discussion on Brazilians' construction of Australia as a classless society, see Wulfhorst (2011).
6. In her study of Hillsong in Amsterdam and New York City, Klaver (2021: 125) remarked how volunteers desired to become full-time employees at the megachurch but "in practice, there is a small chance of realizing this dream, as paid positions at Hillsong Church are very limited."
7. Vision is important as a sign that pastors have spiritual discernment. They are able to differentiate between what is God's and the Devil's doing. In its embrace of the business world, at Hillsong, vision is also about setting goals for the church. Every year, the Hillsong Senior Pastor will lay out his vision for the church on Vision Sunday in early February.
8. As mentioned earlier, Carl Lentz was the celebrity pastor of New York City at the time. He was fired for having affairs and misuse of church funding in 2020. Judah Smith, the senior pastor of Churchome, is frequently invited to preach at Hillsong conferences and extends this invitation for Hillsong Global Senior Pastor to preach at his church. Taya Gaukrodger (née Smith) is the worship leader of Hillsong United.

Chapter 7

1. The lead pastor in charge of opening the Hillsong in Sweden explained that "A DNA Night is essentially a night where you talk about leadership and the vision and culture of your church. This is so important before launching a new campus because it's a great way to get people on board with the vision and the heartbeat of the church." See https://hillsong.com/collected/blog/2016/06/3-foundations-of-a-new-campus/
2. https://www.facebook.com/hillsongsaopaulo/posts/1639591689666772:0
3. However, it is worth noting that Globo and the Brazilian megachurch UCKG have had a tempestuous relationship as media competitors. See Rosas (2015: 135–148) for a good analysis of these conflicts.
4. For more on Christian 'conviction', see Harding (1987).
5. Spiritism is a French offshoot of the US and British Spiritualism. It has flourished in Brazil since the late nineteenth century due to its focus on healing. For more on Spiritism, see Aubrée and Laplantine (1990) and Hess (1994).
6. Here he uses the neologism *crentense*—derived from the word *crente* (believer) as Protestants are called in Brazil—to denominate the particular Protestant jargon.
7. Such jokes associate the Portuguese with ignorance or stupidity, probably as a reaction to the colonizers who saw Brazilians as inferior.
8. For a good analyses of Pentecostalism and politics in Brazil, see Almeida (2020) and Burity (2021).
9. James 5:13–20 (NIV): "Is anyone among you in trouble? Let them pray. Is anyone happy? Let them sing songs of praise. 14 Is anyone among you sick? Let them call the elders of the church to pray over them and anoint them with oil in the name of the Lord. 15 And the prayer offered in faith will make the sick person well; the Lord will raise them up. If they have sinned, they will be forgiven. 16 Therefore confess your sins to each other and pray for each other so that you may be healed. *The prayer of a righteous person is powerful and effective . . .*"

Conclusion

1. https://www.youtube.com/watch?v=W3LCrpp9m_M
2. "Heart for the House" takes place annually on a June weekend across all Hillsong churches. On this occasion, the followers are asked to make donations toward the Hillsong Foundation. For more, see https://hillsong.com/australia/foundation/hfth/
3. "Holy, Holy, Holy; Our God is on the throne; So firm is His foundation; No power can overthrow; And He shall reign Forever and ever; One name outlasts the ages; Through time His truth revealed; While kings may pass like shadows; Our God is sovereign still; To the Lamb upon the throne; Hallelujah hallelujah . . . The day I stand before Him; What praise will fill my soul; And there behold His glory And praise Him all the more." Words and music by Ben Fielding and Reuben Morgan © 2019 Hillsong Music Publishing Australia CCLI: 7134997.

4. Psalm 23:1–6 (KJV): "The LORD is my shepherd; I shall not want. He maketh me to lie down in green pastures: He leadeth me beside the still waters. He restoreth my soul: He leadeth me in the paths of righteousness for his name's sake. Yea, though I walk through the valley of the shadow of death, I will fear no evil: for thou art with me; Thy rod and thy staff they comfort me. Thou preparest a table before me in the presence of mine enemies: Thou anointest my head with oil; my cup runneth over. Surely goodness and mercy shall follow me all the days of my life: And I will dwell in the house of the LORD for ever."
5. Intercession refers to the act of praying to God on behalf of another person.
6. The spelling of *accountability* is a pun using the abbreviation for the Australian Christian Churches (AAC), previously the Assemblies of God in Australia, of which Hillsong was a member until 2018. This social media account aspires to call out not only Hillsong but also the AAC.
7. The Hillsong 2021 annual report is published online here: https://issuu.com/hillsong/docs/annualreview_a4_finalw_v7?fr=sZDJiMTQ0MDIxMzY

References

Abraham, I. 2018. Sincere Performance in Pentecostal Megachurch Music. *Religions* 9 (6): 192.
ABS. 2022a. Cultural Diversity. Released on June 28, 2022. Available at https://www.abs.gov.au/statistics/people/people-and-communities/cultural-diversity-census/latest-release. Accessed June 29, 2022.
ABS. 2022b. Religious Affiliation in Australia. Released on July 4, 2022. Available at https://www.abs.gov.au/articles/religious-affiliation-australia. Accessed July 4, 2022.
Adogame, A. 2013. *The African Christian Diaspora: New Currents and Emerging Trends in World Christianity*. New York: Bloomsbury.
Aguiar, T. 2020. *A "Cultura" para o Reino: Materialidades e Sentidos da Adoração em uma Juventude Evangélica em Porto Alegre*. Master's thesis, Department of Anthropology, Federal University of Rio Grande do Sul.
Allen, K., H. Mendick, L. Harvey, and A. Ahmad. 2016. Cultural Transitions: Celebrity and Young People's Aspirations. In A. Furlong (ed.), *Routledge Handbook of Youth and Young Adulthood*, pp. 229–236. Abingdon: Routledge.
Almeida, R. 2009. *A Igreja Universal e Seus Demônios: Um Estudo Etnográfico*. São Paulo: Editora Terceiro Nome.
Almeida, R. 2019. Bolsonaro Presidente: Conservadorismo, Evangelismo e a Crise Brasileira. *Novos Estudos do CEBRAP* 38 (1): 185–213.
Almeida, S. 2019. *Racismo Estrutural*. São Paulo: Pólen.
Almeida, R. 2020. Evangélicos à Direita. *Horizontes Antropológicos* 26 (58): 419–436.
Alves, J. 2018. *The Anti-Black City: Police Terror and Black Urban Life in Brazil*. Minneapolis: University of Minnesota Press.
Anderson, A. 2010. Varieties, Taxonomies, and Definitions. In A. Anderson, M. Bergunder, A. Droogers, and C. van der Laan (eds.), *Studying Global Pentecostalism: Theories and Methods*, pp. 13–29. Berkeley: University of California Press.
Anderson, A. 2013. *To the Ends of the Earth: Pentecostalism and the Transformation of World Christianity*. Oxford: Oxford University Press.
Angelo, M. 2017. Caiuá, a Ong de R$ 2 Bilhões que se Tornou Dona da Saúde Indígena no Brasil. *The Intercept*, September 30. Available at https://theintercept.com/2017/09/30/caiua-a-ong-de-r-2-bilhoes-que-se-tornou-dona-da-saude-indigena-no-brasil/. Accessed July 1, 2020.
Antunes, A. 2013. The Richest Pastors in Brazil. *Forbes Magazine*, January 17. Available at https://www.forbes.com/sites/andersonantunes/2013/01/17/the-richest-pastors-in-brazil/#2f3cc4df5b1e. Accessed July 28, 2017.
Arweck, E., and W. Keenan (eds.). 2016. *Materializing Religion: Expression, Performance and Ritual*. Abington: Routledge.
Aubrée, M., and F. Laplantine. 1990. *La Table, Le Livre et Les Esprits*. Paris: JC Lattès.
Baeyer, S. 2020. *Living Transnationally between Japan and Brazil: Routes Beyond Roots*. Lanham, MD: Lexington Books.

REFERENCES

Balloussier, A. 2020. Cara típica do evangélico brasileiro é feminina e negra. *Folha de São Paulo*, January 13. Available at https://www1.folha.uol.com.br/poder/2020/01/cara-tipica-do-evangelico-brasileiro-e-feminina-e-negra-aponta-datafolha.shtml. Accessed January 13, 2020.

Barreto, R., and J. Chaves. 2023. The Shared Religious Roots of Twin Insurrections in the U.S. and Brazil. *The Washington Post*, January 18. Available at https://www.washingtonpost.com/made-by-history/2023/01/18/brazil-insurrection-evangelical-christianity. Accessed January 25, 2023.

Bauman, Z. 2008. *Consuming Life*. Cambridge: Polity Press.

BBC. 2017. More Than Half in UK are Non-religious, Suggests Survey. *BBC News*, September 4. https://www.bbc.com/news/uk-41150792. Accessed November 14, 2017.

Beck, U. 1992. *Risk Society: Towards a New Modernity*. London: Sage.

Beck, U., and N. Sznaider. 2006. Unpacking Cosmopolitanism for the Social Sciences: A Research Agenda. *British Journal of Sociology* 57 (1): 1–23.

Bergson, H. 1911. *Laughter: An Essay on the Meaning of the Comic*. Translated by C. Brereton and F. Rothwell. London: Macmillan.

Billings, B. 2020. *Megachurches Can Have Mega Problems: Insights from Toxic Leadership in Modern Megachurches*. Honors Thesis, Belmont University. https://repository.belmont.edu/honors_theses/7.

Blair, L. 2021. How she fought back after assault by Hillsong Church administrator. *The Christian Post*, April 6. https://www.christianpost.com/news/after-assault-by-hillsong-church-administrator-she-fought-back.html. Accessed May 2, 2021.

Blyth, C. 2021. *Rape Culture, Purity Culture, and Coercive Control in Teen Girl Bibles*. London: Routledge.

Boaz, D. 2020. "Spiritual Warfare" or "Crimes against Humanity"? Evangelized Drug Traffickers and Violence against Afro-Brazilian Religions in Rio de Janeiro. *Religions* 11 (12): 640.

Bourdieu, P. 1984. *Distinction: A Social Critique of the Judgement of Taste*. Translated by Richard Nice. Cambridge, MA: Harvard University Press.

Bourdieu, P. 1986. The Forms of Capital. In J. Richards (ed.), *Handbook of Theory and Research in the Sociology of Education*, pp. 46–58. Westport, CT: Greenwood Press.

Bowler, K. 2013. *Blessed: A History of the American Prosperity Gospel*. Oxford: Oxford University Press.

Bowler, K. 2019. *The Preacher's Wife: The Precarious Power of Evangelical Women Celebrities*. Princeton, NJ: Princeton University Press.

Bowler, K., and W. Reagan. 2014. Bigger, Better, Louder: The Prosperity Gospel's Impact on Contemporary Christian Worship. *Religion and American Culture* 24 (2): 186–230.

Boykoff, M., and M. Goodman. 2009. Conspicuous Redemption? Reflections on the Promises and Perils of the "Celebritization" of Climate Change. *Geoforum* 40: 395–406.

Bräunlein, P. 2016. Thinking Religion through Things. *Method and Theory in the Study of Religion* 28 (4–5): 365–399.

Brenneman, R., and B. Miller. 2016. When Bricks Matter: Four Arguments for the Sociological Study of Religious Buildings. *Sociology of Religion* 77 (1): 82–101.

Brodesser-Akner, T. 2016. Hillsong: What It's Really Like Inside the Pentecostal Megachurch. *GQ Australia*, June 6. Available at http://www.gq.com.au/success/opinions/hillsong+what+its+really+like+inside+the+pentecostal+megachurch. Accessed June 2016.

Bullivant, S. 2018. *Europe's Young Adults and Religion*. Benedict XVI Centre for Religion and Society. Available at https://www.stmarys.ac.uk/research/centres/benedict-xvi/docs/2018-mar-europe-young-people-report-eng.pdf. Accessed April 13, 2019.

Burity, J. 2020. Conservative Wave: Religion and the Secular State in Post-impeachment Brazil. *International Journal of Latin American Religions* 4: 83–107.

Burity, J. 2021. The Brazilian Conservative Wave, the Bolsonaro Administration, and Religious Actors. *Brazilian Political Science Review* 15 (3): 1–19.

Butticci, A. 2016. *African Pentecostals in Catholic Europe: The Politics of Presence in the Twenty-First Century*. Cambridge, MA: Harvard University Press.

Caldeira, T. 2000. *City of Walls: Crime, Segregation, and Citizenship in São Paulo*. Berkeley: University of California Press.

Campbell, H. 2012. Understanding the Relationship between Religion Online and Offline in a Networked Society. *Journal of the American Academy of Religion* 80 (1): 64–93.

Cannell, F. 2006. Introduction. In F. Cannell (ed.), *The Anthropology of Christianity*, pp. 1–50. Durham, NC: Duke University Press.

Capler, R. 2022. Porque milhões de evangélicos estão abandonando suas igrejas. *Veja*, May 12. Available at https://veja.abril.com.br/coluna/matheus-leitao/por-que-milhoes-de-evangelicos-estao-abandonando-suas-igrejas/. Accessed May 13, 2022.

Capriglione, L. 2014. Tudo o que você queria saber sobre a inauguração do Templo do Rei Salomão, mas não tinha ninguém que lhe contasse. August 5. Available at https://br.noticias.yahoo.com/blogs/laura-capriglione/tudo-o-que-voc%C3%AA-queria-saber-sobre-inaugura%C3%A7%C3%A3o-025715044.html. Accessed September 15, 2015.

Carrança, T. 2022. Jovens "sem religião" superam católicos e evangélicos em SP e Rio. *BBC News Brasil*, May 9. Available at https://www.bbc.com/portuguese/brasil-61329257. Accessed May 10, 2022.

Cartledge, M. 2020. Megachurches as Educational Institutions. In S. Hunt (ed.), *Handbook of Megachurches*, pp. 172–192. Leiden: Brill.

Casanova, J. 1994. *Public Religion in the Modern World*. Chicago: University of Chicago Press.

Castles, S., M. Kalantzis, B. Cope, and M. Morrissey. 1990. *Mistaken Identity: Multiculturalism and the Demise of Nationalism in Australia*. Sydney: Pluto Press.

Cerqueira, D., H. Ferreira, S. Bueno, P. Palmieri Alves, R. de Lima, D. Marques, F. Barbosa da Silva, I. Lunelli, R. Imanishi Rodrigues, G. de Oliveira Accioly Lins, K. Chacon Armstrong, P. Lira, D. Coelho, B. Barros, I. Sobral, D.Pacheco, A. Pimentel. 2021. *Atlas da Violência*. São Paulo: Fórum Brasileiro de Segurança Pública. Available at https://forumseguranca.org.br/wp-content/uploads/2021/12/atlas-violencia-2021-v7.pdf. Accessed November 15, 2022.

Chagas, T. 2014. Convertida? Bruna Marquezine vai a culto da Hillsong Los Angeles acompanhada da modelo Stephannie Oliveira. *Gospel Mais*, August 20. Available at https://noticias.gospelmais.com.br/bruna-marquezine-hillsong-stephannie-oliveira-70546.html. Accessed October 2, 2014.

Chakrabarty, D. 2000. *Provincializing Europe: Postcolonial Thought and Historical Difference*. Princeton, NJ: Princeton University Press.

Chaves, J. 2021. *Migrational Religion: Context and Creativity in the Latinx Diaspora*. Waco: Baylor University Press.

Chaui, M. 2012. Democracia e Sociedade Autoritária. *Comunicação e Informação* 15 (2): 149–161.

Chen, T. 2019. A Man Created an Instagram About Church Leaders in Expensive Designer Shoes. It's Sending People Down an Existential Morality Spiral. *BuzzFeed*, April 5. https://www.buzzfeednews.com/article/tanyachen/a-man-created-preachersnsneakers-instagram-to-feature. Accessed April 7, 2019.

Coleman, S. 2000. *The Globalisation of Charismatic Christianity: Spreading the Gospel of Prosperity*. Cambridge: Cambridge University Press.

Coleman, S. 2015. Borderlands: Ethics, Ethnography, and "Repugnant" Christianity. *Hau: Journal of Ethnographic Theory* 5 (2): 275–300.

Coleman, S., and S. Chattoo. 2020. Megachurches and Popular Culture: On Enclaving and Encroaching. In S. J. Hunt (ed.), *Handbook of Megachurches*, pp. 84–102. Leiden: Brill.

Coleman, S., and R. Hackett. 2015. Introduction: A New Field? In S. Coleman and R. Hackett (eds.), *The Anthropology of Pentecostalism and Evangelicalism*, pp. 1–37. New York: NYU Press.

Connell, J. 2005. Hillsong: A Megachurch in the Sydney Suburbs. *Australian Geographer* 36: 315–332.

Connell, R., and T. Irving. 1980. *Class Structure in Australian History: Documents, Narrative and Arguments*. Melbourne: Longman Cheshire.

Cool, J. 2012. The Mutual Co-construction of Online and Onground in Cyborganic. In N. Whitehead and M. Wesch (eds.), *Human No More: Digital Subjectivities, Unhuman Subjects, and the End of Anthropology*, pp. 11–32. Boulder: University Press of Colorado.

Corcoran, K. E., and J. K. Wellman Jr. 2016. People Forget He's Human: Charismatic Leadership in Institutionalized Religion. *Sociology of Religion* 77 (4): 309–333.

Cunha, M. 2007. *A Explosão Gospel: Um Olhar das Ciências Humanas sobre o Cenário Evangélico no Brasil*. Rio de Janeiro: Mauad e Instituto Mysterium.

DaMatta, R. 1979 *Carnavais, Malandros e Heróis: Para uma Sociologia do Dilema Brasileiro*. Zahar: Rio de Janeiro.

Dantas, B. 2010. A Dupla Linguagem do Desejo na Igreja Evangélica Bola de Neve. *Religião e Sociedade* 30 (1): 53–80.

Da Silva Moreira, A. 2018. The Aestheticization of Religion in Brazil (and Probably Elsewhere). *International Journal of Latin American Religion* 2: 125–141.

Dawson, A. 2013. Entangled Modernity and Commodified Religion: Alternative Spirituality and the "New Middle Class." In F. Gauthier and T. Martikainen (eds.), *Religion in Consumer Society: Brands, Consumers and Markets*, pp. 127–142. London: Routledge.

Delanty, G. 2006. The Cosmopolitan Imagination: Critical Cosmopolitanism and Social Theory. *British Journal of Sociology* 57 (1): 25–48.

Department of Education and Training. 2020. International Student Data Summary. Available at https://internationaleducation.gov.au/research/international-studentddata/Documents/MONTHLY%20SUMMARIES/2020/Full%20year%20summary.pdf. Accessed June 18, 2021.

Department of Education. 2022. International Education Data and Research International Student Numbers by Country, by State and territory. Available at https://www.dese.gov.au/international-education-data-and-research/international-student-numbers-country-state-and-territory. Accessed August 23, 2022.

Driessens, O. 2012. The Celebritization of Society and Culture: Understanding the Structural Dynamics of Celebrity Culture. *International Journal of Cultural Studies* 16 (6): 641–657.

Duarte, F. 2006. Exploring the Interpersonal Transaction of the Brazilian Jeitinho in Bureaucratic Contexts. *Organization* 13 (4): 509–527.

Elder, C. 2007. *Being Australian: Narratives of National Identity*. Sydney: Allen and Unwin.
Ellingson, S. 2013. Packaging Religious Experience, Selling Modular Religion: Explaining the Emergence and Expansion of Megachurches. In F. Gauthier and T. Martikainen (eds.), *Religion in Consumer Society: Brands, Consumers, and Markets*, pp. 59–74. Farnham, UK: Ashgate.
Engelke, M., and J. Robbins (eds.). 2010. Global Christianity, Global Critique. *Special issue, South Atlantic Quarterly* 109 (4): 623–631.
Eskridge, L. 2013. *God's Forever Family: The Jesus People Movement in America*. New York: Oxford University Press.
Evans, M. 2015. Hillsong Abroad: Tracing the Songlines of Contemporary Pentecostal Music. In M. Ingalls and A. Yong (eds.), *The Spirit of Praise: Music and Worship in Global Pentecostal-Charismatic Christianity*, pp. 179–198. University Park: Penn State University Press.
Evans, M. 2017. Creating the Hillsong Sound: How One Church Changed Australian Christian Music. In T. Riches and T. Wagner (eds.), *The Hillsong Movement Examined: You Call Me out upon the Waters*, pp. 63–81. New York: Palgrave Macmillan.
FBI Arrests Two Brazilian Bishops in Miami. 2007. N/A. *Religion News Blog*, January 9. Available at https://www.religionnewsblog.com/17121/fbi-arrests-two-brazilian-bishops-in-miami. Accessed October 20, 2010.
Featherstone M., and S. Lash. 1995. Globalization, Modernity, and the Spatialization of Social Theory: An Introduction. In M. Featherstone, S. Lash, and R. Robertson (eds.), *Global Modernities*, pp. 1–24. London: Sage.
Feltrin, R. 2017. Globo exibe documentário sobre igreja evangélica e ganha elogios nas redes. *UOL Notícias*, January 2. Available at http://tvefamosos.uol.com.br/noticias/ooops/2017/01/02/globo-exibe-documentario-de-igreja-evangelica-e-ganha-elogios-nas-redes.htm. Accessed January 2, 2017.
Feltrin, R. 2022. Opinião: Série do Discovery+ contra igreja Hillsong é rasa e forçada. May 20. Splash UOL. Available at https://www.uol.com.br/splash/noticias/ooops/2022/05/20/opiniao-serie-do-discovery-contra-igreja-hillsong-e-rasa-e-forcada.htm. Accessed August 31, 2023.
Fewkes, J. H. 2019. Piety in the Pocket: An Introduction. In J. H. Fewkes (ed.), *Anthropological Perspectives on the Religious Uses of Mobile Apps*, pp. 1–16. London: Palgrave Macmillan.
Fórum Brasileiro de Segurança Pública. 2022. 16th *Anuário Brasileiro de Segurança Pública*. São Paulo: FBSP. Available at https://forumseguranca.org.br/anuario-16/. Accessed September 17, 2022.
Foucault, M. 1997. The Birth of Biopolitics. In P. Rabinow (ed.), *Ethics: Subjectivity and Truth*, pp. 73–80. New York: New Press.
Frank, T. 1997. *The Conquest of Cool: Business Culture, Counterculture, and the Rise of Hip Consumerism*. Chicago: University of Chicago Press.
French, A., and D. Adler. 2021. Carl Lentz and the Trouble at Hillsong. *Vanity Fair*, February. Available at https://www.vanityfair.com/style/2021/02/carl-lentz-and-the-trouble-at-hillsong. Accessed May 11, 2021.
Freston, P. 1995. Pentecostalism in Brazil: A Brief History. *Religion* 25: 119–133.
Freston, P. 1997. Charismatic Evangelicals in Latin America: Mission and Politics on the Frontiers of Protestant Growth. In S. Hunt, M. Hamilton, and T. Walter (eds.), *Charismatic Christianity: Sociological Perspectives*, pp. 184–204. London: Macmillan Press.

Freston, P. 2008. The Religious Field among Brazilians in the United States. In C. Jouet-Pastre and L. Braga (eds.), *Becoming Brazuca: Brazilian Immigration to the United States*, pp. 255–268. Cambridge, MA: Harvard University Press.

Freston, P. 2010. Reverse Mission: A Discourse in Search of Reality? *PentecoStudies* 9 (2): 140–152.

Frishberg, H. 2020. "It's a Cult": Ex-Hillsong Members Claim Church Demanded "Slave Labor." *NY Post*, December 23. Available at https://nypost.com/2020/12/23/ex-hillsong-members-claim-church-is-cult-with-slave-labor/amp/?__twitter_impression=true. Accessed March 5, 2021.

Galloway, A. 2022. Tens of Thousands of International Graduates to Work in Australia Longer. *Sydney Morning Herald*, September 3. Available at https://www.smh.com.au/politics/federal/tens-of-thousands-of-international-graduates-to-work-in-australia-longer-20220902-p5betx.html. Accessed September 3, 2022.

Gamson, J. 1994. *Claims to Fame: Celebrity in Contemporary America*. Berkeley: University of California Press.

Gauthier, F., L. Woodhead, and T. Martikainen. 2013. Introduction: Consumerism as the Ethos of Consumer Society. In F. Gauthier and T. Martikainen (eds.), *Religion in Consumer Society: Brands, Consumers and Markets*, pp. 1–24. London: Routledge.

Gaw, K. F. 2000. Reverse Culture Shock in Students Returning from Overseas. *International Journal of Intercultural Relations* 24 (1): 83–104.

Giddens, A. 1991. *Modernity and Self-Identity: Self and Society in the Late Modern Age*. Cambridge: Polity.

Glick Schiller, N., and N. Salazar. 2013. Regimes of Mobility across the Globe. *Journal of Ethnic and Migration Studies* 39 (2): 183–200.

Glick Schiller, N., T. Darieva, and S. Gruner-Domic. 2011. Defining Cosmopolitan Sociability in a Transnational Age: An Introduction. *Ethnic and Racial Studies* 34 (3): 399–418.

Goh, R. 2008. Hillsong and "Megachurch" Practice. *Material Religion* 4 (3): 284–304.

Goldstein, D. 2009. The Aesthetics of Domination: Class, Culture, and the Lives of Domestic Workers in Rio de Janeiro. In K. Hall (ed.), *Studies in Inequality and Social Justice*, pp. 149–195. Meerut: Archana.

Gonçalo, R. 2020. Megatemplos Evangélicos na Experiência Urbana. *Caderno Eletrônico de Ciências Sociais* 8 (1): 60–90.

Gonçalves Pereira, R. 2019. "Deixa o menino rodar": O Carisma Reteté em uma Igreja Pentecostal da Periferia. *Debates do NER* 19 (36): 267–305.

Goodwin, M. 2020. *Abusing Religion: Literary Persecution, Sex Scandals, and American Minority Religions*. New Brunswick, NJ: Rutgers University Press.

Gordon, L. 2020. Shifting the Geography of Reason in Black and Africana Studies. *The Black Scholar* 50 (3): 42–47.

Grieser, A., and J. Johnston. 2017. *Aesthetics of Religion: A Connective Concept*. Berlin: Walter de Gruyter.

Grossberg, L. 1992. Is There a Fan in the House? The Affective Sensibility of Fandom. In L. A. Lewis (ed.), *Fan Culture and Popular Media*, pp. 50–68. New York: Routledge.

Guerreiro, C. 2018. "Hoje à Noite Vai Ter Reteté, Pô!" Evidências de Conflitos Cotidianos em Rituais Pentecostais. *Debates do NER* 19 (34): 123–154.

Habermas, J. 2006. Religion in the Public Sphere. *European Journal of Philosophy* 14 (1): 1–25.

Halafoff, A., H. Shipley, P.D. Young, A. Singleton, M. L. Rasmussen, and G. Bouma. 2020. Complex, Critical and Caring: Young People's Diverse Religious, Spiritual and Non-Religious Worldviews in Australia and Canada. *Religions* 11 (4): 166.

Hannerz, U. 1990. Cosmopolitans and Locals in World Culture. In M. Featherstone (ed.), *Global Culture*, pp. 237–51. London: Sage.

Hardaker, D. 2021. The Hillsong Way: Where Free Labour for God Is Just the Beginning. *Crickey*, August 30. Available at https://www.crikey.com.au/2021/08/30/hillsong-free-labour-for-god/?utm_campaign=CrikeyWorm&utm_medium=email&utm_source=newsletter. Accessed August 31, 2021.

Hardaker, D. 2022. "How Do We Move Forward?": Edited Transcript of Hillsong's March 18 All-Staff Meeting. *Crickey*, March 23. Available at https://www.crikey.com.au/2022/03/23/hillsong-staff-meeting-transcript/. Accessed March 23, 2022.

Harding, S. 1987. Convicted by the Holy Spirit: The Rhetoric of Fundamental Baptist Conversion. *American Ethnologist* 14 (1): 167–181.

Harding, S. 1991. Representing Fundamentalism: The Problem of the Repugnant Cultural Other. *Social Research* 58 (3): 373–393.

Hardy, E. 2022. Brand or Church? How Hillsong Is Facing a Day of Reckoning. *The Guardian*, April 8. Available at https://www.theguardian.com/world/2022/apr/08/brand-or-church-how-hillsong-is-facing-a-day-of-reckoning. Accessed April 8, 2022.

Hardy, E. 2023. Hillsong and the Life of Brian. *The Monthly*, February. Available at https://www.themonthly.com.au/issue/2023/february/elle-hardy/hillsong-and-life-brian#mtr Accessed February 3, 2023.

Harris, E. 2017. Tattoos, Bieber, Black Lives Matter and Jesus. *New York Times*, October 26. Available at https://www.nytimes.com/2017/10/26/books/hillsong-church-carl-lentz-book-justin-bieber.html?action=click&module=RelatedLinks&pgtype=Article. Accessed August 2017.

Hazard, S. 2013. The Material Turn in the Study of Religion. *Religion and Society* 4: 58–78.

Hebdige, D. [1979] 2002. *Subculture: The Meaning of Style*. London: Routledge.

Hess, D. 1994. *Samba in the Night: Spiritism in Brazil*. New York: Columbia University Press.

Hess, D. and R. DaMatta. 1995. *The Brazilian Puzzle: Culture on the Borderlands of the Western World*. New York: Columbia University Press.

Hillsong College Course Guide. 2022–2023. Available at https://workdrive.zohoexternal.com/external/687117a1780a0c2b5c80055df4b58781a0bccb9447e943c3f6044736b607d2a3. Accessed May 12, 2013.

Hjarvard, S. 2008. The Mediatization of Society: A Theory of the Media as Agents of Social and Cultural Change. *Nordicom Review* 29 (2): 105–134.

Hodkinson, P. 2016. Spectacular Youth? Young People's Fashion and Style. In A. Furlong (ed.), *Routledge Handbook of Youth and Young Adulthood*, pp. 266–272. London: Routledge.

Hofbauer, A. 2016. Blackness, Inequality and Religion: The Case of Candomblé. In S. Engler and B. Schmidt (eds.), *Handbook of Contemporary Religions in Brazil*, pp. 448–472. Leiden: Brill.

Houston, B. 2016. The Church I Now See. October 12. Available at https://www.facebook.com/hillsongsaopaulo/posts/1631637017128906:0. Accessed October 13, 2016.

Hunt, S. 2020. Introduction: The Megachurch Phenomenon. In S. Hunt (ed.), *The Handbook of Megachurches*, pp. 1–20. Leiden: Brill.

Hutchinson, M. 2017. "Up the Windsor Road": Social Complexity, Geographies of Emotion, and the Rise of Hillsong. In T. Riches and T. Wagner (eds.), *The Hillsong Movement Examined*, pp. 39–61. New York: Palgrave Macmillan.

Ingalls, M., and A. Yong. 2015. *The Spirit of Praise: Music and Worship in Global Pentecostal-Charismatic Christianity*. University Park: Penn State University Press.

Ikeuchi, S. 2019. *Jesus Loves Japan: Return Migration and Global Pentecostalism in a Brazilian Diaspora*. Stanford, CA: Stanford University Press.

Jackson, J. 2003. *Pastorpreneurs*. Friendswood: Baxter.

Jenkins, P. 2002. *The Next Christendom: The Rise of Global Christianity*. New York: Oxford University Press.

Jennings, M. 2014. Imagining Jesus Doing a Whole Lotta Shakin': Pentecostal Worship, Popular Music and the Politics of Experience. *Culture and Religion* 15 (2): 211–226.

Jobes, P. 2022. Faith through the Furnace: Hillsong, Exit Wounds and Keeping the Faith. *Sixty Stadia*. May 4, Available at http://www.sixtystadia.com/2022/05/faith-through-the-furnace/. Accessed May 10, 2022.

Johnson, J. 2017. Megachurches, Celebrity Pastors, and the Evangelical Industrial Complex. In B. D. Forbes and J. H. Mahan (eds.), *Religion and Popular Culture in America*, pp. 159–176. Oakland: University of California Press.

Johnson, J. 2018. *Biblical Porn: Affect, Labor, and Pastor Mark Driscoll's Evangelical Empire*. Durham, NC: Duke University Press.

Johnson, J. 2020. The Fall of Mars Hill Church in Seattle: How Online Counter-Narratives Catalyzed Change. In M. Stausberg, S. Wright, and C. Cusack (eds.), *The Demise of Religion: How Religions End, Die, or Dissipate*, pp. 119–134. London: Bloomsbury.

Kapferer, B. 1988. *Legends of People, Myths of State: Violence, Intolerance and Political Culture in Sri Lanka and Australia*. Washington, DC: Smithsonian Institution Press.

King-O'Riain, R. C. 2020. "They Were Having So Much Fun, So Genuinely...": K-pop Fan Online Affect and Corroborated Authenticity. *New Media & Society* 23 (9): 2820–2838.

Klaver, M. 2015. Pentecostal Pastorpreneurs and the Global Circulation of Authoritative Aesthetic Styles. *Culture and Religion* 16: 146–159.

Klaver, M. 2018. Global Church Planting in the Media Age: Hillsong Church. *Zeitschrift für Missionswissenschaft und Religionswissenschaft* (ZMR) 102 (3/4): 227–235.

Klaver, M. 2021. *Hillsong Church: Expansive Pentecostalism, Media and the Global City*. Cham: Palgrave Macmillan.

Köhrsen, J. 2016. *Middle-Class Pentecostalism in Argentina: Inappropriate Spirits*. Leiden: Brill.

Laneri, R. 2019. How Religious Celebs Like Kanye West Inspired Sunday "Church" Fashion. *New York Post*, May 20. Available at https://nypost.com/2019/05/20/how-religious-celebs-like-kanye-west-inspired-sunday-church-fashion. Accessed May 21, 2019.

Larkin, B. 2013. The Politics and Poetics of Infrastructure. *Annual Review of Anthropology* 42: 327–343.

Lehmann, D. 1996. *Struggle for the Spirit: Religious Transformation and Popular Culture in Brazil and Latin America*. Oxford: Polity Press.

Levine, R. 1997. *Brazilian Legacies*. New York: ME Sharpe.

Levitt, P. 2007. *God Needs No Passport*. Boston: The New Press.

Levitt, P. 1998. Social Remittances: Migration Driven Local-Level Forms of Cultural Diffusion. *International Migration Review* 32 (4): 926–948.

Levitt, P., and N. Glick Schiller. 2004. Conceptualizing Simultaneity: A Transnational Social Field Perspective on Society. *The International Migration Review* 38 (3): 1002–1039.

Lin, W., J. Lindquist, B. Xiang, and B. Yeoh. 2017. Migration Infrastructures and the Production of Migrant Mobilities. *Mobilities* 12 (2): 167–174.

Lipka, M. 2015. A Closer Look at America's Rapidly Growing Religious "Nones." May 13. Available at https://www.pewresearch.org/fact-tank/2015/05/13/a-closer-look-at-americas-rapidly-growing-religious-nones. Accessed July 30, 2021.

Lofton, K. 2018. Revisited: Sex Abuse and the Study of Religion. *The Immanent Frame*. Available at https://tif.ssrc.org/2018/08/24/sex-abuse-and-the-study-of-religion/ Accessed November 21, 2022.

Luhrmann, T. M. 2012. *When God Talks Back: Understanding the American Evangelical Relationship with God*. New York: Random House.

Maddox, M. 2012. "In the Goofy Parking Lot": Growth Churches as a Novel Religious Form for Late Capitalism. *Social Compass* 59: 146–158.

Maddox, M. 2013a. "Rise Up Warrior Princess Daughters": Is Evangelical Women's Submission a Mere Fairy Tale? *Journal of Feminist Studies in Religion* 29 (1): 9–26.

Maddox, M. 2013b. Prosper, Consume and Be Saved. *Critical Research on Religion* 1 (1): 108–115.

Madianou, M. 2016. Ambient Co-Presence: Transnational Family Practices in Polymedia Environments. *Global Networks* 16 (2): 183–201.

Madianou, M., and Miller, D. 2012. *Migration and New Media: Transnational Families and Polymedia*. London: Routledge.

Maranhão, E. 2013. *A Grande Onda Vai Te Pegar—Marketing, Espetáculo e Ciberespaço na Bola de Neve Church*. São Paulo: Fonte.

Marcus, B. 2015. Exclusive: Is This the Most Fashionable Church Ever? *Harper's Bazaar*, August 13. Available at http://www.harpersbazaar.com/culture/features/news/a11853/hillsong-church. Accessed August 2015.

Mariano, R. 2014. *Neopentecostais: Sociologia do Novo Pentecostalismo no Brasil*. São Paulo: Loyola.

Mariz, C. 1996. Pentecostalism and Confrontation with Poverty in Brazil. In B. Gutierrez and D. Smith (eds.), *In the Power of the Spirit: The Pentecostal Challenge to Historic Churches in Latin America*, pp. 129–146. Online, PC (USA), AIPRAL/CELEP. Available at https://www.religion-online.org/book-chapter/chapter-4-pentecostalism-and-confrontation-with-poverty-in-brazil-by-cecilia-loreto-mariz. Accessed March 15, 2006.

Martí, G. 2017. The Global Phenomenon of Hillsong Church: An Initial Assessment. *Sociology of Religion: A Quarterly Review* 78 (4): 377–386.

Martin, D. 1990. *Tongues of Fire: The Explosion of Protestantism in Latin America*. Oxford: Blackwell.

Martin, D. 2002. *Pentecostalism: The World Their Parish*. Oxford: Blackwell.

Martin, B. 2006. The Aesthetics of Latin American Pentecostalism: The Sociology of Religion and the Problem of Taste. In E. Arweck and W. Keenan (eds.), *Materialising Religion: Expression, Performance and Ritual* (pp. 138–160). Abington: Routledge.

Mason, M., A. Singleton, and R. Webber. 2010. Developments in Spirituality among Youth in Australia and Other Western Societies. In G. Giordan (ed.), *Annual Review of the Sociology of Religion*, pp. 89–114. Leiden: Brill.

Massey, D. 1993. Power-Geometry and a Progressive Sense of Place. In J. Bird, B. Curtis, T. Putnam, and L. Tickner (eds.), *Mapping the Futures: Local Cultures, Global Change*, pp. 59–69. London: Routledge.

Massey, D. 1994. *Space, Place and Gender*. Cambridge: Polity Press.

Massumi, B. 2002. *Parables for the Virtual: Movement, Affect, Sensation*. Durham, NC: Duke University Press.

Mazzarella, W. 2009. Affect: What Is It Good for? In S. Dube (ed.), *Enchantments of Modernity: Empire, Nation, Globalization*, pp. 291–309. New Delhi: Routledge.

McCracken, B. 2010. *Hipster Christianity: When Church and Cool Collide*. Grand Rapids, MI: Baker.

McCracken, B. 2014. Hipster Christianity, Revisited. *Converge Media*, September 3. https://convergemagazine.com/hipster-christianity-revisited-14394/. Accessed September 10, 2015.

McGinnis, K. 2022. Should We Keep Singing Hillsong? *Christianity Today*, May 2. Available at https://www.christianitytoday.com/ct/2022/may-web-only/hillsong-church-music-sing-worship-scandal-documentary.html. Accessed May 5, 2022.

McGregor, C. 2001. *Class in Australia*. Ringwood, Vic.: Penguin.

McIntyre, E. 2007. Brand of Choice: Why Hillsong Music Is Winning Sales and Souls. *Australian Religion Studies Review* 20 (2): 175–194.

Meyer, B. 2009. Introduction: From Imagined Communities to Aesthetic Formations: Religious Mediations, Sensational Forms, and Styles of Binding. In B. Meyer (ed.), *Aesthetic Formations: Media, Religion and the Senses*, pp. 1–28. New York: Palgrave Macmillan.

Meyer, B. 2010a. Pentecostalism and Globalization. In A. Anderson, M. Bergunder, A. Droogers, and C. S. van der Laan (eds.), *Studying Global Pentecostalism: Theories and Methods*, pp. 113–130. Berkeley: University of California Press.

Meyer, B. 2010b. Aesthetics of Persuasion: Global Christianity and Pentecostalism's Sensational Forms. *South Atlantic Quarterly* 109 (4): 741–763.

Meyer, B. 2011. Mediation and Immediacy: Sensational Forms, Semiotic Ideologies and the Question of the Medium. *Social Anthropology/Anthropologie Sociale* 19 (1): 23–39.

Meyer, B., and D. Houtman. 2012. Introduction. Material Religion: How Things Matter. In D. Houtman and B. Meyer (eds.), *Things: Religion and the Question of Materiality*, pp. 1–27. New York: Fordham University Press.

Meyer, B., and A. Moors (eds.). 2006. *Religion, Media, and the Public Sphere*. Bloomington: Indiana University Press.

Meyer, B., and J. Verrips. 2008. Aesthetics. In D. Morgan (ed.), *Key Words in Religion, Media and Culture*, pp. 20–30. New York: Routledge.

Meyer, B., D. Morgan, C. Paine, and S. B. Plate. 2010. The Origin and Mission of Material Religion. *Religion* 40 (3): 207–211.

Miller, D. 1997. *Reinventing American Protestantism: Christianity in the New Millennium*. Berkeley: University of California Press.

Miller, D., and T. Yamamori. 2007. *Global Pentecostalism: The New Face of Christian Social Engagement*. Berkeley: University of California Press.

Miller, E. 2015. *A Planting of the Lord: Contemporary Pentecostal and Charismatic Christianity in Australia*. Unpublished PhD dissertation, University of Sydney, Australia.

Moseley, R. 2005. "Introduction." In R. Moseley (ed.), *Fashioning Film Stars: Dress Culture and Identity*, pp. 1–8. London: BFI.

REFERENCES

Novaes, L. 2015. Hillsong Church São Paulo poderá ser inaugurada no início de 2016. *Guiame*, May 13. Available at http://guiame.com.br/gospel/mundo-cristao/hillsong-church-sao-paulo-podera-ser-inaugurada-no-final-de-2015.html. Accessed March 2016.

O'Dougherty, M. 2002. *Consumption Intensified: The Politics of Middle-Class Daily Life in Brazil*. Durham, NC: Duke University Press.

Oliveira, E. 2021. Brasil regride em meta para acabar com o analfabetismo e não alcança objetivo de investir mais na educação, diz relatório Plano Nacional de Educação. *G1*, June 24. Available at https://g1.globo.com/educacao/noticia/2021/06/24/brasil-regride-em-meta-para-acabar-com-o-analfabetismo-e-nao-alcanca-objetivo-de-investir-mais-na-educacao-diz-relatorio.ghtml. Accessed June 1, 2022.

Oliven, R. 2000. Brazil: The Modern in the Tropics. In V. Schelling (ed.), *Through the Kaleidoscope: The Experience of Modernity in Latin America*, pp. 53–71. London: Verso.

Ong, A. 1999. *Flexible Citizenship: The Cultural Logics of Transnationality*. Durham, NC: Duke University Press.

Oosterbaan, M. 2015. Mediating Culture: Charisma, Fame and Sincerity in Rio de Janeiro, Brazil. In S. Coleman and R. Hackett (eds.), *The Anthropology of Pentecostalism and Evangelicalism*, pp. 161–176. New York: NYU Press.

Openshaw, K. 2018. *I Am Universal: Transnational Material Networks of Spiritual Capital in the Australian Universal Church of the Kingdom of God*. Unpublished PhD dissertation, Western Sydney University.

Openshaw, K. 2019. The Universal Church of the Kingdom of God in Australia: Local Congregants and a Global Spiritual Network. *Journal for the Academic Study of Religion* 32 (1): 27–48.

Openshaw, K. 2021. The Universal Church of the Kingdom of God in Australia: A Church of Non-Brazilian Migrants. *Social Compass* 68 (2): 231–244.

Oro, A. 2012. *Religião no Espaço Público: Atores e Objetos*. São Paulo: Terceiro Nome.

Oro, A. 2014a. Igrejas evangélicas brasileiras na Itália: recorrências e tensões. *Estudos de Religião* 28 (2): 102–114.

Oro, A. 2014b. South American Evangelicals' Re-conquest of Europe. *Journal of Contemporary Religion* 29 (2): 219–232.

Orsi, R. 2017. What Is Catholic about the Clergy Sex Abuse Crisis? In K. Norget, V. Napolitano, and M. Mayblin (eds.), *Anthropology of Catholicism: A Reader*, pp. 282–292. Oakland: University of California Press.

Ortiz, R. 2000. Popular Culture, Modernity and Nation. In V. Schelling (ed.), *Through the Kaleidoscope: The Experience of Modernity in Latin America*, pp. 127–147. London: Verso.

Pacheco, R. 2023. Missões evangelizadoras têm que entrar no rol de investigados pelo genocídio Yanomami. *The Intercept*, February 10. Available at https://theintercept.com/2023/02/10/genocidio-yanomami-missoes-evangelizadoras-tem-que-ser-investigadas/. Accessed February 2023.

Peres, E. 2020. Pastor Everaldo chora e pede clemência ao depor sobre fraudes no Rio. *Correio Braziliense*, December 12. Available at https://www.correiobraziliense.com.br/politica/2020/12/4895536-pastor-everaldo-chora-e-pede-clemencia-ao-depor-sobre-fraudes-no-rio.html. Accessed January 5, 2021. Accessed January 2022

Pew Research Center. 2021. About Three-in-Ten U.S. Adults Are Now Religiously Unaffiliated. December 14. Available at https://www.pewresearch.org/religion/2021/12/14/about-three-in-ten-u-s-adults-are-now-religiously-unaffiliated/. Accessed January 2022.

Pinezi, A., and A. Chesnut. 2019. Pentecostal Gangs in Rio de Janeiro Ratchet Up Their Persecution of Afro-Brazilian Religions under President Bolsonaro. *The Global Catholic Review*, August 29. Available at https://www.patheos.com/blogs/theglobalcatholicreview/2019/08/pentecostal-gangs-in-rio-de-janeiro-ratchet-up-their-persecution-of-afro-brazilian-religions-under-president-bolsonaro/. Accessed September 30, 2019.

Pinheiro-Machado, R., and L. Scalco. 2014. Rolezinhos: Marcas, Consumo e Segregação no Brasil. *Revista Estudos Culturais* 1 (1): 1–21.

Porter, M. 2017. Singing Beyond Territory: Hillsong and Church Planting in Oxford, UK. In T. Riches and T. Wagner (eds.), *The Hillsong Movement Examined: You Call Me out upon the Waters*, pp. 163–179. New York: Palgrave Macmillan.

Pountain, D., and D. Robins. 2000. Cool Rules: Anatomy of an Attitude. *New Formations* 39: 7–14.

Prandi, R. 1996. Religião Paga, Conversão e Serviço. In A. Pierucci and R. Prandi (eds.), *A Realidade Social das Religiões no Brasil: Religião Sociedade e Política*, pp. 257–273. São Paulo: Hucitec.

Premawardhana, D. 2012. Transformational Tithing Sacrifice and Reciprocity in a Neo-Pentecostal Church. *Nova Religion* 15 (4): 85–109.

Rede Nova São Paulo. 2021. Mapa da Desigualdade 2021 é Lançado. October 21. Available at: https://www.nossasaopaulo.org.br/2021/10/21/mapa-da-desigualdade-2021-e-lancado/ Accessed October 20, 2022.

Riches, T. 2010. *Shout to the Lord: Music and Change at Hillsong 1996–2007*. M.Phil. Dissertation, Department of Music, ACU.

Riches, T. 2017. The Sisterhood: Hillsong in a Feminine Key. In T. Riches and T. Wagner (eds.), *The Hillsong Movement Examined: You Call Me out upon the Waters*, pp. 85–105. New York: Palgrave Macmillan.

Riches, T., and T. Wagner. 2012. The Evolution of Hillsong Music: From Australian Pentecostal congregation into Global Brand. *Australian Journal of Communication* 39 (1): 17–36.

Riches, T., and T. Wagner (eds.). 2017. *The Hillsong Movement Examined. You Call Me Out Upon the Waters*. London: Palgrave Macmillan.

Robbins, J. 2003. What Is a Christian? Notes toward an Anthropology of Christianity. *Religion* 33 (3): 191–199.

Robbins, J. 2007. Continuity Thinking and the Problem of Christian Culture: Belief, Time, and the Anthropology of Christianity. *Current Anthropology* 48 (1): 5–38.

Robbins, J. 2010. Anthropology of Religion. In A. Anderson, M. Bergunder, A. Droogers, and C. van der Laan (eds.), *Studying Global Pentecostalism: Theories and Methods*, pp. 156–178. Berkeley: University of California Press.

Robbins, J. 2014. The Anthropology of Christianity: Unity, Diversity, New Directions. *Current Anthropology* 55 (S10): 157–171.

Robertson, J. 2015. Queensland Barrister Tony Morris QC Loses Appeal on $146 Speeding Fine. *The Guardian*, June 23. https://www.theguardian.com/australia-news/2015/jun/23/queensland-barrister-tony-morris-qc-loses-appeal-on-146-speeding-fine. Accessed June 23, 2015.

Robertson, S. 2014. Time and Temporary Migration: The Case of Temporary Graduate Workers and Working Holiday Makers in Australia. *Journal of Ethnic and Migration Studies* 40 (12): 1915–1933.

Robertson, S., and A. Runganaikaloo. 2014. Lives in Limbo: Migration Experiences in Australia's Education–Migration Nexus. *Ethnicities* 14 (2): 208–226.

Robins, D. J. 2019. Lifestyle Migration from the Global South to the Global North: Individualism, Social Class, and Freedom in a Centre of "Superdiversity." *Population, Space and Place* 25 (6): e2236.

Rocha, C. 2006a. *Zen in Brazil: The Quest for Cosmopolitan Modernity*. Honolulu: Hawaii University Press.

Rocha, C. 2006b. Two Faces of God: Religion and Social Class in the Brazilian Diaspora in Sydney. In P. Kumar (ed.), *Religious Pluralism in the Diaspora*, pp. 147–160. Leiden: Brill.

Rocha, C. 2013. Transnational Pentecostal Connections: An Australian Megachurch and a Brazilian Church in Australia. *Pentecostudies* 12 (1): 62–82.

Rocha, C. 2014. Triangular Circulation: Japanese Brazilians on the Move between Japan, Australia and Brazil. *Journal of Intercultural Studies* 35 (5): 493–512.

Rocha, C. 2016. A Megaigreja Hillsong no Brasil: A constituição de um campo religioso transnacional entre o Brasil e a Austrália. *Plural: Revista de Ciências Sociais USP* 23 (2): 162–181.

Rocha, C. 2017a. *John of God: The Globalization of Brazilian Faith Healing*. New York: Oxford University Press.

Rocha, C. 2017b. "The Come to Brazil Effect": Young Brazilians' Fascination with Hillsong. In T. Riches and T. Wagner (eds.), *The Hillsong Movement Examined: You Call Me out upon the Waters*, pp. 125–143. New York: Palgrave Macmillan.

Rocha, C. 2019. "God Is in Control": Middle-Class Pentecostalism and International Student Migration. *Journal of Contemporary Religion* 34 (1): 21–37.

Rocha, C. 2020a. How Religions Travel: Comparing the John of God Movement and a Brazilian Migrant Church. In L. van de Kamp, M. Oosterbaan, and J. Bahia (eds.), *Global Trajectories of Brazilian Religions: Lusospheres*, pp. 23–36. London: Bloomsbury.

Rocha, C. 2020b. "Living the Dream": Post-Millennial Brazilians at Hillsong College. In C. Rocha, M Hutchinson, and K. Openshaw (eds.), *Australian Pentecostal and Charismatic Movements: Arguments from the Margins*, pp. 217–235. Leiden: Brill.

Rocha, C. 2021. Cool Christianity: The Fashion-Celebrity-Megachurch Industrial Complex. *Material Religion* 17 (5): 580–602.

Rocha, C., and M. Barker (eds.). 2010. *Buddhism in Australia: Traditions in Change*. London: Routledge.

Rocha, C., and K. McPhillips. 2019. '#MeToo catches up with spiritual healers: the case of Brazil's John of God.' *The Conversation*, February 22. Available at https://theconversation.com/metoo-catches-up-with-spiritual-healers-the-case-of-brazils-john-of-god-112215. Accessed February 23, 2019.

Rocha, C., and M. Vásquez (eds.). 2013. *The Diaspora of Brazilian Religions*. Leiden: Brill.

Rocha, C. M. Hutchinson, and K. Openshaw (eds.). 2020. *Australian Pentecostal and Charismatic Movements: Arguments from the Margins*. Leiden: Brill.

Rocha, C., K. Openshaw, and R. Vokes. 2021. "Middle-class" Africans in Australia: Choosing Hillsong as a Global Home. *Culture and Religion* 22 (1): 25–45.

Rosas, N. 2015. *Cultura evangélica e "dominação" do Brasil: música, mídia e gênero no caso do Diante do Trono*. Unpublished PhD dissertation, Department of Sociology, Federal University of Minas Gerais.

Rovisco, M. and M. Nowicka. 2011. Introduction. In M. Rovisco and M. Nowicka (eds.), *The Ashgate Research Companion to Cosmopolitanism*, pp. 1–14. London and New York: Routledge.

Ruic, G. 2018. Estas são as 20 melhores cidades do mundo para se viver. *Exame*, March 21. https://exame.com/mundo/estas-sao-as-20-melhores-cidades-do-mundo-para-se-viver/. Accessed January 11, 2022.

Rutherford, D. 2016. Affect Theory and the Empirical. *Annual Review of Anthropology* 45: 285–300.

Sanchez, Z., D. Locatelli, A. Noto, and S. Martins. 2013. Binge Drinking among Brazilian Students: A Gradient of Association with Socioeconomic Status in Five Geo-economic Regions. *Drug Alcohol Dependence* 127 (1–3): 87–93.

Sanders, G. 2014. Ironically Religious, Blandly Fashionable. *Critical Sociology* 40 (4): 495–498.

Sandler, L. 2006. *Righteous: Dispatches from the Evangelical Youth Movement*. New York: Viking.

Sargeant, K. 2000. *Seeker Churches: Promoting Traditional Religion in a Nontraditional Way*. New Brunswick, NJ: Rutgers University Press.

Schäfer, A. 2020. "High on Jesus": US Evangelicals and the Counterculture. *Horizonte* 18 (57): 924–954.

Scheikowski, M. 2008. Ex-judge Einfeld Admits Lying in Court. *SMH*, October 31. https://www.smh.com.au/national/exjudge-einfeld-admits-lying-in-court-20081031-5f0s.html. Accessed October 31, 2008.

Shanahan, M. 2018. *Australian Neo-Pentecostal Churches: Incorporating Late Modernity in a New Religious Form*. Unpublished PhD dissertation. Department of Modern History, Politics, and International Relations, Macquarie University.

Sheppard, J., and N. Biddle. 2017. Class, Capital, and Identity in Australian Society, *Australian Journal of Political Science* 52 (4): 500–516.

Sheringham, O. 2013. *Transnational Religious Spaces Faith and the Brazilian Migration Experience*. London: Palgrave Macmillan.

Silva, V. G. 2016. Crossroads: Conflicts between Neo-Pentecostalism and Afro-Brazilian Religions. In S. Engler and B. Schmidt (eds), *Handbook of Contemporary Religions in Brazil*, pp. 489–507. Leiden: Brill.

Souza, J. 2018. *A Classe Média no Espelho: Sua História, Seus Sonhos e Ilusões, Sua Realidade*. Rio de Janeiro: Estação Brasil.

Souza Martins, J. 2000. The Hesitations of the Modern and the Contradictions of Modernity in Brazil. In V. Schelling (ed.), *Through the Kaleidoscope: The Experience of Modernity in Latin America*, pp. 248–275. London: Verso.

Stieg, C. 2019. Kanye West's Sunday Service Isn't Exactly Church, but It Is Christian. April 4. https://www.refinery29.com/en-us/2019/04/228821/kanye-west-sunday-service-religion-christian-church. Accessed April 10, 2019.

Stolow, J. 2005. Religion and/as Media. *Theory, Culture & Society* 22 (4): 119–145.

Strazzery, J. 2011. "Hillsong College." Brazil-Australia Blog, September 11. Available at www.brazilaustralia.com/hillsong-college. Accessed September 20, 2011.

Thompson, E. P. 1967. Time, Work-Discipline, and Industrial Capitalism. *Past & Present* 38: 56–97.

Thornton, D. 2020. A Match Made in Heaven: Why Popular Music Is Central to the Growth in Pentecostal Charismatic Christianities. In T. Riches and T. Wagner (eds.), *The Hillsong Movement Examined: You Call Me out upon the Waters*, pp. 109–125. New York: Palgrave Macmillan.

Threadgold, S., and J. Gerrard, eds. 2022. *Class in Australia*. Melbourne: Monash University Press.
Thumma, S., and W. Bird. 2015. Megafaith for the Megacity: The Global Megachurch Phenomenon. In S. D. Brunn (ed.), *The Changing World Religion Map: Sacred Places, Identities, Practices and Politics*, pp. 2331–2352. Dordrecht: Springer.
Tietjen, A. 2017. Pastor Carl Lentz Talks Preaching in Ripped Jeans, Bonding with Bieber. *Women's Wear Daily*, November 1. Available at https://wwd.com/eye/people/carl-lentz-talks-preaching-in-jeans-bonding-with-bieber-11037192. Accessed August 2017.
Turner, G. 2006. The Mass Production of Celebrity. "Celetoids," Reality TV and the "Demotic Turn." *International Journal of Cultural Studies* 9 (2): 153–165.
Tweed, T. 2002. *Our Lady of the Exile: Diasporic Religion at a Cuban Catholic Shrine in Miami*. New York: Oxford University Press.
Twitchell, J. 2004. *Branded Nation: The Marketing of Megachurch, College Inc., and Museumworld*. New York: Simon and Schuster.
Twitchell, J. 2007. *Shopping for God: How Christianity Went from in Your Heart to in Your Face*. New York: Simon and Schuster.
Valentinsson, M. C. 2020. Stars: They Talk Just Like Us! *Anthropology News* 61 (1): 3–6.
Van de Kamp, L. 2016. *Violent Conversion: Brazilian Pentecostalism and Urban Women in Mozambique*. Oxford: James Currey.
Van de Kamp, L. 2017. The Transnational Infrastructures of Luso-Pentecostal Mega-Cities. *New Diversities* 19: 1–17.
Van Wyk, I. 2014. *The Universal Church of the Kingdom of God in South Africa: A Church of Strangers*. New York: Cambridge University Press.
Vásquez, M. 2011. *More Than Belief: A Materialist Theory of Religion*. New York: Oxford University Press.
Vásquez, M. 2014. From Colonialism to Neo-liberal Capitalism: Latino/a Immigrants in the U.S. and the New Biopolitics. *Journal for Cultural and Religious Theory* 13 (1): 81–100.
Vásquez, M., and M. Marquardt. 2003. *Globalizing the Sacred: Religion across the Americas*. New Brunswick, NJ: Rutgers University Press.
Vásquez, M., and L. Ribeiro. 2007. "A Igreja é Como a Casa da Minha Mãe": Religião e espaço vivido entre brasileiros no condado de Broward. *Ciencias Sociales y Religion/ Ciências Sociais e Religião* 9 (9): 13–29.
Wade, M., and M. Hynes. 2013. Worshipping Bodies: Affective Labour in the Hillsong Church. *Geographical Research* 51: 173–179.
Wade, M. 2015. Seeker-Friendly: The Hillsong Megachurch as an Enchanting Total Institution. *Journal of Sociology* 52 (4): 661–676.
Wagner, T. 2017. The "Powerful" Hillsong Brand. In T. Riches and T. Wagner (eds.), *The Hillsong Movement Examined. You Call Me Out Upon the Waters*, pp. 253–269. London: Palgrave Macmillan.
Wagner, T. 2020. *Music, Branding and Consumer Culture in Church: Hillsong in Focus*. Abington: Routledge.
Ward, R. 1992. The Australian Legend. In G. Whitlock and D. Carter (eds.), *Images of Australia*, pp. 179–190. Brisbane: University of Queensland Press.
Ward, P. 2020. *Celebrity Worship: Media, Religion and Culture*. Abington, UK: Routledge.
Weber, M. (1922) 1968. *On Charisma and Institution Building: Selected Writings*. Edited by S. N. Eisenstadt. Chicago: University of Chicago Press.

Wellman, J. K., Jr., K. E. Corcoran, and K. J. Stockly. 2020. Megachurches as Total Environments. In S. Hunt (ed.), *Handbook of Megachurches*, pp. 152–171. Leiden: Brill.

Vertovec, S., and R. Cohen (eds.). 2002. *Conceiving Cosmopolitanism: Theory, Context, and Practice*. Oxford: Oxford University Press.

Vincett, G., E. Olson, P. Hopkins, and R. Pain. 2012. Young People and Performance Christianity in Scotland. *Journal of Contemporary Religion* 27 (2): 275–290.

Windle, J., and Q. Maire. 2019. Beyond the Global City: A Comparative Analysis of Cosmopolitanism in Middle-Class Educational Strategies in Australia and Brazil. *Discourse: Studies in the Cultural Politics of Education* 40 (5): 717–733.

Wolf, C. 2020. Jerry Lorenzo Takes the Next Step Towards His Fashion Revolution. *GQ Magazine*, December 23. https://www.gq.com/story/fear-of-god-jerry-lorenzo-adidas-basketball-real-hoopers-know. Accessed January 25, 2021.

Wulfhorst, C. 2011. *Intimate Multiculturalism: Blurred Boundaries between Brazilians and Australians in Sydney*. Unpublished PhD dissertation, Institute for Culture and Society, Western Sydney University.

Wuthnow, R. 2009. *Boundless Faith: The Global Outreach of American Churches*. Berkeley: University of California Press.

Yip, J. 2015. Marketing the Sacred: The Case of Hillsong Church, Australia. In J. James (ed.), *A Moving Faith: Mega Churches Go South*, pp. 106–126. Delhi: Sage.

Index

For the benefit of digital users, indexed terms that span two pages (e.g., 52–53) may, on occasion, appear on only one of those pages.

abuse. *See also* scandals involving pastors
   bullying and, vii–viii
   Cool Christianity and, 51
   financial abuse and, 9–10, 24
   Hillsong churches and, vii–viii, 102–3, 148, 189–92
   sexual abuse and, vii–viii, 9–10, 24, 104, 189–92
   spiritual abuse and, 102
accountability
   cosmopolitanism and, 4
   Global North and, ix
   Hillsong churches and, ix, 147–48, 191, 193, 194–95
adulthood transition
   among Brazilian diaspora in Australia, 73–74, 77, 85–87, 89
   autonomy and, 101, 109–10
   binge drinking and sex during, 86–87, 88, 140–41
   Cool Christianity and, 20, 28, 50–51
   Hillsong churches and, 7–8, 11
   Hillsong College and, 100–1, 105–12
   mattering maps and, 65, 121–22
   volunteerism and, 12, 170
aesthetics. *See also* style
   affective aesthetics and, 3
   aisthesis and, 7–8, 28–29
   beauty and, 29
   the body and, 28–29, 46
   "Cool Christianity" and, 9, 32–33, 51
   Hillsong churches and, 7–8, 11, 20, 22–23, 24, 43–44, 180–81, 182, 184
   Pentecostalism and, 28–29, 42–43, 47–48, 51
   of religion, 7–8, 28–31, 32–33
   Seeker churches and, 8–9, 12, 176

   standardization of, 123
   taste and, 42–43
affect
   affective labor and, 100, 101–3, 121–22, 126–27
   affective transnational community and, 3, 54–55
   the body and, 53–54
   branding and, 33–34, 50–51
   Cool Christianity and, 9, 12
   emotion compared to, 53
   excitement and, 2, 3, 12, 22, 52–53, 66
   Hillsong churches and, 11, 22, 52–53, 54–55, 102–3, 126–27, 141, 186–87, 189, 194–95
   Hillsong College and, 21–22, 101–2, 141–42
   mattering maps and, 53–54, 100
   music and, 54–55, 59, 63
   pleasure and, 3, 12, 53–54, 89–90, 117, 174, 194–95
   pride and, 3, 12, 22, 66, 90–91, 125, 135, 142
   shame and, 7, 135
Afro-Brazilian religious communities, 6–7, 45
Almeida, Silvio, 45–46
Alphacrucis College, 105, 111–12
Alves, Jairo, 5, 45
anthropology of Christianity, 17–18
anti-Black racism in Brazil
   Catholic Church and, 45
   segregation and, 4–5, 45
   social class construction and, 4–5, 43, 45–46
   violence and, 45, 198–99n.8
Argentina, 6, 43–44, 46–47, 75–76

INDEX

Aristotle, 28–29
Assemblies of God churches, 13–14, 47, 55–56, 105, 109
Australia. *See also* Brazilian diaspora in Australia
  anti-authoritarianism in culture of, 154–55, 161
  Brazilians' nostalgia for their time in, 16, 52–53, 119, 150–51, 158–59, 162
  Brazilian tourists in, 68–69
  Brazil's cultural affinities with, 177–78
  census data from, 80–81, 82, 197–98n.1
  class differentiation in, 148
  Covid-19 pandemic and restrictions in, 14–15, 68–69, 80–81, 82, 131–32
  Department of Home Affairs in, 84
  dreams among Brazilians regarding, 52–53, 64–66, 67–69, 70, 73–74, 86, 92, 96, 97
  English language and, 21, 72–73, 78–81
  Global North and, 54–55, 80, 147–48, 156
  imagination regarding, 20–21, 52–53, 54–55, 62–63, 64, 71–72
  immigration policies in, 21, 77, 78–79, 80–81, 87, 89, 92–94, 96–97
  multiculturalism in, 75, 118
  Olympic Games (2000) in, 67–68
  partying and binge drinking in, 86–87, 88, 140–41
  Pentecostalism in, 10, 13–14
  perfection associated with, 67–68
  permanent residency status in, 77, 78–79, 81–83, 84, 91, 92–94, 96
  promotion of education and tourism to Brazilian audiences by, 68–69
  Universal Church of the Kingdom of God in, 56–57
Australian Planetshakers, 181
authoritarianism
  Brazilian culture and, 146–47, 154, 174
  Brazilian Pentecostalism and, viii–ix, 4, 11, 150, 157–58, 163–64, 173–74
  pastoral authority and, 4, 109, 145–47, 154, 155, 173–74

Baldwin, Hailey, 37

Baptist churches, 57, 59, 131. *See also* Evangelicals; Pentecostalism; *specific churches*
Baptist Church of Água Branca (São Paulo), 131
belief, embodiment of, 115
Bergson, Henri, 47–48
Bethel churches, 57–58, 181, 182
Bieber, Justin, 24, 37, 71–72, 160, 167–68, 192
Black Lives Matter movement, 18–19, 41
the body
  aesthetics and, 28–29, 46
  affect and, 53–54
  crentes and, 46
  Holy Spirit and, 28–29, 44
  longing and, 53
  Pentecostalism and, 28–29, 42–43, 44, 51
Bola de Neve church, 1–2, 152–53
Bolsonaro, Jair, 6–7, 19, 171–72
Bourdieu, Pierre, 8, 42
Bowler, Kate, 36, 37, 126
branding
  affective experience and, 33–34, 50–51
  architecture and, 128–29
  community cohesion and, 33
  "Cool Christianity" and, 8–9, 22–23, 26, 50–51
  Hillsong churches and, 3, 7–8, 10, 18–19, 20, 33–34, 59, 67–68, 70, 106, 112, 126–27, 128–29, 163–64
  Hillsong College and, 98, 99–100, 107–8
  music and, 59
  pastors and, 36–37
Brasa Church (Porto Alegre), 131, 182
Brasília cathedral, 130
Brazil. *See also* social class in Brazil
  Australian Embassy in, 68–69
  Australian Festival in, 68–69
  Australia's cultural affinities with, 177–78
  authoritarianism in culture of, 146–47, 154, 174
  census data from, 4, 80–81
  cosmopolitanism and, viii–ix, 3–4
  economic crises in, 79–80
  illiteracy in, 49
  inequality levels in, 79–80

INDEX   223

jeitinho ("clever dodge") in the culture of, 112–14
race in, 4–5, 43, 45–46
segregation and inequality in, 4–6
US culture's influence in, 57, 177, 179
violence in, 4–5, 45, 56, 198–99n.8
Brazil for Christ Church, 55–56
Brazilian diaspora in Australia
  adulthood transition among, 73–74, 77, 85–87, 89
  Australian immigration policies and, 21, 77, 78–79, 80–81, 87, 89, 92–94, 96–97
  binge drinking among, 86–87, 88, 140–41
  Brazilian diasporic churches and, 72–73
  downward mobility among, 73–74, 77, 78, 86, 90–92, 97, 100, 149, 156
  English language learning and, 21, 72–73, 78–79, 81
  Hillsong churches and, 1–3, 72, 94–96
  overall size of, 80–81
  Pentecostalism and, 11, 21, 77, 97
  precarity among, 21, 73–74, 77, 78–79, 82–84, 97, 99, 149
  racism against, 77
  return migration to Brazil and, 16, 22, 52–53, 62–63, 66, 81, 143, 148–62
  social class and, 72–73
  student migration and, 7, 16, 21, 77, 78–79, 80–81, 83–84, 85–88, 91, 94–95, 97, 139–42, 143 (*See also* Hillsong College)
Brazilian diaspora in Japan, 89–90, 149
Brazilian diaspora in London, 149
Brazilian Pentecostalism. *See also* Pentecostalism
  architecture and, 130–31
  authoritarianism and hierarchy in, viii–ix, 4, 11, 150, 157–58, 163–64, 173–74
  Brazilian diaspora communities in Australia and, 11, 21, 77, 97
  foreign missionaries and, 55–56
  Global North Pentecostalism and, 57–58
  growth during twenty-first century of, 4
  patriarchy in, 151, 153–54
  Prosperity Theology and, 56–57
  reteté (ecstatic rituals) in, 43–44, 51, 152, 153
  return migrants from Australia's struggle to reacclimate to, 151–58, 161, 178
  sensational forms and, 41–42, 48, 157–58
  social class and, 4, 6, 20, 22, 28, 44–45, 46–49, 123, 142
Brazilian Universal Church of the Kingdom of God, 58, see Universal Church of the Kingdom of God
Buddhism, 6, 17
Bullock, Geoff, 193–94

C3 churches, 15, 21, 77, 86–87, 93–94
Caldeira, Teresa, 4–5
Cannell, Fenella, 17–18
Cartledge, Mark J., 105
Catholic Church
  anti-Black racism and, 45
  Brasília cathedral and, 130
  Brazilian military coup (1964) and, 17
  decline in influence in Brazil of, 56, 157
  magical religion and, 29–30
  patriarchy in, 17, 143–44
celebrity culture
  in Brazil, 3
  consumerism and commodification in, 34–35
  Cool Christianity and, 8, 25–27, 37–38, 50–51, 99
  English language and, 69
  fandom and, 55
  fashion industry and, 35
  Global North and, 36–37, 144
  Hillsong churches and, 3, 9–10, 20, 22–23, 24–25, 34–35, 36–38, 55, 70–72, 73, 126–27, 160, 165–66, 195
  mediatization and, 34–35
  modernity and, 34–35
  pastors as celebrities and, 34–35, 36–37, 51, 67, 70–71, 101, 160–61, 184–85
  Prosperity Theology and, 37
  social media and, 3, 34–35, 36–37, 66–67, 71–72
  in the United States, 37–38
Charismatic Christianity, 7, 10, 26–27. *See also* Pentecostalism

224 INDEX

Chaui, Marilena, 146–47
Christian Congregation churches, 13–14, 55–56
"Christians Abroad" (pseudonym for study abroad company), 139–42, 156
Churchome, 177
CityCare (Hillsong social justice arm), 188
CJC churches, 21, 72–73, 77, 83–84, 88, 90
Coachella Festival (2019), 26–27
Coleman, Simon, 13–14, 18–19, 129
Colour Conference, 103–4
commodification, 31, 34–35, 36–37, 50–51
consumerism
    celebrity culture and, 34–35
    commodification of the self and, 31, 34–35
    cool and, 31–32
    Hillsong churches and, 10, 27–28
    modernity and, 31, 36
    prosumption and, 36–37
    Seeker churches and, 100–1
    youth culture and, 27–28, 32, 33
contemporary Christian music (CCM), 59–60
Cool Christianity
    abuse and, 51
    adulthood transition and, 20, 28, 50–51
    aesthetics and, 9, 32–33, 51
    branding and, 8–9, 22–23, 26, 50–51
    celebrities and celebrity culture in, 8, 25–27, 37–38, 50–51, 99
    clothing and fashion in, 24, 25–28, 32–33, 40, 138
    cosmopolitanism and, 4, 20
    criticisms of, 38–42, 51
    Hillsong churches and, viii, 9, 11–12, 13, 20, 22–23, 24, 28, 31, 34, 38–39, 53, 123, 127, 138, 195
    hipsters and, 25–26, 38
    Jesus People movement and, 8, 25–26
    modernity and, 12, 28
    music and, 20–21, 26, 32–33, 51
    power asymmetries and, 9
    sensational forms and, 20, 28, 30–31, 34, 42
    sexuality and, 40–41, 42
    social class and, ix, 8, 20
    social media and, 26–27
    youth culture and, 9, 26–28, 31, 51
co-presence
    aesthetics and, 13
    connect groups and, 96
    Covid-19 era and, 22, 123–24, 132
    Hillsong Family network and, 174–75
    Hillsong Leadership network and, 135–38
    infrastructures that sustain, 11, 22, 123–24, 142
    polymedia and, 14
    social media and, 131–35
Corcoran, Katie E., 192–93
Corden, James, 26–27
cosmopolitanism
    accountability and, 4
    Cool Christianity and, 4, 20
    definition of, 3
    English language and, 3, 81, 135, 150–51, 167, 175–76
    Global North and, 28, 150–51
    Hillsong churches and, viii–ix, 12–13, 23, 51, 135, 158, 195
    Hillsong College and, 101–2, 118–21
    identity formation and, 158–61
    sociability and, 158
Covid-19
    Australia's restrictions due to, 14–15, 68–69, 80–81, 82, 131–32
    co-presence in the era of, 22, 123–24, 132
    Hillsong churches and, 22, 123–24, 131–32, 188
    labor shortages and, 82
    polymedia in the era of, 14–15, 131–32
crentes (Pentecostal believers)
    the body and, 46
    class-oriented prejudices against, 44–45, 46–48, 51, 153
    clothing and, 47
    social distinction and, 46
    worship styles among, 152
culture. *See* celebrity culture; youth culture
Cunha, Magali, 59, 60–61

DaMatta, Roberto, 146–47
Dawson, Andrew, 36

INDEX

Diante do Trono, 60–61, 63, 179–80
Dooley, Lucinda, 138, 189–90, 194
Dooley, Phil, vii, 25, 138, 189–90, 194, 195
Douglass, Jonathon "JD," 71, 193
dreams. *See also* imagination
   Cool Christianity and, 9
   fandom and, 62–63
   of former life in Australia, 52–53, 66, 97
   of future in Australia, 64–66, 67–69, 70, 73–74, 86, 92, 96
   God and, 65–66
   of Hillsong churches, 63–64, 65–66, 69, 70
   of Hillsong College, 21–22, 64, 69, 100, 101–2, 116–17
   of "other life," 8–9, 19, 54–55, 64, 89
Driscoll, Mark, vii–viii, 102, 193

embodiment. *See* the body
English language
   Brazilian diaspora in Australia and, 21, 72–73, 78–79, 81
   Brazilian society's valuing of, viii–ix, 12–13, 19, 125, 135, 175–76, 181
   celebrity culture and, 69
   cosmopolitanism and, 3, 81, 135, 150–51, 167, 175–76
   Global North and, 116, 144, 183
   Hillsong churches and, 1–2, 13, 23, 75, 135, 167, 183, 185, 194–95
   Hillsong College and, 101–2, 117, 159
Evangelicals. *See also* Pentecostalism
   celebrity culture and, 70–71
   "church shopping" among, 157
   discerning God's will and, 94
   lifestyle and, 33
   links between United States and Brazil and, 57–58

Falwell Jr., Jerry, vii–viii
fandom
   celebrity culture and, 55
   criticisms of, 70–73
   dreams and, 62–63
   fashion choices and, 36–37
   Hillsong churches and, 3, 11, 20–21, 22–23, 51, 52, 55, 62, 63–64, 67–68, 70, 72, 163–64, 168–69, 195

Hillsong United and, 61–63, 64–65, 126–27
K-Pop music and, 66–67
mattering maps and, 73–74, 100
pastors and, 36–37, 52, 54–55
popular praise music bands and, 3, 20–21, 36–37, 52, 54–55, 70, 72–73, 126–27, 158, 164
sensational forms and, 53
as site of optimism, 53–54
social media and, 36–37, 54–55, 66–67, 70, 126–27
fashion industry
   celebrity culture and, 35
   Fashion-Celebrity-Megachurch industrial complex and, 26–27
   Fear of God label and, 26–27, 198n.2
   Hillsong's clothing line and, 27–28, 41
favelas, 45
Fear of God fashion label, 26–27, 198n.2
Featherstone, Mike, 4–5
Foursquare church, 55–56
Freston, Paul, 6, 55–57

Galante, Raphael, 186, 187–88
Gateway church, 60–61, 181
Gaukrodger, Taya, 71, 72, 160, 193
Gauthier, François, 31, 33
Glick Schiller, Nina, 3, 14–15, 121, 158
global cities, 4–5, 13, 123–24
globalization, 13–14, 17–18, 31, 69, 125, 195
Global North
   Australia and, 54–55, 80, 147–48, 156
   Brazilian culture's valuing of, 12–13, 19, 60–61, 112–14, 125, 183
   celebrity culture and, 36–37, 144
   cool and, 9, 20, 31, 70, 144
   cosmopolitanism and, 28, 150–51
   English language and, 116, 144, 183
   excellence seen as a virtue of, 112–13, 114, 116–17
   global Christianity and, 7, 58
   imagination and, 22–23, 54–55
   modernity and, 8, 54–55, 145, 182
   power asymmetries and, 23, 60–61, 69, 195
   sensational forms and, 48
Global South, 7, 17–18, 19, 58, 182, 185

God
　agency and plan attributed to, 21, 65–66, 77, 78–79, 84, 87–88, 89, 90–94, 95–97, 148–49, 188
　as caring father, 89–90, 95–96
　dreams and, 65–66
　miracles attributed to, 65–66, 77, 89, 117
　relational God and, 50, 88
　unmediated relationships with, 77
God is Love Church, 55–56
Goldstein, Donna M., 85
Gomez, Selena, 71–72, 192
Grossberg, Lawrence, 53–54, 64
Grupo Globo network, 167–68

habitus, 8, 42, 58
Hagin, Kenneth, 57–58
Harding, Susan, 17–18
Harvest Bible Chapel, 102
Hebdige, Dick, 32
Hillsong churches. *See also* Hillsong College
　abuse scandals at, vii–viii, 9–10, 24, 102–3, 148, 189–92
　aesthetics and, 7–8, 11, 20, 22–23, 24, 43–44, 180–81, 182, 184
　affect at, 11, 22, 52–53, 54–55, 102–3, 126–27, 141, 186–87, 189, 194–95
　in Amsterdam, 164, 166
　branding and, 3, 7–8, 10, 18–19, 20, 33–34, 59, 67–68, 70, 106, 112, 126–27, 128–29, 163–64
　Brazilian diaspora in Australia and, 1–3, 72, 94–96
　in Buenos Aires, 164–65, 188
　celebrities and celebrity culture at, 3, 9–10, 20, 22–23, 24–25, 34–35, 36–38, 55, 70–72, 73, 126–27, 160, 165–66, 195
　Christmas Spectacle services and, 103–4, 186–89
　Church Elders at, 190
　clothing and fashion at, 24–25, 27–28, 41, 43–44, 128, 152, 174–75, 186
　connect groups at, 94–96, 192
　consumerism and, 10, 27–28
　Cool Christianity and, viii, 9, 11–12, 13, 20, 22–23, 24, 28, 31, 34, 38–39, 53, 123, 127, 138, 195
　cosmopolitanism and, viii–ix, 12–13, 23, 51, 135, 158, 195
　Covid-19 era and, 22, 123–24, 131–32, 188
　critical documentaries and media coverage of, vii, 160–61, 172–73, 190, 191–92
　Diversity Month at, 75
　dreams and, 63–64, 65–66, 69, 70
　Easter spectacle services and, 133–35
　English language and, 1–2, 13, 23, 75, 135, 167, 183, 185, 194–95
　establishment (1983) of, 9–10
　excellence emphasized at, 38–39, 67–68, 112, 116–17, 137, 156–57, 161, 164–65, 184–85, 195
　fandom and, 3, 11, 20–21, 22–23, 51, 52, 55, 62, 63–64, 67–68, 70, 72, 163–64, 168–69, 195
　Global Board of, 190–91
　grace emphasized over legalism at, 49–50, 192–93
　"Heart for the House" campaign, 187–88
　Hills Christian Life Centre as original name of, 126–27
　Hillsong Conference and, 103–4, 129
　Hillsong Family and, 135–36, 138–39, 149–50, 174–75, 185
　Hillsong Men group at, 103–4
　Hillsong Network and, 135–38, 149–50, 153, 174, 185
　Hillsong Publishing and, 62
　holy communion and baptism at, 173, 186–87
　infrastructures of transnational circulation and, 123–24
　Latino Night at, 75–77
　leadership development emphasis at, 12–13
　length of services at, 152–53
　LGBTQI+ individuals and, 40–41, 50, 165
　in London, 13, 33–34, 71–72, 128, 129, 133–35, 164
　in Los Angeles, 3, 71–72, 160
　mattering maps and, 148–49, 175–76
　Mega Prayer nights and, 132
　in Monterrey, 188
　in Montevideo, 186–87, 188

neoliberalism and, 49, 147, 174
in New York City, viii, 13, 24, 25, 37–38,
    71–72, 128, 164, 165, 166, 182
"Out-of-the-Boat" sessions and, 99, 117
in Oxford, 165–66
in Paris, 71–72, 128, 164
pastors' preaching at, 49–50, 53
popular worship music and, 2, 9–10, 20,
    41, 52–53, 54–55, 59–62, 65–66,
    72–73, 126–28
Prosperity Theology and, 37, 126–27
in São Paulo, 9–10, 11, 20, 22–23, 39,
    75–76, 113–14, 128, 148–49,
    150–51, 153–54, 163–74, 184–85,
    186–89, 191, 194
as Seeker church, 12
sensational forms at, 7–8, 11, 41, 52–54,
    66, 157–58, 161, 184–85
Sisterhood group at, 103–4
social media and, 3, 9–10, 13, 16–17,
    18–19, 20, 22, 27–28, 34–35, 67,
    71–72, 131–35, 148, 158, 164–65,
    167, 169–70, 175–76, 180, 187,
    190, 191–92
in Stockholm, 164
in Sydney, vii, 1–2, 9–10, 13, 15, 24, 47,
    52–53, 65–66, 69–70, 72, 75–77,
    118, 129, 163, 175–76, 186
Team Box and, 27–28
as template for other churches, 10, 11,
    179–84
tolerance and inclusivity emphasized at,
    12, 18–19, 50, 165, 171–72, 173
transnational connection and, 127–28
volunteering at, 12, 37–38, 96, 102–3,
    150, 160, 163–64, 168–69, 170–72,
    174–75, 184–85, 194–95
youth culture and, 12, 24, 27–28, 72,
    178–79
Hillsong College
    adulthood transitions at, 100–1, 105–12
    affective experiences and, 21–22, 101–2,
        141–42
    alumni reunions in Brazil for, 159
    aspiration to change the world among
        students at, 115–17
    behavioral expectations and
        nondisclosure agreements at, 106–
        7, 110–11
    branding at, 98, 99–100, 107–8
    Chapel services at, 98–99
    "Christians Abroad" (pseudonym for
        study abroad company), 141
    clothing and fashion at, 99
    cosmopolitanism and, 101–2, 118–21
    creative arts education at, 12–13,
        101–2
    dreams and, 21–22, 64, 69, 100, 101–2,
        116–17
    English language and, 101–2,
        117, 159
    excellence emphasized at, 112–15
    leadership emphasis at, 12–13, 21–22,
        100–1, 106–8, 161
    neoliberalism and, 106–7
    pastoral education at, 9–10, 185
    pastors at, 21–22, 100–1, 117
    precarity among students at, 99
    Prosperity Theology and, 112
    sexual assault scandal (2021) at, 104,
        200n.5
    tolerance emphasized at, 111
    volunteering at, 100–1, 103–6, 108–10,
        121–22
Hillsong United (band)
    Brazilian music industry and, 16, 60,
        167–68
    concerts and touring by, 61–62, 64–65
    fandom and, 61–63, 64–65, 126–27
    middle-class fan base of, 61–62
    piracy of the music of, 62
    social media and, 9–10, 61, 64–65,
        167–68
    success in Brazil of, 60–61, 167–68
    translations into Portuguese of songs by,
        62, 63, 182
Hillsong Young & Free (band), 71,
    175–76
Hinn, Benny, 57–58
Holy Spirit
    the body and, 28–29, 44
    Pentecostalism and, 8–9, 26, 28–29, 44
    popular praise music and, 63, 126
    transformation and, 173
    transnationalism and, 123
    worship services and, 98–99
Houston, Ben, 154
Houston, Bobby, 9–10, 27–28, 133, 138

Houston, Brian
  abuse scandals at Hillsong and, vii–viii, 102, 148, 189–92
  accountability and, 147–48
  books by, 57–58, 164–65, 174–75, 178–79
  Brazil visit by, ix
  Cool Christianity and, 38–39
  founding of Hillsong (1983) and, 9–10
  on Hillsong and LGBTQI+ individuals, 40–41, 50
  Hillsong College and, 111, 118–19
  Hillsong Family and, 138–39
  Hillsong Leadership Network, 136–37
  Hillsong São Paulo church, 164–65, 166–67, 168–69
  Hillsong United and, 63, 64
  institutional charisma and, 193–94
  resignation from Hillsong (2019) by, vii, 27–28
Houston, Frank, vii–viii
Houston, Joel, 25, 64, 71–72, 193
Hutchinson, Mark, 193–94
Hybels, Bill, vii–viii, 102, 178–79

identity formation, 20, 28, 45–46
Igreja Batista da Lagoinha (Belo Horizonte), 60–61. *See also* Lagoinha church
Igreja Brasa church (Porto Alegre), 182
Igreja da Capital church (Brasília), 131
Igreja no Cinema (Church in the Cinema), 183
Ikeuchi, Suma, 89–90, 176–77
imagination. *See also* dreams
  Australia and, 20–21, 52–53, 54–55, 62–63, 64, 71–72
  Cool Christianity and, 9
  Global North and, 22–23, 54–55
  grounded imaginaries and, 11–13
  Hillsong churches and, 52–53, 62, 63, 72–73
Indigenous peoples, 19, 29–30, 68–69
infrastructures of religion
  aesthetics of, 125
  architecture and, 128–31, 142
  "Christians Abroad" and, 139–42, 156
  co-presence sustained through, 11, 22, 123–24, 142
  cosmopolitanism and, 142
  mobility and, 124–25
  social media and, 131–32, 142
Integrity Music, 60–61
International Church of the Grace of God, 56

jeitinho (clever dodge), 112–14
Jenner, Kendall, 71–72
Jesus Culture (band), 182
Jesus Is King (Kanye West), 26–27
Jesus People movement, 8, 25–26
John of God (Brazilian faith healer), vii–viii, 19

Kant, Immanuel, 29
Kenoly, Ron, 60
Kingdom of God churches (UCKG). *See* Universal Church of the Kingdom of God (UCKG)
King of Heaven (Hillsong Easter spectacle film, 2020), 133–35
King-O'Riain, Rebecca, 66–67
Kirby, Ben, 40
Klaver, Miranda, 131–32, 139, 153–54, 166, 170, 191–92
Köhrsen, Jens, 6, 43, 44
K-pop (Korean popular music), 66–67

Lagoinha church
  aesthetics at, 180–81, 182–83
  Belo Horizonte campus of, 130–31
  Diante do Trono praise band and, 63
  Hillsong churches as a model for, 179–81
  Niterói campus of, 131, 180, 182–83
  volunteerism at, 179–80
Lei de Gérson (Gérson's Law, Brazil), 145
Lentz, Carl
  abuse scandals of, ix, 24, 37–38, 102–3
  celebrities courted by, 37–38, 71–72
  celebrity status of, 160–61
  clothing of, 24, 26–27
Let Hope Rise (documentary film), 167–68
Levitt, Peggy, 14–15, 69
LGBTQI+ people, 18–19, 40–41, 50–51, 111, 165
Lula da Silva, Luis Inácio, 57

MacDonald, James, 102

March for Jesus, 61
Mariano, Ricardo, 57, 59
Marquezine, Bruna, 3, 71–72, 134
Mars Hill church, vii–viii, 102, 181, 193–94
Martí, Gerardo, 179
Martin, Berenice, 6–7, 42–43, 77, 129–30
material religion and the "material turn," 7–8, 29–30, 124–26
mattering maps
   adulthood transition and, 65, 121–22
   affect and, 53–54, 100
   fandom and, 73–74, 100
   Hillsong churches and, 148–49, 175–76
Mauss, Marcel, 33
Maxwell, John, 106–7, 145, 200n.6
Mazzarella, William, 53
McCracken, Brett, 38–40, 41
McPhillips, Kathleen, vii–viii
mediatization, 10, 14, 31, 34–35, 59
megachurches. *See also specific churches*
   affective labor and, 100, 121–22
   architecture of, 13, 129–31
   connect groups at, 94–95
   as educational institutions, 105
   encroaching and enclaving at, 129
   Fashion-Celebrity-Megachurch industrial complex and, 26–27
   "performing the mega" and, 118, 135–36, 186–87
   Prosperity Theology and, 37
   team leadership model and volunteering at, 102
   theology of immediacy at, 131–32
   as total social institutions, 78, 150
   young people's attraction to, 20
Mendez, Chris
   abuse scandals at Hillsong churches and, 190–91
   on Argentina under military dictatorship, 75–76
   Brazilian Pentecostal pastors' discussions with, 165
   on the church's relationship "in the world," 172
   clothing and hairstyle of, 25, 137–38, 186
   on discrimination against immigrants in Australia, 76–77
   on fandom and Hillsong churches, 169
   Hillsong church in São Paulo and, 75–76, 165–66, 167–69, 186–88, 194
   as Hillsong's lead pastor for South America, 25, 75–76, 138, 153, 164, 168–69
   on pastors' roles within the church, 174
Mendez, Lucy, 168–69, 187–88, 194
Meyer, Birgit, 7–8, 29–31, 126, 161
Miller, Brian J., 128
Miller, Donald E., 8–9, 84
modernity
   autonomous subjects and, 11
   Brazil's aspirations regarding, viii–ix, 8
   celebrity culture and, 34–35
   consumerism and, 31, 36
   Cool Christianity and, 12, 28
   globalization and, 8
   Global North and, 8, 54–55, 145, 182
   reflexive modernity and, 4, 12, 101
Moen, Don, 60
money
   offerings and, 48–49
   Prosperity Theology and, 48–49, 144
   tithing and, 6, 56–57
Moseley, Rachel, 35
music. *See also popular praise and worship music*
   contemporary Christian music and, 59–60
   Cool Christianity and, 20–21, 26, 32–33, 51
   Hillsong churches and, 2, 9–10, 20, 41, 52–53, 54–55, 59–62, 65–66, 72–73, 126–28
   música gospel (praise and worship music) and, 59
   Pentecostalism and, 28–29, 59, 126

neoliberalism
   Hillsong churches and, 49, 147, 174
   Hillsong College and, 106–7
   immigrant student workers and, 82
   individual autonomy and, 49, 110
   Seeker churches and, 100–1, 106
   Universal Church of the Kingdom of God and, 56–57
Neo-Pentecostal churches, 59. *See also* Pentecostalism

230　INDEX

New Life churches, 56
New Paradigm churches, 8–9
Nigerian Christ Embassy church, 58
"nones," 26, 157
North Point church, 57–58
Novaes, Regina, 157

O'Dougherty, Maureen, 5, 45–46

Passion City Church, 57–58
pastors. *See also* scandals involving pastors
　authority and authoritarianism of, 4, 11, 109, 145–47, 154, 155, 173–74
　branding and, 36–37
　celebrity and, 34–35, 36–37, 51, 67, 70–71, 101, 160–61, 184–85
　clothing and fashion of, 24–25, 35, 40, 75–76, 186
　electoral politics and, 6–7
　entrepreneurism and, 36
　fandom and, 36–37, 52, 54–55
　Hillsong College and, 21–22, 100–1, 117
　Hillsong conferences and, 57–58, 149–50
　as influencers, 25
　mobility of, 128–29, 138
　personalized charisma as basis of power for, 191–93
　Prosperity Theology and, 48–49
　social media and, 16–17, 36–37, 40, 57–58, 67
　US seminaries and, 57–58
　volunteerism in the service of, 37–38, 103
　wives of, 36
patriarchy, vii–viii, 17, 143–44, 153–54, 155
Pentecostalism. *See also* Brazilian Pentecostalism
　aesthetics and, 28–29, 42–43, 47–48, 51
　anthropology of Christianity and, 17–18
　architecture and, 129–31
　in Argentina, 6
　in Australia, 10, 13–14
　the body and, 28–29, 42–43, 44, 51
　counterculture and, 25–26
　exorcism and, 6, 42–43
　faith healing and, 6
　Holy Spirit and, 8–9, 26, 28–29, 44
　local heterogeneity within, 13–14
　migration and, 84
　music and, 28–29, 59, 126
　Prosperity Theology and, 6, 37, 189
　renovadas (renewed) and, 57
　sexuality and, 40–41, 42–43
　shame and, 7
　social class and, 17, 43, 51
　stigma and, 7, 48
　tithing and, 6
　youth culture and, 26
perfection, 67–68, 145, 147–48, 156–57
Pinheiro-Machado, Rosana, 5–6
polymedia, 14–15
the poor in Brazil
　favela slums and, 45
　illiteracy and, 49
　Pentecostal churches and, 4, 41–43, 48–49
　Prosperity Theology and, 37
　violence against, 4–5, 45
popular praise and worship music. *See also specific bands*
　Brazilian market for, 59–60
　Brazilian music industry and, 59–61
　celebrity culture and, 70–71
　concerts and, 59, 61
　fandom for specific bands and, 3, 20–21, 36–37, 52, 54–55, 70, 72–73, 126–27, 158, 164
　Hillsong's role in promoting, 2, 9–10, 20, 41, 52–53, 54–55, 59–62, 65–66, 72–73, 126–28
　Holy Spirit and, 63, 126
　social media and, 16–17, 61, 64–65, 67
　US bands and, 60
Pountain, Dick, 31–32
Preachers 'n' Sneakers Instagram account, 40
precarity. *See under* Brazilian diaspora in Australia
Prince, Joseph, 174–75
Prosperity Theology
　academic research on, 18
　Baptist churches and, 59
　celebrity culture and, 37
　church growth seen as sign of God's favor in, 144

"hard" versus "soft" prosperity and, 18–19
Hillsong College and, 112
Pentecostalism and, 6, 37, 189
the poor in Brazil and, 37
Universal Church of the Kingdom of God and, 48–49, 56–57, 144
Psalms 23:1–6, 190–91, 203n.4

racism. *See* anti-Black racism in Brazil
Rebustini, Edson, 60
Redeemed Christian Church of God, 58
religion
 aesthetics and, 7–8, 28–31, 32–33
 magical *versus* salvation religion, 29–30
 material religion and, 7–8, 29–30
 transnational nature of, 78
Renascer em Cristo church, ix, 59, 130–31, 144–45
reteté (ecstatic rituals in Pentecostal churches), 43–44, 51, 152, 153
reverse culture shock, 145, 149–50, 155, 159, 201n.3
Ribeiro, Lúcia, 78
Rio de Janeiro (Brazil), 56, 157
 violence in, 56

Saddleback church, 57–58, 177
Sandler, Lauren, 32–33
Santiago, Valdemiro, 144–45, 201n.1
São Paulo (Brazil)
 favela slums and, 45
 Hillsong church in, 9–10, 11, 20, 22–23, 39, 75–76, 113–14, 128, 148–49, 150–51, 153–54, 163–74, 184–85, 186–89, 191, 194
 lower-class residents of, 5
 religious demography of, 157
 social polarization and segregation in, 4–5
 urbanization in mid-twentieth century of, 55–56
scandals involving pastors
 financial abuse and, 24, 144–45
 narcotrafficking and, 6–7
 Renascer church and, ix, 144–45
 sexual abuse and, vii–viii, 24, 189–90

Schäfer, Axel, 25–26
Seeker churches. *See also specific churches*
 aesthetics of, 8–9, 12, 176
 consumerism and, 100–1
 Hillsong as, 12
 music and, 8–9
 neoliberalism and, 100–1, 106
 openness to secular world at, 128–29
 welcoming attitude emphasized at, 171
sensational forms
 Brazilian Pentecostalism and, 41–42, 48, 157–58
 Cool Christianity and, 20, 28, 30–31, 34, 42
 definition of, 7–8, 30
 fandom and, 53
 Global North and, 48
 Hillsong churches and, 7–8, 11, 41, 52–54, 66, 157–58, 161, 184–85
 negotiations regarding new forms and, 30–31
 social class and, 8
 standardization of, 11, 30
 style and, 30
Sheringham, Olivia, 89–90, 149, 159
"Shout to the Lord" (song), 60–61, 63
Silva, Vagner Gonçalves da, 45
Smith, Chelsea, 177
Smith, Judah, 160, 177
Smith, Taya. *See* Gaukrodger, Taya
social class in Brazil
 Cool Christianity and, ix, 8, 20
 health outcomes correlated with, 5
 lower class and, 4–6, 20, 41–42, 79–80, 106, 129–31
 middle class and, 3, 4–6, 7–8, 12–13, 19, 20, 28, 31, 41–42, 43, 46–47, 49, 51, 72–73, 79–80, 81, 85, 97, 106, 130–31, 135, 141–42, 158, 179–80
 Pentecostalism and, 4, 6, 20, 22, 28, 44–45, 46–49, 123, 142
 performance of, 5–6
 race and, 4–5, 43, 45–46
 sensational forms and, 8
 style and, 8
 taste and, 6, 42
 upper class and, 4–6, 81, 108, 128, 130

social distinction
  clothing and, 5
  English language and, 150–51
  habitus and, 42
  performance and, 8
  style and, 3, 30
social media
  celebrities and celebrity culture on, 3, 34–35, 36–37, 66–67, 71–72
  Cool Christianity and, 26–27
  co-presence and, 14, 131–35
  Covid-19 era and, 131–32
  fandom and, 36–37, 54–55, 66–67, 70, 126–27
  fieldwork and, 14–15
  Hillsong churches and, 3, 9–10, 13, 16–17, 18–19, 20, 22, 27–28, 34–35, 67, 71–72, 131–35, 148, 158, 164–65, 167, 169–70, 175–76, 180, 187, 190, 191–92
  Mars Hill Church and, 193
  pastors and, 16–17, 36–37, 40, 57–58, 67
  Pentecostal churches and, 7
  praise music bands and, 16–17, 61, 64–65, 67
  youth culture and, 27–28
Spiritism, 1–2, 6, 171
Stanley, Andy, 178–79
Stolow, Jeremy, 125–26
style. *See also* aesthetics
  boundaries and, 30
  sensational forms and, 30
  shared style and, 30–31, 51
  social class and, 8
  social distinction and, 3, 30
Summit conferences, 57–58

taste, 6–7, 8, 42–43, 131
Theology of Prosperity. *See* Prosperity Theology
transnationalism
  affective transnational community and, 3, 54–55
  Hillsong churches and, 123–24, 127–28
  Holy Spirit and, 123
  immobile transnationalism and, 14–15
  infrastructures of circulation and, 123
  mediatization and, 14
  siting of religious services as means of reinforcing connections of, 128–29, 131

United States
  Brazilian culture influenced by culture of, 57, 177, 179
  Brazilian students in, 19, 80
  celebrity culture in, 37–38
  economic hegemony of, 81
  Hillsong churches in, vii
Universal Church of the Kingdom of God (UCKG)
  in Australia, 56–57
  criticisms of, 48–49, 144
  establishment of church in Rio de Janeiro by, 56
  headquarters in São Paulo of, 130
  media conglomerate owned by, 56–57
  neoliberalism and, 56–57
  overall reputation of Brazilian Pentecostalism and, 7
  political influence of, 56–57
  the poor and, 7, 56–57
  Prosperity Theology and, 48–49, 56–57, 144
  schisms in, 56–57
  tithing and donations at, 56–57

Valadão, Ana Paula, 60
van de Kamp, Linda, 123
Vásquez, Manuel, 78
Villagio JK (São Paulo nightclub), 128, 130–31
Vocational Education and Training (VET), 81
volunteerism
  adulthood transition and, 12, 170
  autonomy and, 12
  exploitation and, 102–5, 160–61, 195
  fandom as an obstacle to, 168–70
  at Hillsong churches, 12, 37–38, 96, 102–3, 150, 160, 163–64, 168–69, 170–72, 174–75, 184–85, 194–95
  at Hillsong College, 100–1, 103–6, 108–10, 121–22

Hillsong Conference and, 103–4
at Lagoinha churches, 179–80
pastors as beneficiaries of, 37–38, 103

Wagner, Peter, 33–34, 57–58, 70–71, 169
Ward, Russel, 154–55
Warren, Rick, 174–75
Weber, Max, 29–30, 191–92
Wellman Jr., James K., 192–93
West, Kanye, 26–28
Willow Creek church, vii–viii, 57–58, 102, 177, 181
Wuthnow, Robert, 58

Yanomami genocide (Brazil), 19

Yeezy Sunday Service fashion line, 26–27
youth culture
consumerism and, 27–28, 32, 33
"Cool Christianity" and, 9, 26–28, 31, 51
Hillsong churches and, 12, 24, 27–28, 72, 178–79
Pentecostalism and, 26
social media and, 27–28
spectacular subcultures and, 32
style and, 32

Zschech, Darlene, 60–61, 64, 70–71, 193–94